The Future of the Library

Lance Strate
General Editor

Vol. 3

The Understanding Media Ecology series is part
of the Peter Lang Media and Communication list.
Every volume is peer reviewed and meets
the highest quality standards for content and production.

PETER LANG
New York • Bern • Frankfurt • Berlin
Brussels • Vienna • Oxford • Warsaw

ROBERT K. LOGAN *with* MARSHALL MCLUHAN

The Future of the Library

From Electric Media to Digital Media

PETER LANG
New York • Bern • Frankfurt • Berlin
Brussels • Vienna • Oxford • Warsaw

Library of Congress Cataloging-in-Publication Data

Names: Logan, Robert K., author. | McLuhan, Marshall, 1911–1980, author.
Title: The future of the library: from electric media to digital media / Robert K. Logan.
Description: New York: Lang, [2016] | Series: Understanding media ecology,
ISSN 2374-7676 (print), ISSN 2374-7684 (online); vol. 3 |
"All the chapters of this book were co-authored by Marshall McLuhan and
Robert K. Logan with the exception of 2015 Preface, Chapters 6 and 7 and Part 2
of Chapter 13, which were authored by Robert K. Logan in 2015. The original material
co-authored by Marshall McLuhan and Robert K. Logan circa 1979 is presented
unedited exactly as it was written then. However Robert K. Logan has inserted
parenthetical remarks to this material to bring it up to date where necessary or to
comment on the 1979 material from a 2015 perspective. These parenthetical remarks
are encased in {curly brackets}." |
Includes bibliographical references and index.
Identifiers: LCCN 2015035203 | ISBN 9781433132643 (paperback: alk. paper) |
ISBN 9781453917701 (e-book)
Subjects: LCSH: Libraries—Forecasting. | Libraries—Aims and objectives. |
Libraries—Information technology. | Libraries and the Internet. |
Libraries and society. | Digital media.
Classification: LCC Z665.L785 2015 | DDC 027—dc23
LC record available at http://lccn.loc.gov/2015035203

Bibliographic information published by **Die Deutsche Nationalbibliothek**.
Die Deutsche Nationalbibliothek lists this publication in the "Deutsche
Nationalbibliografie"; detailed bibliographic data are available
on the Internet at http://dnb.d-nb.de/.

Cover Design by Clear Point Designs

© 2016 Peter Lang Publishing, Inc., New York
29 Broadway, 18th floor, New York, NY 10006
www.peterlang.com

CONTENTS

A NOTE TO READERS

All the chapters of this book were co-authored by Marshall McLuhan and Robert K. Logan with the exception of 2015 preface, chapters 6 and 7, and part 2 of chapter 13, which were authored by Robert K. Logan in 2015. The original material co-authored by McLuhan and Logan circa 1979 is presented unedited exactly as it was written then. However, Robert K. Logan has inserted parenthetical remarks to this material to bring it up to date where necessary or to comment on the 1979 material from a 2015 perspective. These parenthetical remarks are encased in {*curly brackets*}, with the bracketed text in italic. This book was rescued from the National Archive of Canada and is missing the page numbers of many of the quotes, for which I apologize. McLuhan and I were not very careful about those details in our first draft of the book. I am afraid that information was lost in the 36 years it took to make this book public.

ORIGINAL 1979 PREFACE

This is the original preface McLuhan and Logan wrote sometime in 1979, to which has been added the mention of the two new chapters 6 and 7.

In part I (chapters 1–3), we develop the tools of media study, drawing upon McLuhan's earlier work. This section also contains historical sketches of the development of the alphabet, literature, and the library, using the tools of media study.

Part II (chapters 4–7) examines the effects of modern technology and information overload on the contemporary library. The impact on the library of the media of electronic telecommunications and the new information environment they create is also studied {*including in chapters 6 and 7 the new digital media that McLuhan never had a chance to witness*}. In view of the changed environment in which the library now functions, it is necessary to rethink and redefine the notion of the library. The future of the library, while constrained to a certain extent by its technology and social context, will be determined by what librarians wish it to become.

In part III (chapters 8–12), we outline the directions for the future development of the library that we would like to see occur. Our proposals include the incorporation of the oral tradition in the libraries' activities, the return to human scale, and the creation of and widespread dissemination of the compact library, a collection of approximately 2,000 volumes that survey and review all the learning of mankind. Our suggestions are presented as probes for further debate, deliberation, and consideration, and not as a detailed blueprint for revamping the library.

In part IV (chapter 13), we summarize our findings.

2015 PREFACE

Robert K. Logan

A history of how this book came into being is important for readers to understand before they tackle the reading of this book co-authored by Marshall McLuhan and me in two stages. The book is a hybrid of the book that Marshall McLuhan and I wrote in the years between 1976 and 1979 and the supplemental text that I wrote in 2015. The original book lay untouched during the thirty-six years between 1979 and 2015. Let me share how this current edition of the book came into being, beginning with how I came to collaborate with McLuhan in the first place.

The story begins in 1974 when I first met Marshall McLuhan as a physics professor whose research up to that point had been almost entirely in elementary particle physics but with interests in interdisciplinary studies. I was organizing at that time a seminar on future studies at New College in the University of Toronto, having just spent three months working with Ivan Illich in Cuernavaca, Mexico. I called the seminar the Club of Gnu after the college mascot, the gnu, and the hot futures studies nongovernmental organization (NGO) at the time, the Club of Rome, which had just commissioned the study titled Limits to Growth. I first recruited Arthur Porter, a systems thinker, the Chair of Industrial Engineering, and, as I later learned, the Associate Director of McLuhan's Centre for Culture and Technology. Porter was happy to join the seminar and help in its organization. He immediately suggested including McLuhan. Porter telephoned McLuhan and told him that I was organizing a futures seminar, which McLuhan eventually joined. McLuhan immediately asked Porter if I was the Bob Logan who taught the course The Poetry of Physics and the Physics of Poetry. Once this was confirmed McLuhan told Porter, "Send Logan over for lunch; I want to talk to him."

As we two sat at lunch McLuhan asked me what I had learned teaching my course, The Poetry of Physics. I responded by saying I was trying to understand why abstract science began in Europe despite the fact that the Chinese invented so much of technology as I had learned by reading Joseph Needham's book *The Grand Titration*, where Needham documents the many contributions the Chinese made to the development of the Scientific Revolution. I told McLuhan I was working on the idea that perhaps abstract science arose in Europe because it was in Europe that there was a tradition of monotheism and codified law, which in turn gave rise to the notion of universal law, a key ingredient for abstract science. The Chinese are spiritual but not monotheistic and they have laws but they are not codified. McLuhan nodded approvingly and then asked, "What else do we have in the West that is not present in China?" I was so intimidated by this great scholar that I suffered a brain freeze and told McLuhan I did not know. When he blurted out, "The alphabet, of course," I let out a great groan because I immediately remembered how he had connected alphabetic writing to abstract science and deductive logic. During the remainder of that lunch we sketched out our first paper together, *Alphabet, Mother of Invention* (McLuhan & Logan, 1977), which is described in the next chapter. We basically suggested that codified law, the alphabet, monotheism, abstract science, and deductive logic created an environment for their mutual development. That was the beginning of our collaboration that lasted to the end of his life.

Neil Postman, the editor of the journal *ETC: A Review of General Semantics*, published by the International Society for General Semantics, quickly accepted the article, "Alphabet, Mother of Invention," for publication. Marshall and I planned to write a book based on this article. Then one day he announced that he had found a publisher interested in our planned book and that I was to come to the Coach House the following Monday to meet the publisher. At that meeting an acquisition editor from Bowker Publishing, a publisher of books about libraries as well as books for librarians, asked us to describe our project. McLuhan described our alphabet project to which the acquisition editor retorted, "I think we have two books here, the one you want to write and the one I came to commission you to do on the future of the library." In desperation I asked, "Well how could one organize a library without an alphabet?" McLuhan seized on this remark and spent the next fifteen minutes connecting the operations of the library to the alphabet. When he was finished the editor said, "Well I think we have three books now, the third being a book on the future of the library and its relation to the alphabet." He commissioned us to do that book right on the spot.

Marshall and I began to work on this project, which resulted in the first incarnation of this book. Sadly, he fell to a stroke in the fall of 1979 that left him aphasic, and he passed away on December 31, 1980. I stopped work on the library project and instead turned to our original plan to write about the alphabet and as a consequence wrote *The Alphabet Effect*, which was first published in 1984 and again in 2004. I never returned to the library project because the alphabet study led to a series of studies and books including *The Fifth Language* (1995); *The Sixth Language* (2004b); *The Extended Mind* (2007); *Understanding New Media* (2010a); *McLuhan Misunderstood* (2012); and *What Is Information?* (2014).

Our original manuscript lay fallow. The National Archive of Canada collected it, where it sat unnoticed until last year when I had two requests to share it by scholars who had discovered it, I assume, through using a search engine. In 2014 Matthew Lamb, the editor of the Australian journal *Island*, based in Hobart, Tasmania, commissioned me to write an article about the library manuscript McLuhan and I wrote. That article appeared in 2015 in volume 140 of the *Island*. With the newfound expression of interest in *The Future of the Library*, I decided to return to our library project, something I had always intended to do. Naturally much has happened in the world of libraries in the thirty-six years since work on the project was halted.

The most significant changes to the library, as well as the ground or environment in which it operates, has been the emergence of digital media, by which I mean the personal computer, the Internet, the World Wide Web, the highly portable notebook computer, the smartphone, the tablet, and the many Internet and Web applications such as email, Web sites, search engines, blogs, YouTube, Flickr, Instagram, Facebook, and Wikipedia to mention a few of the more popular ones. It is the emergence of these new media that require the many additions to the manuscript that I have added given the radical impact these digital media have had on libraries. In 1979 McLuhan prophetically foreshadowed the transformative effect that computing would have on "mass library organization" when he wrote the following lines:

A computer as a research and communication instrument could enhance retrieval, obsolesce mass library organization, retrieve individual encyclopedic function and flip into a private line to speedily tailored data of a saleable kind. (1995, pp. 295–296)

These prophetic lines not only announce the coming of the Internet, Wikipedia, and Google but also indicate that the library will undergo major changes. When McLuhan writes mass library organization will be obsolesced one must remember he also said, "Obsolescence never meant the end of anything, it's just the beginning." And so once again the library will have a new beginning just as it did when the printing press emerged. I will certainly address the changed role and the new beginning of the library in the current digital age in this revised manuscript, but keep all of the original text that McLuhan and I wrote in 1979.

The emergence of the many new forms of digital media and their impact on the library present two challenges for retaining the spirit of the manuscript McLuhan and I wrote and at the same time to bring the manuscript up to date.

The first challenge and the easiest one to resolve is one of nomenclature and what we mean by and how we treat the terms we used in 1979 when we coupled the terms "electric," "electronic," and "new" with the terms "media," "technology," "environment," and "ground" and what we mean now when we couple the term "digital" with the terms "media," "technology," "environment," and "ground." The solution is simple. We shall continue to use "electric" and "electronic" to refer to the electric or electronic mass media such as telegraph, telephone, radio, recorded music, television, and movies with which McLuhan was familiar. The digital term will be used to refer to the interactive media that emerged after 1979, the year when the original manuscript for this book was written. The only digital technologies that we referred to in the original manuscript and which McLuhan was familiar with were mainframe and mini computers. These media naturally made use of digital technology but they were not and still are not as interactive as personal computers, tablets, and smartphones, so that by and large we will use the adjective "digital" when we are referring to the post-1979 media such as personal computers, tablets, smartphones, the Internet, and the Web.

The second challenge is how to organize the new updated book. I rejected the idea of publishing the 1979 manuscript just as we wrote it and then adding an update section taking into account the impacts of the digital media that have surfaced since 1979. I rejected this course because as I read over our 1979 manuscript I realized that many of the points that McLuhan and I made in the era of "electric media" are still valid in the era of "digital media." So rather than dividing the book into two separate sections—the original text and a section devoted to the effects and impacts on the library of the digital media—I have decided to go with the original manuscript and integrate comments about the impacts of digital media in the flow of the original manuscript. Some sections are brand new, but the bulk of the book is the original manuscript still intact. In other words, instead of leaving the manuscript in its original state and then adding an addendum, I have decided to intersperse the updates in the context of the original text by inserting between {*curly brackets with the text in italic*} the impact on libraries of the digital media that did not exist before 1979. This preserves the flow of the original manuscript and at the same time provides updates in the context of the original study. It also avoids a lot of repetition that would have resulted if I had chosen the ad seriatim approach. For short comments I will merely enclose my remarks between {*curly brackets like so*} and for longer entries I will use the curly brackets again but I will add my initials {*like so, RKL*}. I have also invoked poetic license and added bracketed comments to some of the quotes that we originally made use of to bring them up to date. The one exception to this procedure is that I have added two new chapters. Chapter 6 provides a LOM (Laws of the Media) treatment of the new post-McLuhan digital media, and chapter 7 discusses the impact of these media on today's library. I have also added part 2 to the concluding chapter 13 to update some of the conclusions that McLuhan and I reached in 1979.

I have also changed the subtitle of the book, which originally was *An Old Figure in a New Ground*. When McLuhan and I wrote the first version of the book circa 1979 the ground was electric media but today's media are digital, hence the new subtitle: *From Electric Media to Digital Media*.

Socializing and Updating This Book

It is now possible in this age of the Internet to socialize this book and easily update it. I would be very interested in entering into a dialog with my readers about the ideas proposed in this book and I have the mechanism in place to achieve this dialog with my readers, as well as a mechanism for the readers to dialog with each other. About five years ago with the help of Dave Gray I started a Google Group titled Rethinking-the-Book, which I would like to also use as a vehicle for a dialog about our book, *The Future of the Library*, or rethinking the library, if you will. If you are interested in commenting on the book or would merely like to lurk on this Google Group, send me an email to logan@physics.utoronto.ca and I will inscribe you in the Google Group. You will then receive emails posted to the Google Group and be able to post comments by sending an email to rethinking-the-book@googlegroups.com. In addition to a dialog about the future of the library, there will also be items about the future of the book, which I am sure will be of interest to you as well. From time to time I will post updates to *The Future of the Library* to keep the book up to date with the latest developments in the world of libraries.

· 1 ·

THE LIBRARY: THE PHYSICAL EXTENSION OF MAN'S MEMORY (MOTHER OF THE MUSES)— A STUDY OF MEDIA

The library is a physical extension of man's memory, a tool, a medium, and a technology that can be studied like all the other extensions of man's body and psyche. It is our intention in this volume to apply to the library the classical notions of media study as developed in Marshall McLuhan's *The Mechanical Bride: The Folklore of Industrial Man* (1951), *The Gutenberg Galaxy: The Making of Typographic Man* (1962), and *Understanding Media: The Extensions of Man* (1964). This will provide us with an overview and an understanding of where the library is today in order to indicate possible directions for its future development. {*In updating the original version of this book, use will also be made of* Understanding New Media: Extending Marshall McLuhan *(Logan, 2010a) and* McLuhan Misunderstood: Setting the Record Straight *(Logan, 2013), both of which extend McLuhan's work into the digital age.*}

There exists a misconception regarding the nature of media study, which should be cleared up at the very outset. To study or examine a phenomenon and to report the trends that exist is not to endorse or condone those trends. The aim of media study is to reveal the effects, almost always hidden, of the various media. Its aim is not to promote one medium over another.

Media study, and those who pursue it, should not be regarded as enemies of the book. On the contrary, media studies have a number of insights to offer those who wish to revitalize the library and increase its effectiveness. Discovering the effects of new technologies such as the computer {here we were referring to mainframe and mini computers}, reprography, microforms, and audio-visual equipment {as well as the various digital media of the Internet, the Web, social media, notebooks, tablets, and smartphone} are essential to understanding the role of the library today and of the future.

William Eshelman's article, "Audio-Visual Aids: Fallout from the McLuhan Galaxy," in which the author defends the traditional library from the purported invasion of audio-visual materials, provides an example of a misinterpretation of McLuhan's work:

> In the sixties the McLuhan galaxy swam into our ken, creating a new cultural shock. We were informed that the long dominance of print had forced us into being linear creatures. Print is made up of words strung together in sentences and paragraphs, separate elements that can be arranged only in linear chains. Thus we think step by step, a clumsy, time-consuming method when contrasted with what is possible through the means of the new electronic media. Now, according to Marshall McLuhan, because of TV, computers and other gear, it behooved everyone to become an involved, simultaneous thinker. (*New York Times*, May 6, 1973)

Nowhere does McLuhan suggest that it behooves anyone to become a simultaneous thinker. Electric media are neither endorsed nor declared superior to print {the same holds for digital media}. Some of the effects of electric media are described in *Understanding Media* and a warning of some of their consequences is made:

> The electric technology is within the gates, and we are numb, deaf, blind, and mute about its encounter with the Gutenberg technology, an aid through which the American way of life was formed. It is, however, no time to suggest strategies when the threat has not even been acknowledged to exist. I am in the position of Louis Pasteur telling doctors that their greatest enemy was quite invisible, and quite unrecognized by them. (McLuhan, 1964)

Hardly an endorsement of electric media. Yet there are some who suggest that McLuhan is the cause of the invasion of electric media. Rulers of ancient times struck down the messengers of bad news as though the messenger were the cause of the disturbing report. It is difficult to argue with those who are angry about the invasion of electric media and wish to place the blame on McLuhan. Perhaps the best response to those who brand McLuhan an enemy of the book, and hence the library, is to remind them of the bumper sticker

that reads: MARSHALL McLUHAN WRITES BOOKS! Or refer them to
Doris Bass's (1969) remarks in the *Library Journal*:

> After all, when he (McLuhan) has something to say, he writes a book. Even Louis
> Shores (1968) an advocate of the multi-media library somehow feels that McLuhan is
> opposed to print: "But don't sell print short, as McLuhan does." (p. 3024)

To study or question a phenomenon is not to be hostile toward it. To discover
and report facts that do not bode well for the future of the book is not to be
its enemy. It is only through understanding the role of the book in our technologically altered society that we can perceive its place in our cultural life.

It was, therefore, a pleasure for us to accept Bowker's offer to do a study
of the future of the library. Our approach is that of two outsiders looking in.
While we are not experts in the area of library science, we are not strangers
to the library. Our respective research in physics and futuristics (Logan), and
English literature and communications (McLuhan) has brought us into intimate contact with many aspects of the library. In addition to our experience
as library users, we also bring to this project an acquaintance of the hidden
effects of technology and media on the social and psychic complex of man.

The hidden effects of man's tools have concomitantly a profound impact
on the future concept and operation of the library. The impact on the library is
of a twofold nature: (1) the direct effect of different technologies used within
the library, and (2) the changed environment in which the library operates
due to the effects of electric {*as well as digital*} media and modern technology.

The figure of the library as a repository of information has changed little
since its earliest inception in Sumer. The original libraries had facilities for
reading, a catalog, and shelves upon which were stored jars containing clay
tablets inscribed with cuneiform writing. The basic organization of the library
has not changed over the years. The jars of clay tablets have been replaced
by books, audio discs, audio tapes, films, slides, and video tapes {*as well as
digital media*}, but otherwise the structure is basically the same, in the sense
that the present library still provides facilities for "reading" the collection
and accessing it through a catalog, as well as collecting and materially storing
information {*with the addition that it now also stores digital information and provides patrons with access to online materials*}. Naturally the present-day library
is infinitely more sophisticated because of the tremendous growth of information. But a library is a library just as a Sumerian house or a twentieth-century
house is still a house. The functions are the same.

One cannot consider a <u>figure</u> in isolation from its <u>ground</u>, that is, the political, economic, technological, social, and cultural context in which it exists. It is the <u>ground</u> of the library that has changed most dramatically over the years, not the <u>figure</u> of the library. It is this changed environment that we shall examine when considering the future of the library, hence our sub-title: "An old <u>figure</u> in a new <u>ground</u>." The ground in which the library first emerged was that of a literate environment. Library services were organized for those who were committed to books and reading. Today this segment of society represents a vanishing race, old guard academics—no longer a con-temporary force. The new ground of the library, the electronically transmitted information environment, is a flip back to the oral ground of preliterate tribal man. Under the impact of electronic media and instantaneous information, youngsters and university students are losing the capacity to read. This is a crucial piece of empirical information librarians must take into account. It cannot be dismissed by attributing it to permissive education or the influence of certain selected writers or thinkers. Our young people are abandoning their literary heritage and returning to an oral world, the world of rock and drugs. {*Digital media has in fact increased the flip back to the oral ground in that the writing of emails, tweets, and text messages have the character of oral communication, but, on the other hand, users of digital media are more involved with the written word than the users of the A-V media of radio, TV, and the movies.—RKL*}

It is perhaps the most alarming, as well as the most difficult, challenge facing educators and librarians today. In order to deal with this crisis, which threatens not only the library and our educational system but also the very fabric of our society, it is essential to understand the effects of media and technology.

It is all too easy to identify enemies of the book, reading, or of libraries but when given to this activity one should bear in mind what is perhaps Pogo's {*a comic strip character circa 1940–1970 created by Walt Kelly*} most famous remark: "We have met the enemy and he is us." Our ignorance of the effects of media, of books, of print, of the alphabet makes us perhaps our own worst enemies. If the heritage of the book and reading has indeed been passed to librarians, as many are ready to claim, then upon these individuals rests the responsibility of understanding the effects of the book and other information media. If we can be of any assistance to librarians in this task, then we will have accomplished one of our goals.

The traditional library—a monument to hardware—now finds itself in the new electronic age of instantaneous information, an age of software {*and*} *two-way interactive digital media}*. The libraries' response to this challenge has been to go multimedia. It is fighting back with audiotapes and discs, video tapes, films, music concerts, plays, art galleries, computer terminals, and centers for continuing study. In short the library is becoming a center for media ecology instead of remaining more tied to the culture of the book. *{This is even more so the case now than when McLuhan and I wrote these words in 1979. Libraries are now fighting back also with the full array of digital media.}*

This is a healthy sign of vitality, one that must be encouraged but also understood. Introducing multimedia activities into the libraries because it is au courant, avant-garde, or groovy will not help us meet the challenges of increasing our inadequate educational systems and lack of communication. We have mass communication systems but we are not communicating with each other. Misunderstanding and alienation are rampant. We have a massive education system but we are not supporting our youth for the challenges of today and tomorrow. *{This is just as true today and maybe more so.}* Understanding the effects of these media and how they can be combined to facilitate learning, communications, and the accessibility of information will help, however.

The increasing importance of the role of information in all of our lives necessitates an increased vitalization of the institution of the library. There has been a shift of emphasis from hardware to software *{even more so today}*. The thesis of Marx that control of the means of production is equivalent to control of the society was a notion that was valid, to some extent, for the times in which it was formulated, the nineteenth century. In the present cybernetic postindustrial age in which we live, it is information that shapes and controls our society *{even more so today}*. Given this reality, it is incumbent upon librarians to be more assertive in the pursuit of their professional activities. Their services and expertise in handling the enormous volume of information required for the maintenance of our society becomes progressively more crucial. Their role in preserving the learning and lore of our culture in view of the disintegration of basic communication skills among the young take on a profound importance. The future for libraries and librarians is filled with challenges and opportunities.

An example of how the study of the medium of communication leads to insights into the nature of educational and library activities is provided by Harold Innis's analysis of the decline of learning that accompanied the fall of the Roman empire. Innis has pointed out that once the Romans lost their supply of Egyptian papyrus, they could no longer maintain their military bureaucracy, which required the rapid transmission of written orders for which papyrus was essential and, as a result, their empire fell. In addition the loss of papyrus also resulted in a decline of learning in Europe. This period, known as the Dark Ages, lasted until the Chinese technique of making paper from pulp arrived in Europe in the thirteenth century as a result of trading contacts.

Papyrus was replaced by animal parchment, which was far more expensive and scarce than papyrus. This naturally reduced the level of literacy and, hence, intellectual activity of the West. Books became much more precious as a result, and library collections were much smaller. Books were so precious that they were frequently chained to the table on which they sat so that no one would take them away.

One of the positive side effects of writing on parchment was the development of the codex, the forerunner of the modern book. In the age of papyrus, writings were collected on scrolls. This form of storing written material has certain advantages of compactness. However, it is difficult to leaf through or thumb through a scroll. Winding and unwinding the scroll to find a particular section is a rather tedious task. A table of contents and an index are virtually impossible with a scroll. With parchment, however, because of its durability, it was possible to sew together quires or signatures (leaves) to form the codex, the forerunner of the book. The codex was usually bound with a thick leather cover to protect the individual leaves.

The next development that stimulated bookmaking and the library was the arrival in Europe of paper, a product invented by the Chinese. The arrival of paper coincided with the beginning of the Renaissance, an event too fortuitous to be coincidental. The next major technological innovation to affect the library was the Gutenberg printing press, which enormously increased the availability of written material. This created a reading audience, which, in turn, demanded still more books. At first, print did not change the private nature of libraries, which were organized primarily for scholars and the privileged. Print, however, changed the social and political attitudes of society, and it was these new social attitudes that created the public library of media studies.

With the arrival of paper, the Renaissance began. On the other hand:

> Eastern Hellenism, unlike its Western counterpart, had no renaissance, because it had no dark ages. There is a straight linear progress from the death of Alexander in B.C. 323 to the fall of Constantinople in the fifteenth Christian century. (Peters, 1970, p. 23)

The East did not experience a dark age because the medium of the written word was parchment and not papyrus. Hence, the interruption of the papyrus supply left their learning establishment unaffected. This example hopefully illustrates the potential usefulness of studying the physical media that affect learning and, hence, the library.

Media Studies

Media studies requires special attention to be fully appreciated. Just as one must struggle with the new idea of modern physics, so must one also struggle with the new ideas of media studies, to which we now turn our attention. A full understanding of ideas such as "the medium is the message" requires looking at media and technology from an altogether new perspective in which the hidden <u>ground</u> of the effect is examined. One must consider what are the actual effects of the medium, not just the intended ones. It is obvious that one effect of the motorcar is to transport people rapidly from one point in space to another. The other effects of the motorcar, such as the way they transform the city, the countryside, our style of life, are less obvious. This is the real message of the motorcar. This way of considering media is not the way we are accustomed to thinking and, therefore, requires a new way of looking at technology. This is the point Deirdre Boyle makes:

> I have long had ambiguous attitudes toward media. For a time I interpreted "understanding media" to mean a wholesale endorsement of media technologies, some sort of *mindless* enthusiasm for kinetic images and groovy sounds. My only brush with media theory in college was a cursory reading of Marshall McLuhan's *Understanding Media*, which, like *many* before and after me, I violently rejected, thinking he was attacking print. Years later perceptions of what McLuhan was expressing have been radically altered, but not without the struggle to understand a startling and revolutionary concept. (1976, p. 125)

Deirdre Boyle's initial rejection of "understanding media" brings to mind the initial resistance on the part of both scientist and layman to the ideas of modern physics. One can draw parallels between media study with Einstein's theory of relativity and the quantum mechanical description of the atomic world. All three of these breakthroughs involved a new understanding and consideration of the way in which information is gathered and/or transmitted. The theory of relativity developed from the realization that information must travel at a finite velocity not faster than the speed of light. Quantum mechanics developed from the realization that the gathering of information or measurement affects and changes any physical system one wishes to study. This effect became apparent studying atomic systems because of their small size. The effects of relativity also became apparent with atomic systems because these tiny particles travel with velocities near the speed of light. As the effects of relativity and quantum mechanics became apparent, resistance to them developed. Scientists could not accept that the manner in which information was gathered or transmitted could effect what was being studied. The reticence of scientists to adopt new positions lead Max Planck, the discoverer of the quantum of energy, to conclude: "A new scientific truth does not triumph by convincing its opponents and making them see the light, but rather because its opponents eventually die, and a new generation grows up that is familiar with it."

A situation similar to the one in modern physics has occurred in the field of media study. The formula "the medium is the message" has met with as much resistance as Einstein's $E = MC^2$. Proponents of the notion that the content of the message is the only information transmitted are as oblivious to the effects of the means of communication as those who opposed relativity or quantum mechanics. {*Although these lines were written in 1979 there are still many who resist McLuhan's insights. But with so many of his predictions having come true, resistance to his ideas is slowly abating. Yet the battle continues, which is why I wrote* McLuhan Misunderstood: Setting the Record Straight *(2013).—RKL*}

The blindness to the effects of a medium is perfectly natural. Fish are completely oblivious to the water in which they live. Scientists were oblivious to the medium of measurements through which they observed nature. It is only by being forced out of the water that fish become aware of their medium. It was only with the rapid decrease in the size of objects observed, and the speedup of the velocities with which these objects moved, that physicists became aware of the effects of their observations. In the same way, it was only with the speed-up of information transmission with electric technologies that we became aware of the effects of the medium. With this insight, perhaps we can understand why Deirdre Boyle describes her coming to grips with McLuhan's revolutionary concepts as a struggle.

Since the literal meaning or content of a medium is not its only message, one must study the effects of a medium to discover its true message. The necessity of studying the effects of the medium of the book is mentioned by Jesse Shera, the former dean of Case Western Reserve University Library School:

If we think of the relationship between book and reader as an equilateral triangle of which the right side represents books, the left people and the base books and people, it is at this base that the function of the library is focused. Yet, despite the fact that librarians have been toying with this relationship for centuries, no one yet really knows the nature of the interaction between the *reader* and the book. Admittedly, some small progress toward understanding is resulting from the work of neurologists, brain specialists, and ophthalmologists, not to mention certain workers in the inter-disciplinary fields of biophysics and related areas but we still have a very long way to go. Some day, no doubt, the scientists will achieve a real understanding of what takes place along, that mysterious path from printed page to eye to brain, and then the implication for library service will be very great indeed.

What is a book that a man may know it, and a man that he may know a book? If we knew the answer to that rhetorical question, if we knew what cognition, learning, comprehension really are, if we understood how human communication really works, we could stop our worrying about what the librarian should be taught and how he should be doing his job. (1971, pp. 21–22)

The Gutenberg Galaxy (McLuhan, 1962) treats in detail the effect of print and the book. We shall review some of this material in later chapters. We shall also examine the <u>ground</u> that made the book possible, namely, the phonetic alphabet. Writing alone does not in itself create the conditions for the book, because it is only with phonetic writing (of which the alphabet is the purest form) that prose emerges and, hence, the necessity for book-length records. Ideographic writing gave rise to stelae, tablets, and proclamations but not to books. In the next section we shall examine the effects of the alphabet on society in general, and the library in particular. But let us resume our review of some of the (highlights) of media study, using the medium of the book to illustrate our ideas.

A comparison of the contrasting attitudes of two librarians toward the book provides us with an opportunity to examine the meaning of "the medium is the message." Lawrence Powell, in his article "My Favorite Four-Letter Word, Or, How I Feel About the Book," defends the book as "a holy icon for the dissemination of information":

I believe that books—those beautiful blends of form and sport—have a future fully as glorious as their past; that to disbelieve this is an act of faithlessness, is dangerous, and could lead to the downfall of the kind of librarianship in which the book is cen-tral and basic. I know that I am not alone in my belief, my faith, my love and I call on book-sellers and librarians to close ranks, face the invaders and give the tricks, preferably in elephant folio. (Powell, 1958)

Powell (ibid.) identifies the enemy as: "idea boys and efficiency experts who tolerate books only as long as there is no more efficient way for recording, preserving, and transmitting knowledge." They are not true librarians, but interlopers to the field:

> They strayed into librarianship mostly from other fields and they have never been at home since, for to them books in large numbers are merely a nuisance, and they spend their time trying to think up substitutes for them, jargonizing about automation, bibliographic control, contact points, mass media, decision-making processes, retrieval of information and the dissemination of knowledge. They will do everything on earth to a book but read it. (ibid.)

In contrast to Powell's confining book chauvinism, we have the view of Louis Shores, former dean of the Florida State University Library School:

> Life must be communicability. And this definition of life all at once gives meaning to the past, present and future of the book. To begin with, I understand the book in the ... generic sense ... the book comprehends all the media of communicability through which mankind gives evidence of life. The term "book" includes hard covers and soft covers, periodicals and pamphlets, pictures and maps, tape and disc recordings, broadcasts and telecasts, and perhaps two score more classes of formats. (Shores, 1955)

{*I am certain that Shores would have added the Net, the Web, and all other forms of digital media.*} Shores believes that the essence of the "book" and the library is communicability. Powell, by contrast, comes off as an archconservative opposed to any other format for information except the classical form of the book. If one reads between the lines, however, one discovers that Powell is also an advocate of "the medium is the message," even though he would probably be loath to use such terminology. He maintains that the content of a communication is not the most important criterion for judging its worth but, rather, the way in which that communication is delivered—that is the medium. Powell further maintains that of all the media presently available, none surpasses the book.

Powell's contention is not without merit. The book is an extremely convenient form of storing information that allows the reader to absorb material at his own rate, to scan through a great deal of material quickly, as well as to repeat material that was not initially understood. Thumbing through a book is a very efficient way of locating information. The book, he claims, is a simple form of technology, easily produced, which does not break down aside from fire, flood, or vandalism. The book is a comfortable format, well suited to our use, as David Mearns, chief of the Manuscript Department of the Library of Congress, points out: "Can you imagine anyone curling up in bed with a microfilm?"

While the book has much to support it, the exclusive role that Powell would have it play in the life of the library does seem a bit extreme. Shores's position, that all means of communicability are books, is likewise extreme but nevertheless worth examining. The telephone creates communicability, yet it is rather far-fetched to consider it a book. The telephone, however, plays an essential role in the life of a library. In fact, new ways to exploit it more in achieving the aims of the library are being explored. One often learns as much from a well-placed telephone call as one does from several books. Telephone reference networks organized by libraries have proven to be a valuable asset to their community and will likely become more widespread in the future. {*Could we have been talking about the possibility of the Internet? Possibly. It is certainly true that libraries use the Internet to network information to their users, but to be fair we did not imagine such a possibility back in 1979, even though we were aware of Local Area Networks.—RLK*}

Shores's provocative definition of the book as any medium of communicability lacks one very important element possessed by the classical format of the book or by the library, and that is <u>storage</u>. Speech, a microphone and loudspeaker, or smoke signals are not books in the sense that they leave no permanent record. Radio and television become books by virtue of audio and videotapes. Speech, coupled with memory, takes on the properties of a book in that information can be passed on from generation to generation by this mechanism. The poets and storytellers of preliterate societies played a role similar to books in a literate society, or discs, films, and tapes in a postliterate society {*and hard drives, servers, and the Cloud in the digital age*}.

The controversy that presently exists between the advocates of the book versus those who would use a multimedia approach to storing information is, in some ways, a replay of the battle that raged between the defenders of the oral tradition versus the new literati. Eric Havelock (1963), in his book *Preface to Plato*, demonstrates that Plato's attack on the poets in his dialog in the *Republic* was one of the many skirmishes *in* that battle between the men of letters like Plato and Aristotle, and those who communicated with the spoken word, like the Sophists and the poets who carried on in the tradition of Homer and Hesiod. Plato's quarrel with the Sophists was partly grounded in this conflict.

Perhaps there is a lesson to be drawn from that ancient era when literacy first challenged the dominance of the oral tradition. The book did not completely subdue poetry or the oral tradition; however, the role of the spoken word in our society has completely changed since the introduction of literacy. So it is with the new electric media. They challenge the dominance of the book. These new media will make further inroads as their use expands, but the bibliophile need not fear; the book will never be completely pushed out. The role of the book in our society will never be the same, however. It is one of the aims of this project to examine the new role that the book must inevitably play. {*With the advent of e-books and e-readers a similar alarm has been raised that the ink-on-paper version of the book would be obsolesced. In fact, what has happened is that after a very rapid increase in the sale of e-books, the percentage of e-book sales has leveled off to approximately 20% of the market. The reports of the demise of the printed book were greatly exaggerated.—RKL*}

Perhaps the views of the fifteenth-century bibliophile Vespasiano, concerning the library of Duke Frederigo of Arbino in Italy, provide some insight into today's conflict between the defender's of the book and the defenders of the multimedia approach for the library: "In his library all the books are superlatively good, and written with the pen, and had there been one printed volume it would have been ashamed in such company" (1926).

How many librarians feel that audio-visual materials should feel ashamed of keeping company with finely printed mass-produced books? {*Far fewer today than was the case back in 1979.*}

User as Content

The cognitive agent is and becomes the thing known.—Aristotle

The twelfth-century German physicist Georg Christoph Lichtenberg wrote: "A book is a mirror; when a jackass looks into it he does not see St. Paul looking back." The eminent librarian Jesse Shera expressed a similar sentiment:

> A book is a "container for things contained" yet what that thing may be depends upon him who reads. For the author the book is the physical embodiment of what he thought he put there, but to the reader its content is a variable. (1971, p. 21)

Both the physicist and the librarian are making the same point, namely, the user is the content. This insight into the nature of the book applies to all media, including the library. The content of a library, paradoxically, is not its books but its users, as a recent study of the use of campus libraries by university faculty revealed. It was found that the dominant criterion for selection of a library was the geographical proximity of the library to the professor's office. The depth of the collection in researcher's field was not as important a criterion as convenience (Dougherty & Blomquist, 1974, pp. 64–65). The researcher was able to convert the nearest library into a research facility that met his needs. In other words, the content of this conveniently located facility was that of its user. Any library can be converted from the facility it was designed to be, into the facility the user wishes it to become. A library designed for research can be used for entertainment, and vice-versa. As we move into greater use of electronic media, the user of the library will change even more. As the user changes, so will the library's content or the use to which the content of the library will be subjected. In other words, as the ground in which the library exists changes, so will the figure of the library. The nineteenth-century notion of the library storing basically twentieth-century material will have to cope with the needs of twenty-first century users.

Figure-Ground

After three thousand years of explosion by means of fragmentary and mechanical technologies, the Western world is imploding. During the mechanical ages we had extended our bodies in space. Today, after more than a century of electric technology, we have extended our central nervous system itself in a global embrace, abolishing both space and time, as far as our planet is concerned. Rapidly, we approach the final phase of the extensions of man—the stimulation of consciousness, when the creative process of knowing will be collectively and corporately extended to the whole of human society, much as we have already extended our senses and our nerves by the various media {especially since 1994 when the Internet and the World Wide Web were first commercialized and made available to the public}. Whether the extension of consciousness, so long sought by advertisers for specific products, will be a "good thing," is a question that admits of a wide solution. There is little possibility of answering such a question about the extensions of man without considering all of them together. Any extension, whether of skin, hand, or foot, affects the whole psychic and social complex. (McLuhan, 1964, p. 3)

The book and the library are examples of extensions of man, which affect the totality of man's experience. In order to study them properly, we must not consider them in isolation from all the other extensions of man. We must consider them together with all the other media and technologies with which they interact. This environment is the ground in which the <u>figure</u> of the library operates, and without which the library is meaningless. The ground for any <u>figure</u> provides the social, political, geographic, technological, and cultural context for it. Studying a <u>figure</u> in isolation from its <u>ground</u> is meaningless, much like studying a fish out of water. Most studies of technologies or institutions suffer from ignoring the <u>ground</u> and focusing almost exclusively on the <u>figure</u>.

Our approach in studying the library is to examine the <u>ground</u> or the environment of the library very carefully. The figure of the library, one of man's oldest media of communication, has not, in fact, changed very dramatically over the years—nor for that matter has the book {*the e-book not withstanding*}. The <u>ground</u> in which they are embedded, however, has changed radically, and this changes and affects the ways in which we interact with, and use, the library.

The library, as a physical extension of man's memory, does not play a passive role with respect to the material collected within its walls. C. S. Bartlett noted that remembering (re-membering) is re-ordering and, hence, changes the material. Turbane, in *The Myth of Metaphor*, demonstrates the naiveté of Locke's model of the mind as a photographic plate (tabla rasa). Karl Ashley's failure to find the engram, the storage place for memory in the brain, reinforces Turbane's conclusion. Pribram likens man's memory to a hologram in which memory is not stored locally but everywhere in the brain. Each memory in Pribram's model is affected by all the other memories stored in the brain, as well as the act of recalling the information. The library functions in a similar way. Each book stored in a library affects all the other books of the collection, for example, the way in which they are stored, the way in which they are classified, and the way in which they are accessed. In a similar way, every request for an item affects the way in which the library deals with all its material.

The Medium Is the Message

Every medium or technology produces new personal and social consequences by virtue of the new scale introduced into our affairs by this new extension of ourselves. The scale and form of human association and action are shaped and controlled by the service environment created by each new medium, and therein lies its message. The content of a medium is all too often taken to be its message, blinding us to the holistic effects and character of that medium.

The message of a medium, therefore, is not only what it says to us but also what it does to us. Let us illustrate this idea by examining the "message" of the following snippet of polite conversation: "Please don't go to the trouble of doing X; I wouldn't want you to bother yourself." The message conveyed by such a statement is not necessarily one of concern for the person to whom it is directed. Depending on the tone with which the statement is made, the message might well be: "I don't want you to do X; it would be a bother for me."

· 2 ·

ALPHABET, MOTHER OF INVENTION

The library, a physical extension of man's memory, like all other media, cannot be studied without considering all the other media since each medium affects the entire psychic and social complex of man's activities. In the previous chapter, we briefly considered the book, the medium with which the library is most concerned. In succeeding chapters we shall reconsider the book along with a number of other extensions of man, which crucially affect the library, such as audio-visual media, computers, reprography, and microforms {and various forms of digital media}.

In this chapter, however, we turn our attention to the alphabet, that extension of man that made possible prose, and hence the book and library as we know it today. Not only did the alphabet directly make possible the book and the library, but it also affected all aspects of Western society and, hence, the <u>ground</u> in which the institution of the modern library developed and flourished. Let us, therefore, turn to a general examination of the alphabet and the historic effect it has had on Western civilization. {An expansion of this chapter can be found in Logan, 1986/2004}.

Language: The Difference of Man

If one should choose the one dominant factor that separates man from the rest of the animal kingdom, it would undoubtedly be language. The ancients said: "Speech is the difference of man." Opposition of the thumbs and fingers and an erect stature were certainly key developments in the separation of man from animals, but the great quantum leap of intellectual capacity took place with speech. Spoken language structures the way in which man thinks and perceives the world. It is the medium of both thought and perception as well as of communication {see Logan, 2010a}. Language also serves as a collective memory.

Until literacy developed, speech was the principal means of communication. With writing, a new medium of communication opened up and man's intellectual development made a second quantum leap "contrary to the ancient view that only old things can come out of change" (Bunge, 1970, pp. 203–204). Breasted (1926) notes,

> The invention of writing and of a convenient system of records on paper has had a greater influence on uplifting the human race than any other intellectual achievement in the career of man. Carlyle, Kant, Mirabel and Renan believed that writing was the beginning of civilization. (p. 23)

The Effect of Literacy

Harold Innis, the Canadian economic historian, was perhaps the first to examine the effects of writing in shaping the intellectual, social, economic, and political life of man:

> The art of writing provided man with a transpersonal memory. Men were given an artificially extended and verifiable memory of objects and events not present to sight or recollection. Individuals applied their minds to symbols rather than things and went beyond the world of concrete experience into the world of conceptual relations created within an enlarged time and space universe. ... Writing enormously enhanced a capacity for abstract thinking. ... Man's activities and powers were roughly extended in proportion to the increased use and perfection of written records. (1972, pp. 10–11)

Innis observed that writing upon stone and clay created priestly bureaucracies and gave command over time because of the permanence of the record. Writing on paper, on the other hand, created military bureaucracies and gave command over space because of the ease with which information written upon paper could be transported and, hence, provide command at a distance. Innis attributed the fall of Rome to the disappearance of its source of paper.

If writing has had the impact that Breasted and Innis suggest, then the particular form a writing system assumes also plays a crucial role in shaping the thought of its users. Not only should one expect a major difference in the thought patterns of literate and preliterate people, but one should also expect a comparable difference in the thought patterns of societies whose writing systems differ significantly.

Innis points out the differences that using a particular medium, such as paper, clay, or stone, has on the organization of a society. Of equal importance in affecting a society's thought patterns is the way in which the spoken word is visually coded. There is a vast difference between ideographic (pictographic) codes, syllabic codes, and the alphabetic code, as well as the thought patterns they encourage (McLuhan, 1962, 1964). Let us compare Chinese and European culture. Western alphabetic literacy and Chinese literacy represent the two extremes of writing. The alphabet is used phonetically to visually represent the sound of a word. Chinese characters are used pictographically to represent the idea of a word {although there are phonetic elements to Chinese writing}. Consequently, they are less abstract and less specialized than alphabetic writing. Eastern and Western thought patterns are as polarized as their respective writing systems.

Western thought patterns are highly abstract compared with Eastern. There developed in the West, and only in the West, a group of innovations that constitute the basis of Western thought. These include (in addition to the alphabet) codified law, monotheism, abstract science, formal logic, and individualism. All of these innovations, including the alphabet, arose within the very narrow geographic zone between the Tigris-Euphrates river system and the Aegean Sea, and within the very narrow timeframe between 2000 B.C. and 500 B.C. We do not consider this to be an accident. While not suggesting a direct causal connection between the alphabet and the other innovations, we would claim, however, that the phonetic alphabet played a particularly dynamic role within this constellation of events and provided the <u>ground</u> or framework for the mutual development of these innovations (McLuhan & Logan, 1977).

The effects of the alphabet and the abstract, logical, systematic thought that it encouraged explains why science began in the West and not the East, despite the much greater technological sophistication of the Chinese, the inventors of metallurgy, irrigation systems, animal harnesses, paper, ink, print-ing, movable type, gunpowder, rockets, porcelain, and silk. Credit must also be given to monotheism and codified law for the roles they played in develop-ing the notion of universal law, an essential building block of science. Almost all of the early scientists—Thales, Anaximenes, Anaximander, Anaxagoras, and Heraclitus—were both lawmakers in their community and monotheisti-cally inclined. They each believed that a unifying principle ruled the universe (Logan, 1979).

Phonetic writing was essential to the intellectual development in the West. No such development occurred in the East. To understand why the alphabet developed in the West and not in the East, we need only consider the nature of the spoken Chinese language. All Chinese words are monosyl-labic. As a consequence of the limited number of sounds possible for a word, there is an enormous amount of redundancy in the sounds of Chinese words. There are 239 words, for instance, with all the same sound *shih*. There is little incentive for the development of an alphabet under these conditions. West-ern tongues, on the other hand, lend themselves to alphabetic transcription because they are more fractured.

All writing systems began as ideographic systems in which the idea of a word is represented by a sign (Diringer, 1947; Gelb, 1963). Although the Chinese writing system has phonetic elements, the two characters that denote a word are basically ideographic. The Sumerian and Egyptian systems, which began in 3500 and 3000 B.C. respectively, evolved into syllabic systems in which the sounds of syllables were represented by signs. The Egyptians retained their hieroglyphs and used a mixed system of ideograms and syllabic signs. In addition to these signs, they also developed twenty-two uniconsonantal signs, which could have served as an alphabet. These signs were restricted to render-ing foreign proper names, however, and, hence, cannot be considered a true alphabet.

The Semitic tribe, the Seirites, who mined copper for the Egyptians in the Sinai desert, developed the first primitive alphabet. They are referred to in Scripture as the Midianites, or Kennites, and are the tribe Moses sojourned with in Sinai. The Seirites adapted the twenty-two Egyptian consonants to their own Semitic tongue. This primitive "alphabet" was used by the Phoeni-cians and Hebrews and spread from the Middle East to the Indian subconti-nent where it formed the basis of the Brahmi, Pali, and Sanskrit alphabets. All of these forms of writing operated on the phonetic principle minus a vowel structure and, hence, fell short of the totally phonetic alphabet.

The Greeks borrowed the Semitic alphabets from the Phoenicians and converted it into a truly phonetic alphabet with the inclusion of vowels. So enriched, the Greek alphabet spread to other cultures and became the basis of all modern Western alphabets, including our own. The alphabet was invented once, and only once, in the history of man, and its effects, as we shall see, were as unique as the thing itself.

By including the vowels, the Greek alphabet became the most sophisticated writing machine developed by man. The impact of the Greek alphabet was naturally much greater than the impact of the earlier and more primitive phonetic writing systems such as the Babylonian syllabary or the Semitic alphabet of consonants only. The effects of these earlier phonetic writing systems, however, cannot be ignored.

The Babylonian syllabary, like the alphabet, encouraged the development of classification. The reform and simplification of the Babylonian syllabary from 600 signs to 60 signs occurred at the same time that the Hammurabic legal code was introduced. In addition to organizing the laws in a systematic manner, the code also promoted uniform and standardized procedure throughout the Babylonian empire, introducing uniform weights and measures.

The Semitic alphabet made its strongest impact on the Hebrew people. The effects of classification are seen clearly in the way they codified their law and also in the systematic way in which they recorded their history, the first people to do so. The abstraction, which the use of the alphabet encouraged, expressed itself in the theological concepts of the Hebrews, the first people to entertain the idea of one, and only one, God. True monotheism begins at Mount Sinai when Moses descends with the tablets of the Law "written by the finger of God" (Exodus 24:12). It is at this moment in the history of the Israelites that they are simultaneously introduced to monotheism, codified law, and systematic alphabetic writing.

By adding vowels to the Semitic alphabet, the Greeks created the first truly phonetic alphabet that is able to accurately and unambiguously transcribe the spoken words of any language, using only twenty to thirty signs or letters. "The original Greek invention achieved the essential task of analysis and it has not been improved upon" (Havelock, 1976, p. 61).

The purely phonetic alphabet had its greatest impact on the Greeks, the very first people to achieve and to use it. The Greek alphabet first came into use around 700 B.C. (Carpenter, 1933, 1938). Within 300 years the Greeks had developed from dependence on an oral tradition based on myths to a rationalistic, logical culture, which laid the foundation for logic, science, philosophy, psychology, history, political science, and individualism. How can one account for this rapid transition from a state of group involvement to individual skepticism? The alphabet served as the operative ground for this rich development, which was characterized by the classification and abstraction of ideas.

The very word *idea* is indicative of the revolution in thinking that took place with literacy. This word, which is not to be found in Homeric Greek, derived from the word *eidos*, indicating "visual image." The alphabet had the mysterious and unique power of separating the visual faculty from the other senses and giving dominant play to the visual. The pervasive use of uniform elements, the phonetic letters that the alphabet entailed, encouraged the additional visual matching of situational elements, which formed the ground for Greek logic, geometry, and rationality. The idea of truth itself, the correspondence of thing and intellect, is based on matching. At a more popular level, the development of realistic representation in the arts is identified with the Greeks in their first age of literacy (see E. H. Gombrich [1960] *Art and Illusion: A Study in the Psychology of Pictorial Representation*).

The phonetic alphabet also served as a paradigm for the process of abstraction, for the written word is an abstraction of the spoken word, which, in turn, is an abstraction from the holistic experience. The word, when written with the phonetic alphabet, represents a double level of abstraction beyond the merely spoken language. First, the spoken word is broken up into its constituents of semantically meaningless phonemes, which, in turn, are represented by meaningless letters. The use of the phonetic alphabet encouraged the development of abstractions:

> With literacy they [the Greeks] suddenly saw their universe as ordered. Their new worldview, however, was in conflict with the vocabulary they inherited from their oral tradition. Their conflict produced essential and permanent contributions to the vocabulary of all abstract thought: body and space, matter and motion, permanence and change, quality and quantity, combination and separation, are among the counters of common currency now available because pre-Socratics first brought them near the level of consciousness. (Havelock, 1963)

Paradoxically, the alphabet enabled the Greeks to reduce the massive polyphonies of their oral culture by selecting and logically (visually) connecting what had been simultaneous and musical. If the Greek means of abstracting and conceptualizing was by logical connection, the abstract art and science of the twentieth century proceeds by the contrary means of pull-ing out the "logical" (visual) connections in space and time. This returns the art and philosophy of today to musical form. If the Greek drive to abstraction had been to eliminate the acoustic and musical in favor of visual and logical connections, our nonrepresentational and abstract art and science assumes a complementary pattern.

The Greek alphabet also provided both the model and the bias for classifi-cation, an essential development in Greek analytic thought during the period from 700 to 400 B.C., especially for logic, science, and history. In addition to serving as a paradigm of abstraction and classification, the alphabet also served as a model for division and separability. With the alphabet, every word is separated into its constituent sounds and constituent letters. Havelock shows that the Greek idea of atomicity—that all matter can be divided up into individual tiny atoms—is related to the use of the alphabet: "They saw the analogy with what the alphabet had done to language and likened their atoms to letters" (Havelock, 1976).

The Greek capacity for divisiveness and separation extends way beyond their atomicity of matter. With writing, what is recorded or remembered becomes separate from the writer, existing in a book or a scroll. Knowledge takes on objective identity, separate from the knower. The Greek, in this way, developed the notion of objectivity and detachment, the separation of the knower from the object of his awareness. This is the beginning of the scientific method and the source of the dichotomy the Greeks created between subjec-tive thinking as found in art and poetry, and objective thinking as exemplified by philosophy and science. In art, percept precedes concept, while in science, method dominates both.

The Greeks invented "nature" (phusis), which is their classification of the objective external world. "Nature" does not include man or any of his artifacts such as the alphabet, which may explain why the Greeks never even studied the effects of their own technology, a radical flaw in their objectivity. It was the separation of man from nature, perhaps, that allowed Western thinkers to consider nature as an object to be studied or a resource to be exploited.

The Greeks did not study the entelechies or formal effects of human arti-facts, but only those of natural forms, whether of mineral, flora, or fauna. When Achilles encounters the ghost of Patroclus, he feels frustrated and says: "I see that we do live on after death, but without entelechies." The entelechy of anything is, as it were, the functional vortex of energy and power, which it manifests by its action. The merely visual or logical connectedness, which the phonetic alphabet fosters in the thought and perception of literate men, is quite unable to relate the environmental and structural forms to their users. Edward T. Hall spots this peculiar gap in "the edifice of Western thought" when he observes: "Quite simply the Western view is that human processes, particularly behavior, are independent of environmental controls and influence" (Hall & Hall, 1975). That which is environmental or ecologically holistic has an acoustic or simultaneous structure inaccessible to the lineal forms of thinking fostered by the alphabet.

Another important split in Greek thinking was the separation of the individual from his society. Plato develops the notion of psyche or soul from which the notion of an individual developed. In *The Republic* Plato "equipped his reader with the doctrine of the autonomous identified it as the seat of rational thought" (Havelock, 1963, p. 207). That the alphabet contributed to this unique event in the history of man was certainly not recognized by Plato or Aristotle. Like other literate Greeks, they avoided the study of the effects of their own artifacts.

Left-Right Split of the Brain and the Role of the Alphabet in Hemispheric Dominance

Recent developments in the field of neurophysiology tend to support the hypothesis that the alphabet produced a situation favorable for the development of logic, rational thought, and science. Neurophysiologists have determined that while there is a certain degree of redundancy and overlap between the two hemispheres of the brain, essentially the left and right hemispheres of the brain perform specialized tasks. The right hemisphere is the locus of the artistic, intuitive, spiritual, holistic, simultaneous, discontinuous, or creative side of our personalities, whereas the left hemisphere controls the lineal, visual, logical, analytic, mathematical, and verbal activities of our psyche.

{*The spirit in which we dealt with the bi-cameral mind was largely metaphoric. What we were suggesting is that cognitive styles can be characterized in terms of left and right brain functions. There is no scientific evidence that there is a clean split between what is called left and right brain functionality. All we know is that certain functions associated with language and analytic thinking are greatly compromised when there is damage to the left half of the brain and similarly damage to the right hemisphere seriously affects spatial co-ordination and musical capabilities.*

I (Logan 1986/2004) returned to this topic in chapter 15 of my book The Alphabet Effect, *where I updated some of the ideas McLuhan and I developed with regard to the bicameral mind. Leonard Shlain (1999) also treated this topic in his book* The Alphabet versus the Goddess.

It is important to bear in mind that there is not a clean break in functions between the two hemispheres. As pointed out by Iain McGilchrist (2012) in his book The Master and His Emissary: The Divided Brain and the Making of the Western World, *damage to the right side of the brain can also affect language skills, such as the ability to use and understand metaphor, sarcasm, and simile and, hence, language is interpreted literally.—RKL.}*

We here suggest that the alphabet created a lineal and visual environment of services and experiences (everything from architecture and highways to representational art), which contributed to the ascendancy or dominance of the left, or lineal, hemisphere. This conjecture is consistent with the results of the Russian neurophysiologist Luria who found that the area of the brain that controls linear sequencing and, hence, logic, mathematics, and scientific thinking, is located in the prefrontal region of the left hemisphere:

> The mental process for writing a word entails still another specialization: Putting the letters in the proper sequence to form the word. Lashley discovered many years ago that sequential analysis involved a zone of the brain different from that employed for spatial analysis. In the course of our extensive studies we have located the region responsible for sequential analysis in the anterior regions of the left hemisphere. (Luria, 1970)

Luria's results show that the expression *linear thinking* is not merely a figure of speech but an actual bona fide activity of the brain, which takes place in the anterior regions of the left hemisphere. His results also indicate that the use of the alphabet, with its emphasis on linear sequence, stimulates this area of the brain. Luria's findings provide an understanding of how the written alphabet, with its lineal structure, was able to create the conditions conducive to the development of Western science, technology, and rationality.

The alphabet separated and isolated visual space from the many other kinds of sensory space involved in the senses of smell, touch, kinesthesia, and acoustics. This made possible the awareness of Euclidean space, which is lineal, homogeneous, connected, and static. When neurophysiologists assign a vague "spatial" property to the right hemisphere, they are referring to the simultaneous and discontinuous properties of audile-tactile and multiple other spaces of the sensorium. The Euclidean space of analytic geometry is a concept of the left hemisphere of the brain, while the multidimensional spaces of the holistic sensorium are percepts of the right hemisphere of the brain.

Mystery of Zero

The Greeks, the first people to develop the totally phonetic alphabet with its continuous and connected spaces, unwittingly excluded the possibility of zero from their culture. One of the great historical paradoxes is that although the Greeks invented logic and formal geometry, they never developed the concept of zero, and thus their algebra was only marginal. The Greeks, guided by Parmenides's logic, simply rejected the notion of nonbeing as being logically inconsistent. Aristotle held that nature abhorred a vacuum. The Greeks were literally too inhibited by their logic to entertain or to conceive zero. The Hindus, on the other hand, regarded nonbeing as the goal of their spiritual life, the way to Nirvana. The Hindus in their oral culture, with almost total disregard for logical rigor but with sheer intuition, invented the notion of zero and the Arabic-Hindu numerals we presently use. They pioneered all of the present-day calculational logarithms or methods for addition, subtraction, multiplication, division, and square rooting, as well as developed algebra into a sophisticated mathematical system. Without the mathematical ideas developed by the Hindus and transmitted to Europe by the Arabs, the scientific revolution of the Renaissance could never have taken place. Hindu algebra laid the foundations for the work of Descartes, Leibnitz, and Newton.

The Intensification of the Effects of the Alphabet with Print

If the phonetic alphabet had created a <u>ground</u> or climate favorable to the intensified activity of the left hemisphere of the brain, the printed word reinforced this effect many times, both for the individual reader and by the spread of the reading habit. The very activity of typesetting became a major *paradigm* of sequential and segmented organization, which fostered the habit of precise measurement so necessary for the development of analytic, experimental technique. Without the development of the experimental and observational technique by Tycho Brahe, Galileo, and others, Renaissance scientists would never have broken out of the constraints of Greek theory with its relative indifference for the imperfections of the physical world. The effects of precise and repeatable diagrams in botany and anatomy brought a completely new dimension to these sciences. Writing in "Early Science and the Printed Book," Stillman Drake (1970) observes that print made available texts from the ancient world, so crucial to the Renaissance of learning and science, and made this material available on a much larger scale. Arabic texts transmitting the Hindu notions of zero, place numeration, and algebra were also more widely circulated as a result of printing. These mathematical developments were essential for the rise of science. Another effect of printing was to spread scientific learning beyond the walls of the university where it had been monopolized and limited by academics. Non-academics like Copernicus, Brahe, and Kepler made many of the breakthroughs in science during the Renaissance.

The Re-emergence of the Oral Tradition with Nonprint Electric Media

If the alphabet and print intensified that lineal activity of the left hemisphere of the brain, the new holistic and simultaneous information environments created by electronic technology brings back into full play the activity of the right hemisphere of the brain. Electricity moves at the speed of light, creating a simultaneous, nonlineal, acoustic environment of interface and resonance rather than connection. The right side of the brain is specially qualified to deal with this figure-ground environment of simultaneous information and pattern recognition. The lineal, segmented, causally connected description of nature, characteristic of the left side of the brain, can no longer cope with the new ecological, nuclear environment.

The clockwork universe of Newton, phased out at the speed of light, is replaced by the holistic nonlinear descriptions of quantum mechanics, general relativity, and the new astronomy. Einstein's general theory of relativity no longer describes the interactions of the individual components of matter placed in the passive container of Newtonian space. In Einstein's world, matter, through its gravitational interactions, creates "space," which, in turn, reacts back on this matter. Lineal, connected, infinite, static Euclidean space gives way to a dynamic, resonating, nonlineal, non-Euclidean, finite, closed universe that folds back on itself—"On a clear day you can see the back of your head." {*This is just one view of how our universe might be structured. A lot has happened in the decades since we described the closed universe as we did above, such as the discovery of dark matter and dark energy, but the point we made still holds in that the universe is no longer regarded as consisting of objects operating in a static Euclidean space.—RKL}*

In the world of atomic physics, the distinction between particles and waves assumes a complementary character. Light and other forms of electromagnetic radiation displays the properties of particles, knocking electrons out of metals (the photo electric effect), while electrons are found to behave like waves (through electron diffraction). According to the Heisenberg uncertainty principle, one can no longer measure simultaneously the exact position and momentum of a particle. One is forced to adopt a probabilistic description of nature, in which particles are represented by waves of probability. The chemical bonds that hold atoms together are resonances of these probability waves (Pauling, 1960). The very elementary particles of which matter is composed are themselves resonating composites of each other.

The electric service environment of simultaneous information, as was first exemplified by the telegraph, provided a new social ground favorable to the rediscovery of oral culture. This was reflected by the interest that developed in the nineteenth century in folk tales, folk culture, and anthropology. These, in turn, relate to the changes that occurred in psychology at the beginning of the twentieth century. Just as Planck was ushering in the idea of the discontinuous quantum of energy, Freud was preparing the demise of the mechanistic psychology that arose during the Enlightenment under the influence of Newtonian physics and print mentality. Freud returned medicine to the oral tradition of curing the sick through the use of words. Lain Entralgo's studies reveal that, as the ancient Greeks established their medicine on a firmer scientific ground, they dropped the verbal elements of their treatment to concentrate solely on somatic cures. Freud's psychotherapy represented a return to the shamanistic traditions of tribal medicine and "the therapy of the word" (Entralgo, 1970).

Evidence for the revival of oral traditions can also be found in the art, music, and literature of the nineteenth and early twentieth century. Examples include Mark Twain's use of local dialects in *Huckleberry Finn*, the symbolists' avoidance of ideological connections in their poetry, Joyce's *Finnegans Wake*, the popularity of jazz and rock whose origins are found deep in the rhythms of African music, the dropping of melodic connections in atonal music, and the use of African motifs and abstract discontinuity in the paintings of Picasso and the cubist school. *{Although electric and digital media have retrieved patterns of oral culture, the orality of the twentieth and twenty-first centuries differs from* *that of preliterate orality, as was pointed out by Walter Ong (1982/2002), who coined the notion of secondary orality described in his book* Orality and Literacy: The Technologizing of the Word. *Ong described secondary orality as "essentially a more deliberate and self-conscious orality, based permanently on the use of writing and print." It is worth noting that before print handwritten books were read aloud. Silent reading only emerged with print.—RKL}*

· 3 ·

THE LIBRARY: A FIGURE IN MANY DIFFERENT GROUNDS

In the last chapter we examined the historic effects on Western society of the phonetic alphabet, including its initial impact on the Ancient Greeks, its amplified impact on Renaissance Europe through print, and its waning influence on the modern world due to its competition with electric media. In this chapter we shall examine the figure of the library in the context of the historically changing ground described in the last chapter. Since each medium is affected by all the other media, or extensions of man, with which it interacts, the nature and the role of the library has changed dramatically with time since its inception.

For the purposes of this exercise we shall not narrowly define the library as a collection of books but rather as an extension of man's memory. In other words, we shall define the library as that device that stores and makes available for easy access the lore and culture of a society.

The Historical Roots of the Library

If we choose to define the library as the institution that catalogs and preserves books, then we would trace the origin of the library back to the origin of the book. This would not include the famous library at Alexandria, however, which preserved the great works of the Greeks in the form of scrolls. If we redefine the library as the institution that preserves written material of a civilization or a culture, then we might trace the origin of the library back to the dawn of writing, which occurred in Sumer about 5,000 years ago. Clay tablets that recorded literary activity of the Sumerian culture indicate that time and effort were devoted to the preservation of the lore and the learning of the culture through writing. Schools were organized to teach the privileged young men of the society the art of writing. It was the duty of these scribes to preserve the learning of the culture. Tablets have been recovered in which the titles of other tablets have been cataloged, indicating the existence of some sort of library system. The tablets do not actually list titles but refer to other tablets by their first line. The authors are not referred to, and no subject catalog has been found. The first lines probably played the same role that key descriptors play in our computer-based cataloging system.

The library is no older than 5,000 years, if one considers the library to be the repository of written material. This definition of the library, however, is based on hardware, namely the physical written material, tablets for the Sumerians, scrolls for the Greeks, and books for our society. If we look at the function of the library, then we will arrive at a much broader interpretation of what we mean by a library. The function of a library is to preserve the learning and the lore of a culture. Using this definition, it *is* possible to consider preliterate libraries by identifying the library with that institution that preserves the traditions of a culture. This role was played in oral society, by the poets who passed on from generation to generation the epics and sagas of their people. Homer was the librarian of preliterate Greece. Language itself is a library in the sense that language serves as a collective memory.

Poet's Resource Known as the Word-Horde and the Library Resource as the Book-Horde

The poets were the librarians of oral society. The very first things that were recorded and preserved by a culture when they acquired the ability to write were its national sagas or epics. This is true of the earliest literature of the Sumerians, the Egyptians, the Akkadians, the Hebrews, and the Greeks.

Eric Havelock (1963), in his book *The Preface to Plato*, has demonstrated that Homer served the preliterate Greeks in the same way that the Library at Alexandria served the Hellenistic world and the U.S. Library of Congress serves the modern world. Although the Homerian epic seems to be only concerned with the exploits and adventure of its heroes, it, in fact, with almost encyclopedic precision provides access to valuable information required for life in archaic Greece. It records everything from the necessary dress for combat, to instructions for sailing ships, and codes of behavior for court life. The library of the oral society is democratic. Every member has equal access to the information, since the epic poems were recited in public for all to hear. It is only with literacy that learning became the domain of the privileged, those who had the leisure to learn the art of reading and writing.

The library of oral society stores its information in the collective memory of the entire society. The form of the poetry is conducive to memorization through devices such as plot, meter, and rhyme. Writing, an extension of man's memory, actually had a deleterious effect on memory. It created a dependency for its users. The ancient Greeks recognized this shortly after they underwent the rapid transition from the oral Homeric tradition to the literate philosophical tradition, as illustrated by the following dialog in Plato's *Phaedrus*:

> "This invention, O king," said Theuth, "will make the Egyptians wiser and will improve their memories; for it is an elixir of memory and wisdom that I have discovered." But Thamus replied, "Most ingenious Theuth, one man has the ability to beget arts, but the ability to judge of their usefulness or harmfulness to their users belongs to another; and now you; who are the father of letters, have been led by your affection to ascribe to them a power the opposite of that which they really possess. For this invention will produce forgetfulness in the minds of those who learn to use it, because they will not practice their memory. Their trust in writing, produced by external characters, which are no part of themselves, will discourage the use of their own memory within them. You have invented an elixir not of memory, but of reminding; and you offer your pupils the appearance of wisdom, not true wisdom, for they will read many things without instruction and will therefore seem to know many things, when they are for the most part ignorant and hard to get along with, since they are not wise, but only appear wise." (Nielsen, 1954, pp. 22–23)

This passage illustrates the typical blindness of a left-brain Oriental technologist (Theuth) to the effects of his invention. Thamus points out that a special type of mentality is required to judge the usefulness or harmfulness of any specialist's art. He is referring to the right-brain oriented holistic approach we discussed earlier. He also recognizes that writing and reading discourage the development of this right-brain mentality, which he calls "wisdom."

Writing necessitates the library, since it destroys memory:

> Every day we seem to be piling heaps of ashes on the divine light within us. Men who read the *Times* every morning or it may be serious works on such different subjects as geology, philology, geography or history are systematically ruining their memories. They are under the suzerainty of books and helpless without them. (Müller, 1901)

Let us trace how the dependency on the book developed. With literacy, the role of the poet as preserver of the culture, passed on to the scribe. With the complicated writing systems of cuneiform and hieroglyphics, learning was strictly for the elite—the "eliterate." The following passage from earlier Egyptian literature illustrates the importance of the role played by the scribe:

> Do not become an officer, a priest or a baker. Become a clerk. He is released from labor, protected against work; he is free from hoeing with the hoe and you need not carry a knife! The officer runs the risk of lying prostrate before his superiors and exposing himself to the danger of losing his life, and the priest may be compelled to do public service; the baker runs the risk of falling into the oven and so perishing in the flames; but the clerk he is fortunate: "He directs all that is done in this country." (Erman, 1923)

The following passage from Nyberg indicates the way in which writing was used during biblical times:

> Writing was principally employed in practical matters, for contracts, covenants, monuments—in these cases doubtless also with magical significance—probably also for official registers and lists, and, above all, for letters. Annals were modeled on the Assyrian annals; legal texts of major importance were possibly committed to writing also. But the actual tradition or history, the epic tales, the cult-legends, doubtless generally the law too, must in the main have been handed down orally. Writers should certainly not be reckoned among the prophets and poets except with the greatest caution. The art of writing was the business of the specialists, not of the common man, as it always has been in the Orient. (Nyberg, 1935)

With literacy it became possible to store knowledge externally. Stone or clay served as the first surfaces upon which writing began. Almost as soon as writing emerged, so did the library, in much the form we know it today. The oldest known writing system is that of the Sumerians. They were also the first to create a library, which, like today, was a collection of writings. Clay tablets were collected together and stored in clay jars, which were placed on shelves. This form of organization is not unlike the collection of pages, which are bound together in a book and stored on shelves. The old Sumerian libraries of clay tablets contained two elements of the modern libraries: a dictionary and a catalog.

Mesopotamian culture became bilingual when the Sumerians, an Aryan people speaking an Indo-European language, were conquered by the Akkadians, who spoke a Semitic language. The Akkadians adapted the Sumerian writing system to their own tongue. Mesopotamian literature was preserved in both languages. The Akkadians eventually simplified the cuneiform system, reducing the number or signs from 600 to 60. The Akkadians, or Babylonians, began to develop some of the techniques of library science. They collected the tablets of the Sumerians. They produced the first bilingual dictionary, translating Sumerian words into Akkadian. Sumerian laws were collected and codified. This codification procedure began in approximately 2100 B.C. and culminated in the famous Hammurabic code of 1700 B.C.

The tablet catalogs contained the titles, or more accurately, the first lines of other tablets, like a modern day poetry index. Two catalogs have been found and are contained in the Louvre and the University of Pennsylvania Museum:

> The Louvre tablet is also divided into four columns. It catalogues sixty-eight titles, six more than the University Museum tablet. Forty-three of the titles are identical on the two tablets, although the order frequently varies. ... As for the principles, which guided the scribe in the arrangement of his catalogue; these are by no means clear. In the first place, since the forty-three titles common to both catalogues differ considerably in the order of their arrangement, it is obvious that the guiding principles were not identical for the two catalogues. A *priori* one might have expected the nature of the contents of the composition to have been the determining criterion. Actually, this is rarely the case. The only very convincing example of arrangement according to content is that of the last thirteen titles of the University Museum tablet, which are all "wisdom" compositions. Interestingly enough, none of these is found on the Louvre tablets. (Kramer, 1959, pp. 218–219)

The classification skills developed by the Akkadian-Babylonian culture became the standard tools of future librarians. The form of the library has not changed much since the days of ancient Sumer. With the advent of paper and the alphabet, more written material appeared. The size and number of libraries increased. The alphabet, by simplifying reading and writing, democratized literacy, making it more available. The production of papyrus, a paperlike material, made the production and transportation of written material easier. This not only created a military bureaucracy, as Innis (1972) points out, but it also stimulated the growth of the library. The Library at Alexandria, for example, contained up to 500,000 volumes.

Perhaps the next important advance in the cataloging and collection of information was the creation of the Holy Scriptures by the Hebrew people. The Hebrews developed the Semitic consonantal alphabet, which was the breakthrough in literacy, for the recording of their tribal history and religious experiences. The Hebrew were the first people to record their national history. The total library of their knowledge was to be found in the Scriptures, which were born in about 500 B.C. and which were not completed until shortly before the Diaspora in 44 A.D. The Scriptures served as the written repository of Jewish tradition:

> It is characteristic of all these traditions that the law is promulgated publicly and orally, and that it is afterwards written down and that this document is deposited in a sanctuary of YHWH (46) ...

> In this connection it would be natural to mention the possibility of interplay between written and oral tradition. Regarding the Homeric epics we have just pointed out two methods of tradition running side by side: the public recitation of the poems by a whole guild of masters of tradition and recitation, and the written copies deposited in different places as a means of control for, and aid to, oral recitation. A similar interplay existed in Ancient Mesopotamia, and we have at least one distinct parallel in the Old Testament; of the 'introduction' in Deut 31 to the song of Moses. (32) ...

> The law tradition is of a double nature. When once the law has been ratified in an assembly of people on the basis of an oral promulgation, it is written down and deposited in the holy place. But this does not mean that the oral recitation of the law ceases. In Deut. 31.9–11 the responsible leaders of the people are commanded to see to it that the law is orally promulgated in the assembly of all Israel when the people are gathered together every seventh year at the feast of tabernacles before the face of YHWH in that place where He lets his name dwell. This double method of tradition reminds one strikingly of the mode of tradition of Homeric poems. (Nielsen, 1954, pp. 46–47)

{This tradition of the mix of the oral and the written tradition persists to this day. In the Jewish tradition the Torah is read orally to the congregation in weekly segments throughout the year from a handwritten scroll that has been copied over and over again for more than 2,500 years. On the holiday of Simchat Torah (Joy of the Torah) that takes place three weeks after Rosha Shannah (the new year or literally the head of the year), the scroll is rewound and the reading of the Torah commences for another year. Reading the Torah is central to the Jewish tradition, which is perhaps why Jews like to refer to themselves as the people of the book. In the Christian tradition, readings from the Bible accompany their church services. A similar *practice takes place in the Moslem mosques with the public reading of their holy book, the Koran.—RKL}*

The mixture of the written and oral tradition is found in the poem with which the book of Proverbs ends. Each stanza of this poem begins with the next letter of the alphabet. This device, also used in Psalms, facilitates the memorization of this material for oral recitation.

Further evidence of the oral-written mixture is found in the diplomatic correspondence from Mari and El-Amarna where the following phrases appear:

(1) "Your tablet which you did sent forth, I have heard."
(2) "Hear it" —that is, acquaint yourself with the contents of a letter I have sent.
(3) "May he hear it." (Nielsen, p. 30)

Diplomatic correspondence was delivered orally by a delegation representing their king. The written letter they carried was used to aid their memory and serve as a control of what they reported. *{The importance of hearing what is written is included in the most sacred prayer of the Jewish tradition, know as the shmah (the Hebrew word for hear): "Hear O Israel, The Lord Our God the Lord is One."}*

The change from oral to written tradition is a gradual one. The transition, Nielsen claims, is due to an external threat to the culture:

> The change from oral to written literature does not take place because cultural summits have been reached, nor because the ability to read and write has become common property, but because the culture itself is felt to be threatened from within by syncretism and from without by political events. This change occurred, for Judah presumably towards the end of the seventh century or at the beginning of the sixth, for northern Israel, perhaps a century and a half earlier. (Nielsen, p. 60)

The transition to a written tradition has never been complete for the Hebrew people despite the central role that Scriptures play in their religious life.

> When once society has been somewhat consolidated thru the incipient formation or a written canon, there is again room for oral tradition and in this case its task will be to adjust an authoritative basis for the life of the community—which is now fixed in writing—to living conditions that have changed in the meantime. (Nielsen, p. 1)

The oral strand within the Hebrew tradition was preserved in two ways. One was the Talmudic disputes that arose over the interpretation of the Law as it is written in Scripture, and the other was the weekly public reading of the law, which enabled the entire community to have access to this information.

The role of culture preservation in the Hebrew society was filled by the synagogue, the congregation of men who gathered once a week to celebrate the Sabbath and read aloud the Holy Book. The role of librarian was played by the rabbi who copied the Holy Scriptures, kept the scrolls in safe keeping in the synagogue, and taught the young men to read the holy script. Even during the times that the Jewish people did not use Hebrew as their vernacular, they learned to read Hebrew before they learned to read their vernacular.

The Vedic Scriptures of the Hindus also provide an example of how the oral tradition survives literacy. The Sanskrit script, or alphabet, is based on an older script, Brahmi, named after the God Brahma. The Brahmi alphabet, like the Semitic alphabet from which it was originally derived, does not contain vowels. After the invention of vowels by the Greeks, vowels were added to this script in much the same manner that they were added to Hebrew. The Vedas were the first material from the Hindu oral tradition to be transcribed. Although the Vedas have been fully preserved in Sanskrit for more than 2,000 years, they are still committed to memory as they were originally before writing was introduced into India. India has never had a break with its oral tradition. This oral tradition survived the introduction of writing in 600 B.C. as well as the alphabetic culture of the British colonizer:

> Cult and religion are always rather immune to technical improvements, are always wedded to tradition. The Vedas were a divine message, handed down orally from one generation to another, without the aid of writing: therefore the oral tradition is continued into the age of writing. (Müller, 1901)

The feature of librarianship in oral or semi-oral literate societies is that it is totally integrated with the educational, religious, and legal institutions of the society. Homer's epics wove together the mores and customs of tribal Greece with stories of the gods. Hebrew scriptures combine legal and moral codes with deeply spiritual and religious writing. Learning and education in this society consist entirely of the study and interpretation of these scriptures.

With the development of a truly literate society, the role of the library changes, becoming less integrated with the other institutions of society. The Greeks were the first people to use an entirely phonetic alphabet in which the vowels were notated. They were also the first society to make a complete break with their oral tradition. One of the impacts of the phonetic alphabet was to create a model or paradigm for division and separation. It was under the influence of this paradigm that the Greeks created specialism, which reflected itself, both in the division of learning into separate subject areas and the division of the religious, educational, and legal activities of society into separate institutions. With the separation of the visual faculty from the rest of the sensorium that the phonetic alphabet encourages, left-hemisphere dominance came into play in Greek thought.

The Greeks were the first society to create the library as a repository of written material separated from the educational and religious functions of society. The Greeks were also the first to introduce the institution of a university (Plato's Academy and Aristotle's Lyceum). The university, from its very inception, was an ivory-tower operation, separated from the mainstream of everyday life. The Greeks were also the first to organize the church as an institution separated from the other institutions in society. The legal system was also operated independently from the library, church, and university. The pattern set by the Greeks has maintained itself to this day in our society. During the age of literacy, particularly with the advent of print, the separation of functions provided by the church, the court, the university, and the library proved quite satisfactory. The fragmentation and specialism of the print world, however, are difficult to maintain in a world of electric media. The isolation of library, church, court, and university no longer proves satisfying. Each of these institutions is undergoing a breakdown. Within each of these institutions there is a cry for more relevancy, for interconnectedness with the rest of society. The library is no exception. There are still a few conservatives who believe that the only business of the library is to collect books and service that constituency that is already turned on to books. The general trend of librarianship, however, in recent times has been toward greater integration of the library with society. This thrust has not yet been thorough enough to really counteract the fragmented role the library has historically played in society, nor to overcome the fragmenting tendency of information overload and the alienating aspects of our greater dependency on technology. {*It must be said that the separation of the library from the other institutions of society is somewhat less than it was in 1979, and one finds today many instances of libraries attempting to integrate their operations with the communities they serve.*}

The Bias of the Library à la Innis

As the store of human thought and perception, libraries are vast armories and arsenals and have been consciously used as such at various times. Through the ages libraries have served to establish great religious bureaucracies. The legal codes of Hammurabi were inscribed on stone. Priestly bureaucracies, using stone or clay as writing material for recording transactions, naturally tended to be static and stable, where as the scribe using papyrus, or even parchment, enjoyed a freedom and mobility that created the organization of political spaces and military structures that could be administered at a distance. In his *The Bias of Communication*, Harold Innis (1951) devotes his principal chapters to the problem of political and historical space and time as they are organized in the ancient world as a result of the availability of various materials for recording information:

> I have attempted to suggest that Western civilization has been profoundly influenced by communication and that marked changes in communications have had important implications. Briefly this address is divided into the following periods in relation to media of communication: clay, the stylus, and cuneiform script from the beginnings of civilization in Mesopotamia; papyrus, the brush, and hieroglyphics and hieratic to the Graeco-Roman period; and the reed pen and the alphabet to the retreat of the Empire from the west; parchment and the pen to the tenth century or the dark ages; and overlapping with paper, the latter becoming more important with the invention of printing; paper and brush in China, and paper and pen in Europe before the invention of printing or the Renaissance; paper and the printing-press under handicraft methods to the beginning of the nineteenth century, or from the Reformation to the French Revolution; paper produced by machinery and the application of power to the printing press since the beginning of the nineteenth century to paper manufactured from wood in the second half of the century; celluloid in the growth of the cinema; and finally the radio in the second quarter of the present century. In each period I have attempted to trace the implications of the media of communication for the character of knowledge *and* to suggest that a monopoly or an oligopoly of knowledge is built up to the point that equilibrium is disturbed. (p. 3)

Innis is considered a very difficult writer. The reason is simple. Understanding is not a point of view, and Innis followed <u>processes</u>. The historians and sociologists of the Western world, whether in economics or architecture or urban studies, have consistently ignored the service/disservice environments created by the products of every technical innovation. A close friend of Harold Innis, Eric Havelock (1963), devoted his *Preface to Plato* to studying the disappearance of the ancient and oral poetic educational establishment under the impact of the phonetic alphabet. He also recognized that the phonetic alphabet not only abolished Homer and the "tribal encyclopedia," but it also retrieved an extremely ancient and long-forgotten human fact, the recognition and awareness of the individual metaphysical substance of the private person. Plato saw that the consequences were basic:

Since he is now equipped, and has equipped his reader, with the doctrine of the autonomous personality and identified it as the seat of rational thought, he is in a position to re-examine "mimesis" from the basis of this doctrine, and he finds the two wholly incompatible. (Havelock, p. 207)

Innis is one of the few economic historians who have ever traced the psychic and social consequences of technological innovation. Even Aristotle was led into the "usury" trap by his failure to see the enormous service environments created by writing and coinage as wealth-makers. From Adam Smith and Ricardo to Karl Marx and Keynes, economists have ignored all service/disservice environments. This blank in their vision "has rendered their analyses sterile and irrelevant."

Yet by supplying the needed insights to complete this blank, Innis became unintelligible. That is to say, he was stating actualities, which most scholars preferred to know nothing about. A "difficult" writer is someone who has something upsetting to say. Most writers instinctively understand that it is their business to say what their readers already know and what they want to hear. Perhaps a major block to the understanding of Harold Innis is the difficulty that the literati have with the facts of acoustic space. Innis understood that acoustic and visual space were antithetic and complementary, like the written and oral traditions. That is why he has such relevance *for* the student of libraries. His work is founded on recognition of the fact that there must be some rapport between the written and the oral traditions—between the visual and the auditory—for *any* society to persist in a state of health. Our current inability to understand the electric revolution or to recognize its reconstitutive powers and effects is a residue of our ancient commitment to visual space. Visual bias commits us to classification and connection, to points of view, and to moral judgments. It warns us away from understanding processes just as it tells us to "shun the punman."

Naturally the electric all-at-once-ness of our time creates acoustic space whose center is everywhere and whose margin is nowhere. Such acoustic or auditory space is now the only available space even for people of visual and literary bias. This condition creates the current sense of total alienation and a feeling of the absurd in all ordinary human affairs.

Today in the age of X-ray awareness and pattern recognition, all monopolies of knowledge have been dissipated with the resulting participation of the total world audience in political action and decision making. There are no more spectators, as it were. Something comparable to this is happening in the book world, when, instead of circulating individual books, it has become possible to circulate entire libraries in the space and volume of a single book. {*This is even more so in the digital age*}. The Innis observations about the polit-ical and social consequences of book collecting are extended and reenforced by John L. Thornton (1941) in *The Chronology of Librarianship*. He recognizes that libraries and civilization are inseparable.

The Pre-Christian Era

Libraries date from the beginning of civilization, and before then if we rely upon mythological material. Dr. E. G. Richardson (1914) in his book *The Beginnings of Libraries* deals exhaustively with this aspect, including tooth necklaces, message sticks, trophies, tattooing, and quipus as records that might possibly be termed libraries. Although they certainly were records of events, in most instances they mean little at the present time. We are unable to "read" quipus, or knotted cords, and Professor Locke asserts that they were merely used for counting, despite opinions to the contrary. These quipus were in use in China as well as Mexico and Peru, and it is possible that they may have had greater significance than is now apparent, but we must ignore these, together with other objects that are now rightly considered as museum pieces.

If libraries had been the sinews of war and empire in the ancient world, they were even more needed by the Christian Church, as Thornton (1941) indicates:

> Ireland was the earliest centre of monastic activity in Great Britain, and its schol-ars were recognized throughout the learned world. Their influence extended to the Continent, and it is to them that England is greatly indebted for the spread of schol-arship to its shores. Mr. Ernest A. Savage, in his *Old English Libraries*, gives a very full account of the formation of the early monastic and academic libraries, and this book is a mine of information to those particularly interested in the period known as the Middle Ages.

> It has been suggested that Canterbury was the home of the first library in England, Augustine having brought nine books with him in 597 to form the nucleus of the library of St. Augustine's Priory. Before this date scholarship had been almost non-existent in the British Isles since 410, when Honorius and his Romans left Britain, and its reformation is not generally considered to have begun until about 670. No doubt the Romans brought literature with them, but they left no trace of it as evidence. (Thornton, 1941, p. 19)

Alfred Hessel's (1950) A *History of Libraries* supplements the war and library perspective with the view of the library role in Plato and Aristotle:

> The true development of the Greek library began, then, in the very decades, which embraced the activity of those two intellectual giants, Plato and Aristotle. The Academy and the Peripatetic school can claim the glory of having created not only the learning of Greece but of classical antiquity as a whole. Here there developed for the first time a large-scale organization of cooperative work under the leadership of a single individual. Plato undertook a methodical investigation into the fields of mathematics and natural science. Aristotle strove, insofar as possible, to collect completely and establish on a sound footing the facts in all the branches of knowledge, and he became the father of the disciplines of philological criticism and literary history. The work of both these men unquestionably presupposes the existence of a considerable library. With regard to Plato we have no definite report of such a library; of Aristotle, on the contrary, we hear that he collected manuscripts systematically, and we know also of the vicissitudes suffered by the library, which he left behind.
>
> Aristotle's pupil, Alexander the Great, opened a new period of ancient history through his campaigns. Greek culture broadened in scope, becoming a world civilization. An international class of educated men came into being. In Hellenistic culture scholarship and erudition became important factors of intellectual life. The seed sown by Aristotle now bore rich fruit, yet there was at the same time a change in the direction of scholarly endeavor. The unifying bond with which the master had connected the special fields of knowledge became more and more relaxed. These individual fields of knowledge became independent; investigations were confined to limited subject matter; and not infrequently the accumulation of knowledge handed down by preceding generations took the place of creative work. (Hessel, 1950, p. 3)

The development of empires and the rise of book communication is a relationship indicated in the Cadmus myth itself where King Cadmus sowed the dragon's teeth and they sprang up armed men. Letters themselves as aggressive weapons seem to have been related to teeth, since teeth are the only repetitive and uniform features of the animal body. Letters permitted the extension of empire to vast distances by the courier system since by this means it was possible to exercise authoritative control at a great distance.

Perhaps the most "imperialistic" book ever produced was *The Domesday Book* of *William the Conqueror*. To this book F. W. Maitland (1897) devotes an entire volume of analysis, titled *Domesday Book and Beyond*. Maitland brings to our attention that the crucial date in British history was not 1066, but 1086. This was the year of *The Domesday Book*, when English landholders large and small had to produce documentary evidence of land ownership. For most people it was, in fact, an act of confiscation, since England was then a nonliterate tribal society. The great monasteries with their teams of scribes were able to fake documents of land tenure that would have done credit to the great nineteenth century scholarly forger, T. A. Wise.

Hessel's narrative relates the role of the library to the conquest of Greece by Rome:

> "Conquered Greece subdued her savage conqueror," says the ancient poet. Modern scholarship sees in the culture of the Roman Empire only a continuation and further development of Hellenistic culture. From the middle of the second century B.C. Roman generals began to bring home Greek libraries along with other booty. The first to do this was Aemilius Paulus, and in the next century Sulla and Lucullus followed his example. Toward the end of the first century B.C. love of books spread among the Roman aristocracy. Cicero valued his collection very highly and saw in it the heart of his home. His friend Atticus was Rome's first large publisher and dared even to compete with the Alexandrian book trade. ...

> At the opening of the fourth century A.D. the public libraries in the capital city numbered twenty-eight. Only a few of them can be identified. Still, we are justified in assuming that collections were hardly wanting at the great forum and baths. *The* most important was the Bibliotheca Ulpia near the column of Trajan. Like the others, it was divided into a Greek and a Latin division, and it served also as the archive for important state documents.

> Heading these libraries at first were distinguished scholars with the rank of procurator. Later there developed a distinction between the administrative officials proper and the scholarly directors. Under them served slaves or freedmen so numerous as to require their own physician. (Hessel, 1950, p. 6)

Perhaps one of the most remarkable testimonies to the power of libraries in the shaping of culture concerns the dividing of ancient and medieval periods in accordance with the shift from papyrus to parchment as the basis for book production and library organization.

The Pagan Papyrus versus the Christian Codex

The pagan library at Alexandria fell victim to Christian rivalry and hostility. The contest between library empires led Emunes II to cut off papyrus supplies from Egypt to Rome. The ensuing story has never been filled in. It was one of the persisting themes of Harold Innis (1972) that the end of the papyrus supply dealt a fatal blow to the Roman military and political establishments, which did not recover until the coming of handmade paper from China in the eleventh century A.D. Their meager supplies of parchment could not possibly sustain their courier systems and bureaucratic organization. It was almost as if gasoline were cut off from the Western world. The diminishing of trade and transport would be drastic. Historians have ignored the fact that paper, as much as coinage, in the ancient world was a basic service environment. In a world that had relatively few service environments of an artificial kind, paper was crucial. Innis insists that the Roman empire was open for business again as soon as the Chinese provided an abundance of handmade paper in the eleventh century and afterward. The Carolingian Renaissance rested on Chinese paper.

Hessel parallels Harold Innis when he makes a division between the ancient and medieval world in terms of papyrus and parchment codex technologies, even though he appears to ignore the causes:

> Historians nowadays avoid drawing a sharp line of demarcation between the ancient world and the Middle Ages; instead they suggest a period of transition lasting a good five hundred years. Accordingly no exact span of years can be specified in which the ancient library ceased to exist and the medieval library had its inception. Scholars must content themselves with identifying each of the main factors, which determined the character of this new type of library and with following the course of its development.

> A signal characteristic of the ancient library is the papyrus roll, of the medieval library, the parchment codex. In the preceding chapter we became acquainted with papyrus as the writing material of ancient times. Even then as a matter of fact, parchment was used for less important purposes, but artistic and literary evidence indicates that it first came into more general use in the third century A.D., and by the fifth century it had almost entirely supplanted papyrus. In this period, therefore, there took place the transcription of most of the extant literature from the one writing material to the other, a process whose importance for the textual criticism carried on in modern philology is well known. And now, corresponding to the substitution of parchment for papyrus, in these centuries the parchment codex with a stiff cover replaced the papyrus roll as the physical form of books. It is to be expected that the infiltration of the parchment codex brought with it certain changes in the internal structure of the library. Still, these could not have been of a revolutionary nature; at least a mosaic of the fifth century … and a miniature of the sixth century show that the codices were kept in chests, just as the rolls had been formerly. … If accommodating the new form of book demanded considerably more space than before, this disadvantage was in a measure compensated for by the fact that a single codex could contain the texts of a whole series of papyrus scrolls. (p. 9)

New technology tends to do more with less. But the first great demonstration of this principle was provided by the unexpected recapture of antiquity by Gutenberg technology. That is why the Renaissance itself was constituted by the innovation of the printed book. The medieval scribe had no means of reproducing the entire literature of antiquity. But the Gutenberg technology scrapped the scribe as well as the oral culture of scholasticism and quickly retrieved pagan antiquity, dumping it en masse into the lap of the Renaissance. The parallel in our own time is the scrapping of industrial hardware by electric circuitry and the retrieval of all modes of primitive awareness with which the twentieth century has now been invested. {*This process is accelerated with digital media, which in addition scraps or greatly reduces some of the practices associated with mass electric media.*}

The battle of the book in the early Middle Ages involved a battle between pagan and Christian cultures, according to Alfred Hessel:

> Thus it seems to have been a time in which the new form of book was propagated by the religious power then coming to the fore, Christianity, while pagan culture, placed on the defensive, was clinging to the form which was on the way out. It was probably about the same time that the Christian library entered into competition with the pagan. (1950, p. 10)

Dean Jonathan Swift's battle of the books is not lacking in echoes of this ancient biblical quarrel between pagan and Christian, but we doubt whether Swift was aware of the parallel events that had occurred 1,000 years before him. Hessel relates how the *translatio studii* had been involved in the rise of Christian scholarship and exegesis:

> The fate of the pagan library was closely tied up with that of ancient culture. With that culture falling into decay, one school of rhetoricians after another shutting down, and the number of unlettered people rapidly increasing, desolation settled upon the places where formerly those interested in pagan science and literature used to foregather. In the fourth century Amianus Marcellinus is already lamenting the "libraries closed forever like tombs" (*bybliothecae sepulchrorum ritu in perpetuum claustrae*). Upon the heels of desolation came destruction. We have practically no trustworthy accounts of the dispersal of manuscripts and the tearing down of buildings. The Alexandrian Library appears to have fallen prey to Christian fanaticism at the end of the fourth century, and it is said that the same Gregory the Great who preached the famous "funeral sermons" to a Rome oppressed by the Lombards caused the imperial book collections to be burned. This comes down, to be sure, as a much later tradition of the Middle Ages, yet it contains the kernel of truth latent in every legend.

In structure Christian libraries copied the pagan ones. As so many of the latter were located within temples, it was natural to bring the former within houses of worship and there with to assure them of the protection of the Church. The books of the Bible (hence also designated *biblia sacra* or *divina*) everywhere formed the basis of the collection. To these were then added liturgical and exegetical writings, and from the time when Christian apologetics began to expand, the works of the theologians and their heathen opponents could no longer be missing. Finally, for studying and gaining proficiency in the language of the Church, be it Greek or Latin, the remaining profane literature was needed.

We have information about many a church library, especially in Africa, even before the reign of Diocletian. Many fell victim to his great persecution. But, from the time the Church was raised by Constantine to the rank of a state institution, the disciplinary, organizational, and dogmatic duties of each bishop forced him at least to maintain a library of moderate compass. At the opening of the fifth century Paulinus of Nola even built at his episcopal seat a Christian reading room and provided it with the inscription: "Here he whose thoughts are on the laws of God may sit and ponder over holy books (Clark 1901, Chapter 2)."

One of the revolutionary features of Gutenberg for libraries was that the printed book was both portable and expendable. Uniform and repetitive or mass-produced commodities had their beginning with the printed book. The Gutenberg technology of uniform, movable types became the pattern and exemplar for all subsequent forms of mass production. It was the first mechanization of complex handwork achieved by multiple steps, that is, the movable type.

The manuscript library was "locked in." Books were irreplaceable and frequently chained to the shelves, somewhat in the manner of the telephone directories in a public phone booth {*circa 1979*}. The reasons for chaining are somewhat different but the effects are not unlike. The idea of exact copies of the same book was quite revolutionary as demonstrated by Margaret Mead's experience years ago when she took a batch of copies of the same book to the Admiralty Islands. When the books were distributed to the local inhabitants they were quite excited to discover that the copies were identical. It was their first experience of industrial mass production. Naturally, it appeared as pure magic to them. This "magical" dimension of exact repetition is lost upon us for whom it has long been an unquestioned service environment. We forget perhaps that the criterion of scientific "proof" for a long time was the power to repeat an effect or an experiment. Since we consider magic and science to be antithetic, it is a little strange to encounter a culture in which magic and repetition are one and the same. Perhaps it would be truer to call Gutenberg a magician or sorcerer than just an inventor or mechanist. The results of his technology have been exactly like those of the Sorcerer's Apprentice, who released forces of abundance far beyond his intent or control.

The effect of the Gutenberg book abundance was to increase the reading public many times. Libraries, in the modern sense of the word, naturally began with the portable, repeatable mass-produced book. Eventually, the printing press became a kind of power plant, steam-propelled, and the result was to turn libraries into vast powerhouses of learning. Book storage soon became a major problem and systems of book classification became ever more complex.

One of the paradoxes of Gutenberg mass production is that as the reading public has enlarged, the point of view of the writer has narrowed. More and more writers tend to select their audiences on a specialist basis, much in the way in which librarians classify the results of the author's endeavors.

In total contrast with the pattern of print production and book storage and classification and usage, there is the world of the newspaper, which is a daily corporate "book." It is a mosaic form with corporate authorship and an existence subsidized by ads that have pushed the cost of the newspaper down to the point where it would actually be cheaper to give it away than to sell it. This same reverse effect of ever-faster production is especially noticeable in the new forms of electric broadcast printing. It is now possible to publish books and newspapers on private TV sets. The day is at hand when a careless set owner might leave the book-button on, only to return to find his house destroyed by a super glut of page copy! Something like this has already tended to happen in the overproduction of books, which now taxes all existing library and librarian powers to contain and to control. {*Thanks to McLuhan's foresight we seem to have anticipated here the Internet, the Web, and e-readers.*}

The situation is not unlike the vast increase of new words in the English language. Neologisms are increasing the language daily beyond the powers of philologists and lexicographers to collect or to define. It is the speed-up of verbal transactions in a whole range of media, which causes the language to expand at this exponential rate. By the same token, speed-up of coding and retrieval is now tending to produce the means of intense compression. What we call the "match-box library," (the one projected by Vannevar Bush [1945] in the *Atlantic Monthly*) represents speed of compression in the interest of space flights and the programming of space capsules. There probably never has been a time when the organization of knowledge as the major form of military and industrial activity has been so manifest as at the present moment. There has been a steady trend, not only to speed the movement of knowledge but also to store it for more and more rapid access.

A full-page ad in the *Wall Street Journal* reveals some basic features of the new "Library":

> Breakthrough! NCR (National Cash Register) introduces practical paperless publishing! A microform system that lets you publish 3,200 pages on a 4" x 6" transparency, send it anywhere for a nickel, and read it full size when it gets there, again and again.

"Paperless publishing"—that should be enough to frighten the paper industry and the publishing trade. But NCR doesn't stop there:

> How does the PCMI Microform System work? The amazing science of photochromics permits the non-photographic reproduction of incredibly small images. The technique, unlike photography, is reversible, so mistakes can be corrected during the recording process. By visually checking each image as it appears, NCR can produce a flawless PCMI master. Then a photographic master is prepared, checked and duplicate positives made and laminated. A single but optically sophisticated reader returns the images to the original (or preferred) size for easy reading.

This is nonphotographic and reversible "photography," a simple but optically sophisticated reader. What would you have done if you were Kodak and Recordak? But what about libraries?

> Extremely inexpensive home viewers are in the offing. The complete works of Shakespeare, the great recipes of the world, an unabridged dictionary would each fit into a single transparency. An encyclopedia would take only eight. These and all the great books of the world can be stored in the corner of a desk drawer.

The second appendix of the National Science Academy's publication *Biology and the Exploration of Mars* (1966) is titled "Potential Applications of Electron-Optical Methods to Storage of Information for Direct Retrieval." After discussing successful experiments that used the electron microscope to demagnify images several thousand times, H. Ferandee-Movan goes on to propose:

> that all of the information obtained during the Mars missions and other extraterrestrial missions be considerably condensed by electron optical demagnification (ratio of demagnification 1:1,000 and 1:50,000 or more). This would mean that bits of information, greater in number by several orders of magnitude, can be imprinted directly onto reels of special ultrathin tape by demagnification electron microscopy. ... The amount of information that could be recorded in a tape reel with a total area the

size of a typewritten page varies from a content of a 1,000,000 volume library (each volume, 500 pages) to approximately a 10,000,000 volume library. (Feeley, 1967, pp. 92–93)

{In today's environment with the Net and the Cloud, these estimates of the storage capacity seem modest. This 1967 report did not anticipate the tools of the digital age but the concerns that they raise are very much an issue that librarians must consider today.}

Mr. Feeley does well to speak of the "library environment" since, with our new means of electrical service environments, information itself becomes not only an environmental service, but it also becomes "software." The paperless, or software library, brings the Gutenberg assembly line of movable types into an altogether new circle of magical effects. The technological tendency to do more and more with less and less could now be exceeded only by putting the information directly into the human nervous system. If an age of "brain transplants" lies ahead, it may become possible to supply each new generation with "brain prints" taken live and directly from the intellects of the age. Instead of buying the works of Shakespeare or Erasmus, one might well become electro-encephalographically imprinted with the actual brain perception and erudition of Shakespeare or Erasmus. The book as a means of intellectual enlargement could then be bypassed. {Although this has a bit of a science fiction feel to it, with the development of wearable computing, these speculations seem less outlandish today.}

What, then, would become the role at libraries? Would they become brain banks instead of book banks? {Today's libraries are still book banks but they are also computer banks.} Instead of "trying on" the mental world of Montaigne or Voltaire by dipping into their works, will we be able to try on the actual brain and perception of such giants? It seems within the range of electronic possibility that this could be done in the foreseeable future. It does not follow that one would approach the problem in the same spirit as deciding between a Cadillac and a Volkswagen.

And what would become of authors and the reading public? Would we all become consigned to the omniscient and all-encompassing awareness of the encyclopedic language of James Joyce's Finnegans Wake? Many would turn in horror from such a prospect as the ultimate mode of "Mission Intolerable." If many people are reluctant to face the prospect of the loss of private status and to meet the new tribal group involvement on its own terms, it may be some comfort for them to know that the beginnings of the more highly developed forms of private individuality in the age of Gutenberg and Montaigne created acute psychic discomfort and bewilderment. The "to be or not to be" of Hamlet was a universal cry of doubt in an age that was being whirled from the medieval corporate condition to the state of extreme individuality. This dilemma confronts electronic man in an exactly reversed prospect from that of the sixteenth century.

In industry there is an old saying: "If it works, it is obsolete." We have been saying that the book and printing are obsolete for some years. Many people interpret this to mean that printing and the book are about to disappear. Obsolescence, in fact, means the exact opposite. It means that a service has become so pervasive that it permeates every area of a culture like the vernacular itself. Obsolescence, in short, ensures total acceptance and ever-wider use.

On the other hand, new speed applied to old forms results in strange alteration of use and function. Thus, when print was new, there were no writers for the printing press and nobody knew what sort of a form it really constituted or what sort of an audience it would call into being. It was not until the reading public had taken a definite and greatly enlarged form, different from anything known to previous ages, that authorship for the printing press began. Montaigne is one of the most notable and self-conscious of this new race of beings, and it is worth a momentary glance at what he considered to be his new role as a writer for the press.

Donald M. Frame (1965), in his splendid new *Biography of Montaigne*, provides ample materials and discussion of the unexpected results of printing on the psyche of society and author alike with the following excerpts from Montaigne's writings:

> If there are any persons, any good company, in country or city, in France or elsewhere, residing or traveling, who like my humors and whose humors I like, they have only to whistle in their palm and I will go furnish them with essays in flesh and bone. (op. cit., p. 130)

The sense of the *Essays* as a kind of bottle, or multitude of bottles, in the sea, is clear in the following call from the depths of loneliness:

> Besides this profit that I derive from writing about myself, I hope for this other advantage, that if my humors happen to please and suit some worthy man before I die, he will try to meet me. I give him a big advantage in ground covered; for all that long acquaintance and familiarity could have gained for him in several years, he can see in three days in this record, and *more* surely and exactly.

Amusing notion: many things that I would not want to tell anyone, I tell the public; and for my most secret knowledge and thoughts I send my most faithful friends to a bookseller's shop. (Frame, op. cit., 82)

The difficulty of selecting an audience from the innumerable available readers troubled Montaigne as it has many later writers:

Letter writing ... is a kind of work in which my friends think I have some ability. And I would have preferred to adopt this form to publish my sallies, if I had had someone to talk to. I needed what I once had, a certain relationship to lead me on, sustain me, and raise me up. ... I would have been more attentive and confident, with a strong friend to address, than I am now, when I consider the various tastes of a whole public. And if I am not mistaken, I would have been more successful. (op. cit., Frame, p. 83)

Next Montaigne was very conscious of the ways in which writing and print had affected his objectives and the way he thought about things.

Montaigne's remarks about his *Essays* are more frequent and candid now. In a "humorous and familiar style" and a rich but unformed language, he writes his book "for few men and for few years." He avoids reading as he writes for fear of its influence, and is glad to work "in a backward region" where no one helps or corrects him, since the book, even if weaker, is more his own, "I go out of my way," he says, "but rather by license than carelessness. My ideas follow one another, but sometimes it is from a distance, and look at each other, but with a sidelong glance." He adds but does not correct, for an author has no right to suppress what he has mortgaged to the public.

He studies himself more than any other subject; that is his metaphysics and his physics. "I would rather be an authority on myself than on Cicero. In the experience I have of myself, I find enough to make me wise, if I were a good scholar." Fortune has placed him too low to keep a record of his life by his actions; he keeps it by his thoughts. He makes no claim to learning: "I speak ignorance pompously and opulently, and speak knowledge meagerly and piteously." (op. cit., p. 253)

He summed it all up in a single phrase:

I owe a complete portrait of myself to the public. The wisdom of my lesson is wholly in truth, in freedom, in reality ... of which propriety and ceremony are daughters, but bastard daughters ...

Whoever would wean man of the folly of such a scrupulous verbal superstition would do the world no great harm. Our life is part folly, part wisdom. Whoever writes about it only reverently and according to *the rules* leaves out more than half of it. (op. cit., pp. 291–292)

The above words of Montaigne superbly delineate this program of self-analysis and self-expression created by the complementary interplay of the private and public sectors. This simultaneous creation of new private and public sectors was a result of the printing press. With the press came intense new stress on both private initiative and private interpretation. Also there came the creation of a vast new reading public, unthinkable in the days of the scribe and the handwritten book.

No less great are the current changes in expression and in the relation between author and public that result from the new electronic means of printing and publishing. With the multitude of new forms of photography and reprography, new diversities of utterance and self-outering have come into being. {And now with digital media, especially social media, today's youth like Montaigne feel they "owe a complete portrait of [themselves] to the public.} On the one hand, pictures supplant a great deal of verbal expression and, on the other hand, the verbal acquires an extraordinary new range of resonance and implication {which is even more the case in the digital age}.

In his celebrated definition of the "auditory imagination," T. S. Eliot (1933) indicates the sudden flip into a new linguistic dimension, a reversal from the dominance of the visual modes of experience and organization to the simultaneous and ecological awareness of the new resonant man of the electro-technical time:

> What I call the "auditory imagination" is the feeling for syllable and rhythm, penetrating far below the conscious levels of thought and feeling, invigorating every word; sinking to the most primitive and forgotten, returning to the origin and bringing something back, seeking the beginning and the end. It works through meanings, certainly, or not without meanings in the ordinary sense, and fuses the old and obliterated and the trite, the current, and the new and surprising, the most ancient and the most civilized mentality. Arnold's notion of "life" in his account of poetry does not perhaps go deep enough.

In terms of authorship this has already meant a return to the corporate participatory and mythic forms of expression heralded in *Finnegans Wake*. The mythic modes of experience resume their ascendency and the lofty private detachment and disinterestedness of the solitary speaker and thinker recede into the twilight zone of group awareness and involvement in acceptance and understanding of inclusive social processes. The *Wake* opens with words that are linked, as in a single sentence, to the last words on the last page:

Riverrun, past Eve and Adam's, from shore to shore to band of bay, brings us by a commodius vicus of recirculation back to Howth Castle and Environs.

With the Wake the world, as it were, ends, not just in a book, but in a sentence; but it is a sentence, which ebbs whichever way it flows.

The Effects of Communication Media on the Nature of the Library

Before literacy, human lore and learning were transmitted by the voice of the poet whose memory served as the repository and storehouse for the culture. The preliterate library was, therefore, the bard or storyteller who served as a "tribal encyclopedia" (Havelock, 1963). One of the principal effects of this form of information storage is that the material stored had to be in a form easily remembered. It is for this reason, Havelock explains, that prose did not develop until there was writing. Preliterate learning is always in the form of narrative poetry. The meter, rhyme, and plot of the narrative poetry serve as mnemonic devices.

The oral transmission of knowledge requires that learning is a corporate and social activity, whereas writing encourages private learning and, indeed, a private point of view. Students learned by sitting at the feet of their master.

The oral tradition also insured the conservation and preservation of material in a static and unchanging form. Change in oral traditions only seems to occur when they are written down. Writing encourages editing, which changes the material. Iona and Peter Opie (1959/2000) collected schoolchildren's playground sayings. They discovered that this material has been transmitted orally over the years from one group of youngsters to another and has remained unchanged over the years.

Another quality of the oral tradition is the immediacy of the transmitter and the audience. Nielsen claims that with writing, something new occurred:

> It is not only a purely technical matter, the inauguration of a different method of transmission, which clearly shows its departure from the usual one by the appearance of a series of different text variants, but an impersonal intermediary link has been introduced between the bearer of the tradition and the receiver. (1954, p. 34)

Perhaps the most obvious effect of the oral transmission is the very fact that the material is spoken, or sounded out. Material that is written to be read silently is much different than material that is to be read aloud. Oral material excites the auditory imagination. The preliterate library of the poet or the bard stored and transmitted the lore and learning of the society in a much more intimate manner than the library or the book.

PART II: UNDERSTANDING THE NEW GROUND OF THE LIBRARY

Introduction

In part I, we reviewed the historical development of writing, alphabet, literacy, and the library. The figure of the library has changed very little over the years. The ground in which the library operates has changed dramatically, however. In part II, we will examine how this change took place. This will provide us with a better understanding of the problems and challenges facing today's library.

In chapter 4 we examine the notion of the Laws of the Media (LOM), which will prove a useful tool in examining the effects of any of man's tools, artifacts, institutions, or rules. We then turn, in chapter 5, to an examination of the new ground of information services in which the old figure of the library now finds itself.

{Chapter 4 will be of interest to the reader on two accounts. The first and most obvious is that it sheds light on our subject, the library. The second point of interest is that it illustrates how McLuhan used the LOM to understand a subject under scrutiny, in this case the library. The idea of the LOM belongs to McLuhan and McLuhan alone and was first published in 1975. I played a secondary role in helping him to formulate the LOM that pertain to the library circa 1977–1979.

Chapter 4, titled "Library LOMs," is the original chapter McLuhan and I composed during the period from 1977 to 1979 with a couple of parenthetical remarks. Chapter 5, titled "Impact of Electricity and Modern Technology on the Library," will discuss the impact of the media described in chapter 4 on the library. Chapter 5 is largely the original chapter we wrote with a few parenthetical remarks. The one exception is that I inserted the statistics for media expenditures in the United States in 2014 immediately following our section on media expenditures in 1969.

A whole host of new media has now emerged since we wrote chapters 4 and 5. I will, for convenience sake, refer to these even newer media as post-McLuhan media. I have elected to write two new chapters: chapter 6, titled "LOM for the New Digital Technology," and chapter 7, titled "The Impact of Digital Technology on the Library." Many of the LOMs for the post-McLuhan media in chapter 6 are based on my book: Understanding New Media: Extending Marshall McLuhan (2010a).—RKL.}

· 4 ·

LAWS OF THE MEDIA (LOM)
AND THE LIBRARY

In order to understand the impact of technologies and media upon the library, we shall review the notion of McLuhan's (1975, p. 74) Laws of the Media (LOM) and then apply them. Media, like the human unconscious, are inaccessible to direct examination since their effects are subliminal. The LOM help identify the properties and actions exerted upon us by our own artifacts. These include our language, our ideas, our laws, our tools, our clothes, our media, our technology—in short, all extensions of our physical human body. The LOM provide a way of observing how new environments created by new technological services disturb an entire population's conventional order to perceive and coerce the development of new models and metaphors of perception.

The Laws of the Media in tetrad form are intended to reveal some of the subliminal and previously inaccessible aspects of technology. To the extent that these observations reveal the hidden effects of artifacts on our lives, they are endeavors of art, bridging between the worlds of biology and technology. Between the artifact and the personal or social response there is an interval of play as between the wheel and the axle. This interval constitutes the figure-ground gestalt of interaction and transformation. The users of any technology at once set up a play toward equilibrium.

Although LOM are called Laws of the Media only a few of them deal with communications media narrowly conceived. Instead, "media" is dealt with in terms of a larger entity of information and perception, which forms our thoughts, structures our experience, and determines our views of the world about us. It is this kind of information flow of media that is responsible for the postulations of a series of insights regarding the impact of certain technological developments. It is only within this information flow that we can arrive at a meaningful overview of the library and the role it is to play within its new information environment.

Every new artifact, or technology, enhances or amplifies some bodily function or activity of man. The knife intensifies the tearing capacity of the hand and teeth. Ideas increase our understanding and awareness of external phenomenon. Whether the artifact or innovation is an extension of the body or mind, it creates new vortices of energy, which exhibit unique patterns of development. Recognizing these patterns is essential to survival in our present world in which human artifacts are massively superimposed upon Nature, and LOM help us to discover these patterns. The LOM pattern applies equally to both hardware and software, since human laws and conventions have the same pattern of social effects as physical tools or technologies. The information environment effects the operation of any figure as much as the physical environment.

The Laws of the Media began with Karl Popper's (1959) suggestion that a scientific hypothesis is one that is capable of falsification, by reducing the "grammars" of the media and technology to four basic aspects:

1. What does it enhance?
2. What does it obsolesce?
3. What does it retrieve that had been obsolesced earlier?
4. What does it flip into when pushed to the limits of its potential?

When these aspects were considered with regard to more than 100 media and technologies, there came a surprising discovery, namely that all the extensions of man, verbal or nonverbal, hardware or software, are essentially metaphoric in structure and that they are in the plenary sense linguistic. Man's outerings are literally "utterings":

Among the Bambara and the Dogon, the gift of weaving is closely associated with that of speech. Soy, the Dogon word for cloth, means "It is the spoken word" (Griaule 1948, 30). Weaving, along with speech, was a gift from the Creator to help man. ... Among the Bambara, weaving, like the other skills, is referred to as "the words of Faro" (Dieterlen 1951, 53). The process of spinning was first revealed to man by the spirit of the crossroads where man would leave his hoe in homage to the god. (Fraser, 1974, p. 88)

The exploration of the Laws of the Media is directly concerned with the grammar and syntax of man's utterings or outerings. The pattern of development of any new artifact or innovation, which we refer to as an LOM, displays the structure of a tetrad, as follows:

1. The innovation enhances some aspect of a situation. This is as true of a law of physics as it is for a bulldozer or a zipper or any human institution such as a school or the library.
2. The innovation obsolesces, pushes aside, or displaces some other activity or artifact.
3. The enhancement of the new activity and the obsolescence of the old activity together affect a recurrence or recall or retrieval of some past action or form that had been displaced or discarded earlier.
4. Finally, the new artifact, when pushed all the way, developed to the limits of its potential, reverses its characteristic manifestations and flips into its opposite. It creates an effect opposite to its original intention.

Apropos of the power of an artifact to amplify or enhance an aspect of a situation we might consider the way in which money speeds transaction or the clock intensifies the sense of time by fragmentation. The second phase of obsolescence or displacement is manifested in the way in which the wheel displaced the foot, the way clothing obsolesces skin, or the manner in which money pushed aside barter.

The third phase by which any artifact restores to currency a kind of action, which had been earlier retired from the scene, is illustrated by any of the forms of "camp" now flourishing. However, most "camp" is not noticed. Snapshots retrieve the past (memory theater); the written word retrieves armed men by action at a distance (the Battle of New Orleans); the mirror retrieves self-idolatry (Narcissus); clothing retrieves corporate mask or fashion in archaic forms.

Any technology pushed far enough eventually creates the opposite effect intended. It flips into its reverse. This fourth phase of reversal is illustrated by "money," which speeds up transactions so that it reverses into credit. Another interesting flip is that of radio, which enhanced access to the entire planet and that, when pushed far enough, flipped into the "global village." Radio, by putting us in touch with the rest of the world, did not ultimately create sophistication and cosmopolitan attitudes. By bringing the sufferings of others across the planet into our living rooms, it created a village mentality but on a global scale.

The fact that all technology presents a basic four-part structure indicates the possibility of an analogical structure resembling language itself. In the *De Anima*, Aristotle says: "It follows that the soul is analogous to the hand; for as the hand is a tool of tools, so the mind is the form of forms and sense the form of sensible things." A four-part analogy is a figure-ground form, like metaphor. There is a ratio between A and B and C and D when we say that A is to B as C is to D. Aristotle is asserting that "the soul is in a way all existing things." By the same token, all technological developments appear to possess these four-part structures of figure-ground, and to that extent may be emanations of the mind itself. The tetrad seems to indicate a relation between the objects of human manufacture and the subjective grounds of intelligence. The tetrad serves as a metaphor. Every metaphor consists of two figures and two grounds. The tetrad of any LOM consists of two figure-ground relations, A to B and C to D.

The LOM are called laws because they represent, as do scientific laws, an ordering of thought and experience that has not yet been disproved. They are laws of the media because the channels and impacts of today's electronic communication systems provide the informational foundation upon which we order, or structure, these experiential perceptions.

In formulating these laws the scientific method has to be used. The laws have been formulated by proceeding by induction, even though in the process of induction one discovers many things that could not be merely inducted. The Laws of the Media have been shaped by studying the effects of media, so there is always a hidden ground upon which these effects stand, and against which they bounce. In other words, the law of a medium is a figure interplaying with a ground. As with a wheel and an axle, there must be an interval between the two in order for the play to exist.

In examining the LOM the reader is invited to play with the ideas, prove or disprove them as they wish, but most important to use them as probes to explore unfamiliar territories and new relationships.

We shall examine in the remainder of this chapter those Laws of the Media that pertain to the library in order to develop a deeper insight into this institution and the various technologies and medias associated with it, such as the spoken, written, and printed word, paper, books, the press, periodicals, electric media, computers, reprography, classification, and catalogs, among others. {*This will also include in chapter 6 the new digital media, which also impact the library.*}

The LOM will be presented in the tetrad format of (1) enhancement, (2) obsolescent, (3) retrieval, and (4) reversal.

Library Laws of the Media

The Spoken Word

1. Enhances uttering of self via a vortex of energy, utterance of thought
2. Obsolesces integral gesture: "I gotta use words when I talk to you."— T. S. Eliot
3. Retrieves perception and experiences via replay—shaping and sharing the world
4. Reverses into cliché—solidifying meanings via recycling

The spoken word is not naturally associated with the library. In fact, for many the library is regarded as a domain in which the nonspoken word dominates reinforced by signs demanding silence. In fact, given today's social alienation and lack of holistic images the retrieval by the spoken word of "shaping and sharing the world" is much needed. The library, therefore, can serve a more useful social role if it can integrate the spoken and written words through programs such as oral readings and storytelling. {*In fact, in today's library there is much more orality and silence is no longer golden. Patrons are now allowed and even encouraged to interact verbally and to collaborate.*}

Myth

1. Enhances narration of new processes
2. Obsolesces old ground
3. Retrieves primal force—collective awareness
4. Flips into cliché, for example, Cadmus

Written Word

1. Amplifies private authorship, the ego
2. Obsolesces vulgar slang, dialects, separates composition and performance
3. Retrieves elitism
4. Reversal comes with the corporate reading public and historical sense

It is precisely the flip of the written word into a historical sense that created the need for the library and the preservation of the culture.

Alphabet

1. Enhances visual faculty, separation, abstraction, logic, scientific thinking
2. Obsolesces the oral and the tribal
3. Retrieves pretribal individualism—"each man for himself"
4. Reverses into electric media; scientific

The alphabet creates the seeds of its own destruction, the electric media, but the library can play an important role in the preservation of the literary-scientific culture that the alphabet made possible.

Paper

1. Enhances spatial range, scope; portability
2. Obsolesces stone, parchment; temple bureaucracy
3. Retrieves general, tribal republicanism
4. Reverses into imperialism, emperor worship

Scroll, manuscript book, and printed book form a set of cascading LOM in which one media flips into another and is thereby obsolesced.

Scroll

1. Enhances storage and usage
2. Obsolesces writing on stone
3. Retrieves oral recitation—carrel
4. Flips into commentators—book—codex

Manuscript Book

1. Enhances community of learning—market for books
2. Obsolesces the scroll
3. Retrieves haggle-barter
4. Flips into the printed book

Printed Book

1. Enhances availability, uniformity, repetition, nationalism
2. Obsolesces the manuscript book, spoken word
3. Retrieves Caesarism by uniform pricing
4. Flips into reading public and extreme individualism

Printing Press

1. Enhances linearity—uniform meanings and printing
2. Obsolesces the handwritten, scribe, individual meaning
3. Retrieves gestalt of one page from many letters à la wine from grapes with the winepress.
4. Flips into reputation and fame

The printing press was the beginning of mass media.

Mass Media

1. Amplifies planet to a single theater
2. Obsolesces private identity and bodily presence
3. Retrieves the occult
4. Reversal of hardware into software: everything is everywhere at once

Press

1. Amplifies today via dateline (Dan Boorstin: "All news is pseudo-event.")
2. Obsolesces yesterday (Communal awareness versus point of view)
3. Retrieves "coverage"—news as corporate clothing for naked egos, for the entire community—"He made the news."
4. Reverses into: "soft news" advertising; garment of abundances; good news

Periodicals

1. Enhances regular coverage and expectation
2. Obsolesces daily banality
3. Retrieves intellectual community
4. Flips into epitomes and abstracts

Electric Media (in general)

1. Amplifies information range, scope, and so forth into status of service environment via the simultaneity of the "speed of light"
2. Obsolesces the visual, connected, discrete, logical, rational
3. Retrieves the subliminal-audiles-tactile-dialog
4. Reversal mode: hardware becomes software; the sender is sent as discarnate information, that is, etherealization

As hardware becomes software the library must come to grips with its investment in hardware, to wit its books. Electric {and digital} media do not mean the end of books but it certainly totally transforms them. The book with electric media can never play the same role it did originally and neither can the library. Each of the following nine media has forever transformed the library for better or worse into a new institution. In chapter 5 we shall examine this transformation.

1. Telephone

1. Amplifies instant access to users: person-to-person
2. Obsolesces privacy by universal cable access
3. Retrieves dialog
4. Reversal: the sender is sent

2. Radio

1. Enhances access to entire planet—everybody, everywhere
2. Obsolesces wires and connections and physical bodies
3. Retrieves tribal ecological environment: trauma, paranoia
4. Reverses into Global Village Theater (Orson Welles' *Invasion from Mars*)

3. TV

1. Amplification of multi-sensuous, using the eye as hand and ear
2. Obsolesces radio, movie, and point of view
3. Retrieves occult—eye as ear
4. Flips into an inner trip; exchange of inner and outer

4. Cassette TV

1. Amplifies program scope
2. Obsolesces the centralized hardware broadcasting
3. Retrieves outer world via processes
4. World goes into role—spectator is actor-producer

5. Instant Replay

1. Enhances awareness of cognitive processes
2. Obsolesces the representational and chronological
3. Retrieves "meaning"
4. Reverses from individual experience to corporate pattern recognition; tradition

6. Phonograph

1. Enhances space-time scope—transcultural
2. Obsolesces amateur performer
3. Retrieves sounds of the past
4. Flips into Muzak (environment)

7. Audiotape

1. Enhances and captures immediate situation
2. Obsolesces stenographer and memorization
3. Retrieves living history
4. Becomes (flips into) time bomb

8. Slides

1. Extends range of perception and users by translucency and sequence
2. Obsolesces the static opaque image of cards
3. Retrieves dreamlike awareness
4. Flips into flick sequence and hence movies

9. Movies

1. Enhances exaggeration of gesture
2. Obsolesces the static world
3. Retrieves mime—mythic
4. Flips into dream fantasy—icon—movie stars

Library LOM

Each artifact has been represented by a single LOM. For the library we shall consider two LOM. The library can be thought of as enhancing storage retrieval and access to information, which is what it does, and it can also be thought of as preserving a culture, which is what it achieves. The first leads to a library that

1. Enhances storage, access, and retrieval of books and other information
2. Obsolesces private possession of books
3. Retrieves the medieval university: "The true university is a collection of books."—Carlyle
4. Flips into information overload

Concomitantly the library also

1. Enhances preservation of culture
2. Obsolesces memory
3. Retrieves the past
4. Flips into the oral tradition (telling stories to children, puppet shows, multimedia)

Each LOM has a lesson for the library, which we shall follow up on later. Let us first scrutinize the various technologies of the library under the lens of LOM.

Classification

1. Enhances access to properties
2. Obsolesces mythic description
3. Retrieves magical metamorphosis
4. Flips into pattern recognition

Card Catalog

1. Enhances access to books, data
2. Obsolesces notebook and memory
3. Retrieves the "hunter," the sleuth
4. Flips into excess-information overload—computer

Computer

1. Amplifies speed of calculations and retrieval
2. Obsolesces sequence, approximation, perception, the present
3. Retrieves perfect memory—total and exact projections
4. Reverses into anarchy via the overlay of bureaucracy—loss of human scale

Computer Journal

1. Amplifies speed of individual composition
2. Obsolesces periodicals—helter skelter notes
3. Retrieves dialog
4. Flips into group—awareness and composition

Xerox

1. Amplifies the speed of the printing process, availability
2. Obsolesces the assembly-line book, copyright
3. Retrieves the oral tradition (committees and council meetings)
4. Reversal mode: everybody becomes a publisher, information overload

Microfilm-Microform

1. Amplifies access
2. Obsolesces book horde, stacks
3. Retrieves manuscript involvement with text—rare books
4. Flip into nonportability of hardware

· 5 ·

THE IMPACT OF ELECTRICITY
AND MODERN TECHNOLOGY
ON THE LIBRARY

In order to understand the changes that the library is presently undergoing and has undergone, it is necessary to appraise the changing information environment in which the library functions. The figure of the library has not changed radically from the way in which it was first organized, but the ground in which it operates has completely changed from a print-dominated eye world to the acoustic simultaneous world of instantaneous electronic {*and digital*} information. We cannot hope to understand the library unless we understand this changed environment of service. A figure isolated from its ground is meaningless. The library has, to a certain degree, lost its sense of purpose, direction, and identity precisely because it has lost touch with its ground, the hidden effects of media. It should come as no surprise that librarians who live in an alphabet-dominated world of print are not always aware of the impact of other media. One of the major effects of the alphabet is that the powers of abstraction and analysis that this technology engenders and encourages, blinds its users to the world of effects of artifacts in general. The Greeks seldom considered the impact of their own technology on themselves or their environment. This limitation in Greek perception has been passed along to those who have worked within the Western tradition of rational abstract thought. {*Although librarians are more aware of the impact of electronic and digital media, the point we raised in 1979 still has validity for today's librarians.}*

The importance of understanding the effects of media and technology increases with time as the number of technological innovations continues to proliferate. At the time the library was first organized information was either communicated orally or by the written word. It is vital to understand the effects of these media as discussed in part I. Since the founding of the first libraries, however, a large number of electric {*and digital*} media have surfaced and have had a major impact on both society and the library. These new media include the telegraph, telephone, electric lights, photography, slides, movies, radio, the phonograph, the tape recorder, television, CATV, videotape, computers, microphotography, holography, fiber optics, dial access retrieval, photocopying, and facsimile transmission {*and, of course, all of the new digital media including the Internet, the Web, social media, Wikipedia, and the Cloud to mention a few, which we will treat in chapters 6 and 7*}. Each of these media has completely transformed and retransformed the library and its operations. The effects of these media on the library are in some cases direct—as with photography, computers, photocopiers, and microforms. In other cases the effects are indirect or side effects. The major impact of radio and television on the library has not been the audio and videotape collections that have appeared in certain libraries, but rather the competition they offer the library as far as providing information and entertainment to mass audiences. Mass media {*and especially digital media*} have all but obsolesced many functions of the library. To remain viable the library has had to search for new ways to be useful in a market glutted with cheap and easily accessible sources of information.

But the library has more than a responsibility to preserve itself and the tradition of the book. Our society is undergoing a major transformation as a result of the impact of electric mass {*and digital*} communication. It is possible that the entire intellectual heritage of Western civilization can be destroyed by our new communication modes, as might befall the Chinese written heritage should they introduce our alphabet. But can the same be said for mass communication? Certainly the record of mass media such as the press, the movies, radio, and television is, on the whole, rather depressing. The question that we must ask ourselves, however, is: Do the media tend to push out literacy and the intellectual activity upon which our culture is based? Or is the effect of the mass media only to provide a form of entertainment for the masses who would not participate in the intellectual development of their culture anyway? One might also ask, do these media in fact create a culture superior to the past and more suited to our present condition of material well-being? These are questions that require careful study by media ecology by librarians, educators, communicators, and all those concerned with the preservation of our cultural heritage.

We cannot assume that technological or material progress necessarily implies cultural progress. History is filled with stories of cultures that were destroyed by their success. Librarians must discover the effects of each of the information formats being offered to their patrons. Each medium has its own patterns for organizing ideas and experiences. The user is usually unaware of these effects. The syntax or grammar of any particular medium is infectious and can color the thought processes of its users. In chapter 2, we examined how this process operated with the use of the phonetic alphabet. Although the alphabet has been with us for about 2,500 years it is only recently that we became aware of its effects. To understand the effects of the new electric {and digital} media may not be as easy if only because of the great variety of media used to transmit information. It will be difficult to separate the effects of radio from television or the audiocassette from the photocopied journal article or {the PDF acquired on the Internet from the print version of the same material}. The mix of media is so rich that isolating an individual medium will be almost impossible. Yet librarians must make this effort if they wish to provide guidance for their clientele. What other way can a rationale be developed for choosing one format over another?

Librarians should also consider the significantly increased flow of information that these new electric technologies make possible and the way in which they enhance certain forms of communication and discourage others. In the last chapter we discovered through the Laws of the Media that when any technology or service is pushed far enough it flips into its opposite. Media of mass communication enhance the flow of information, but if pushed far enough it is possible that their effect can flip so that they contribute to the stagnation of information. As the volume of information increases, our capacity for absorbing it is overwhelmed. We suffer from information overload, a breakdown in communication. Another danger with mass media is that in trying to reach everyone, the level of communication becomes banal, and culture is weakened. {This is less of a problem today as the Internet caters to individual tastes and needs.} In calling attention to these possible dangers we are not necessarily condemning mass media, but we are suggesting that unless we study the effects of these media forces, these will create unintended results.

Let us not forget that we completely underestimated the effects of the automobile. We thought it would merely enhance lineal access. What we got was environmental congestion. The traffic jams and urban sprawl resulting from mass production of the automobile has all but cancelled the originally intended increase in mobility.

Henry Ford predicated that the mass production of his low-cost Model T would permit Americans to get out into the countryside. What he had not counted on was the destruction of the countryside as a result of the automobile. We must learn from this experience and ask ourselves, is it possible that mass communication can destroy communication itself? This is not a trivial concern in an era in which 90% of the messages received by a young person are being simultaneously directed to others. {*This number is considerably less with digital media, which is one of its advantages.*} If one of the prime aspects of communication is interaction, what will be the result of the overwhelming passivity of today's mass audiences? {*This problem that we identified in the late 1970s has abated somewhat because of the interactivity of digital media, but mass communication through radio, TV, movies, and certain aspects of digital media still persists.*}

In order to develop a quantitative notion of the magnitude of this competition of mass media with the book let us examine the following figures on media expenditures in the United States in 1969:

> According to the latest (1969) figures for the publishing industry, sales for adult and juvenile trade books, hardback and paperback came to $380 million. If you want to add to it sales of wholesale paperbacks and sales through book clubs, you come out with $773 million. If you add university press books, you can reach $880 million. How does this compare with the figures for a few other media? Commercial movie sales in 1969 came to 1.1 billion; newspaper advertising expenditures reached $5.85 billion; magazines of all kinds got $1.375 billion in advertising that year. (Geller, 1971, pp. 2048–2053)

{*We can compare the 1969 statistics with those in 2013 (however, we need to take into account that $1 in 1969 is equivalent to $6.47 in 2013 so that to compare 1969 sales to those in 2013 multiply the 1969 figures by 6.47):*

"The US book publishing industry generated $27.01 billion in net revenue in 2013, selling 2.59 billion units, according to a new report from the Association of American Publishers and BISG" (Dilworth, 2014).

Digital movie purchases surged 47% last year to $1.19 billion, according to data released by Digital Entertainment Group, an industry trade group. It was the *fastest-growing category as total home-entertainment revenue inched up 0.7% to $18.22 billion (Fritz, 2014). The total movie box office receipts totaled $10.9 billion (McClintock, 2014).*

Newspaper advertising revenues are $22.3 billion, down from a high of $49 billion in 2006 (Edmonds, Guskin, Mitchell, & Jurkowitz, 2013).

Magazine advertising reached $15.1 billion according to the Web site Statista.

And here is a figure that was zero in 1969: "2013 Internet Ad Revenues Soar to $42.8 Billion, Hitting Landmark High & Surpassing Broadcast Television for the First Time—Marks a 17% Rise Over Record-Setting Revenues in 2012."—RKL}

We wish to refer to the view of Evelyn Geller, former editor of *School Library Journal*, apropos the 1969 figures she reported:

> So, if we (the library) limit our function to serving as institutional outlets for the commercial trade book publisher, we have ignored media of overwhelming importance, in the face of which the publishing industry really shrivels. It is not a question of deferring to these media, but of recognizing, and perhaps countervailing their impact. (1971)

To debate the virtues of print versus the other media for the library is fruitless. We must accept the fact that the book is no longer the major mode of communication in our society {*and that is still the case today as much as it was in 1969, but the relative importance of the book has not changed nor is there any reason to believe it will in the future*}. The book will certainly survive, but its role has changed {*both with the arrival of electric mass media and more recently with digital media*}. The library, because of its special historic role, has an important job to perform in presenting the book, but it can best perform this function by integrating its book services with its function in the other media. In order to achieve this goal, librarians can come to grips with the new challenges facing them by understanding how the competing nonprint, nonbook media act, how they differ from the book, and what is the nature of their effects upon their users. This analysis cannot be confined to individual media. The whole notion of the library must be rethought and redefined in view of the pervasiveness of electric {*and digital*} communication and the altogether new patterns of thought and perception that they promote.

The alphabet creates linear patterns of thought, whereas with electricity and the ensuing speedup and simultaneity of information, pattern recognition emerges {*especially with digital media*}. These new patterns will affect the way in which the library is organized in the future {*and is being organized today*}.

The emergence of pattern awareness and ecological thinking backed by electric information will prove helpful in dealing with environmental problems. Another effect of electricity, however, not quite so manageable, is the fact that electronic information, and TV in particular, discourages reading and, hence, the development of other analytic skills. {*Although digital media encourage reading more so than electric mass media they do not favor deep reading and the reading of book-length texts.*} We are caught in a double bind. Too much print and we are unable to see the patterns crucial to our survival; if we allow our reading skills to deteriorate, we lose our capacity for analytic thought. Librarians and other educators will have to find a middle road, a synthesis, that permits these two crucial activities to coexist and thrive side by side.

The time for the confrontation between the "hard sell" advocates of the "New Media" and the die-hard defenders of the "Book" is over. Each medium has its unique advantages, which can be exploited for the particular education or communication functions to be achieved. The nature of the librarian's task has changed. Lester Asheim captures the spirit of this new librarianship by altering Ortega y Gasset's definition of the librarian as "the filter interposed between man and the torrent of books" by redefining the librarian as:

> "A filter interposed between the users of communication and the torrent of sources of communication content," but the idea remains the same: the librarian has a role to play in identifying the most effective means for the dissemination of different kinds of messages to serve different purposes for different audiences ... . When the book was, to all intents and purposes, the only format that carried intellectual content amenable to wide dissemination, the book was, indeed, the medium of communication, and the librarian was concerned quite literally with finding the right book for the right person at the right time. If the book was not the right medium for some person, then they could not be served by us. But today they can be, for we are able now to see libraries, not as book agencies only, but as agencies of communication: the standards need not be less strict, but the performance of our task can be broader and more varied. Depending on the nature of the needs of the user, and the ways in which the user wants to employ the content, we can provide it in the book form for one purpose, on film for another, on tape recording for a third. (Asheim, 1975, p. 1)

{*One can add to the list compiled by Asheim access to electronic journals that libraries now collect.*}

Not only will librarians have to decide between the book, microform, film, audio, and video formats but there will also be endless combinations of these media with computers, cable television, telephone lines, terminals, and online information services. The information ground of the library is shifting radically with each new technological breakthrough in communication. We are moving into the postindustrial age of instant information. Information traveling back and forth across the land at the speed of light has changed the entire pattern of communication and learning. The age of static information lying on dusty shelves in libraries is over. But the usefulness of the library is not over. New ways will be found for this old institution to fit into the new environment of instantaneous information.

It is not only the speedup of information that has created major changes but also the decentralization of information. Before the revolution of electric communication, information was warehoused or stored in a discrete number of locations, usually institutional libraries and archives. The only major stores of decentralized information during this period were to be found in the memories of individuals or in their private libraries. With the arrival of new media such as newspapers, phonograph records, movies, audio, and videotapes, the centralization of information in a few centers did not change. {*The Internet of course has taken decentralization to a whole new other level.*} The organization of the library that had been developed for books was merely applied to the new media. Phonograph records, tape cassettes, microfilm reproductions of newspapers, film strips, feature films, and the like were stored on shelves, cataloged and lent to users just had been the case with books. In fact, the model of the circulating library was even extended to objects other than information packages. Tools and children's toys have been circulated to users as an extension of the services of the public library.

With the arrival of the computer {*particularly the personal computer and the Internet*} and photocopiers and their integration into the library, the model of the library as a mere acquirer, organizer, and lender of information began to change. The library suddenly found itself able to create new modes to information by using the elements of its collection as resource material to be duplicated and reassembled into new combinations. The repackaging of information goes beyond the organization of immutable packages; it involves creation of new information sources, in the same way that a collection of oral addresses published in book form is a new information package. However, to provide a user with a custom-made list of bibliographic references using online computer facilities, or to assemble a collection of photocopied journal articles on a particular topic requested by the user, is to enter into a new area of activity. It is to engage in the manufacture of new information artifacts.

These types of activities change the role of the library from that of a passive distributor of the information artifacts of others to that of the manufacturer of information on par with a publisher, a filmmaker, or a broadcaster.

While the library is not the primary source of the information that goes into the information packages that it creates, it is still operating on the same level as the other manufacturers of information packages. The publisher, for example, does not create the information in his books, he merely publicizes the thoughts of his authors, using the technology of the printing press. And the authors themselves are not the originators of all the ideas that go into their writing. They assemble ideas from other writers as well as from their own experiences and put these down in a form that readers will find useful.

There is nothing new under the sun.—Ecclesiastes 1:9

There has been reluctance among librarians to enter into the activity of creating new information packages. C. Walter Stone attributes this both to a limited public and also to the professional perception of the library's role, in addition to the inadequacies of the education program for librarians:

> One obstacle to be overcome in bringing more traditional library programs up to date has been their professed philosophy of giving "service on demand." Accepting this philosophy the public often views libraries mainly as separate places, which have but limited responsibilities for acquiring, storing and distributing various types of published information and records. Thus a majority of North American public, academic research and special libraries are envisioned by their constituencies as more or less passive repositories and distributors of knowledge "packages." The recruitment and training of librarians (an information specialist) whose job is conceived as involving primarily acquisition and storage for local distribution of "packages" of pre-recorded information is "grossly inadequate indeed dangerous, in our time." All too often professional education of "library" service personnel still consists chiefly of introducing ways in which knowledge package (e.g. books) may be ordered, described (in cataloguing), arranged on shelves, loaned, shipped and returned, reduced in size and or transferred from one point to another. (Stone, 1975)

Stone is calling for a more dynamic, interactive institution, able to integrate into a large system and at the same time be in better touch with its constituency to determine its information needs and anticipate them. Basically Stone is calling for a reorganization of the library along postindustrial or cybernetic lines. Most libraries still follow the patterns of industrial-age organization in which mass-produced immutable information artifacts are distributed or transported along a linear path that links the author, the publisher, the bookseller or library, and the user. There is little or no feedback along this information-flow path. {*This pattern is changing as we will discover in chapter 13.*}

Tony Schwartz, in "The Responsive Chord," explores how electronic communication differs from the traditional concept of information transportation. The transportation theory involves a sender, a message and a receiver. The sender, or author/publisher, transmits the message, or book, to the receiver, librarian/patron. In this equation, all communications information is contained in the message. A transportation theory of communication is useful only when the movement of information is a central problem. But, when someone is overloaded with information, as we are of late, the transportation theory ceases to be meaningful. What we are really dealing with is information flow, a much more complex process than the mere transportation of messages. (Boyle, 1976)

The transportation theory of messages corresponds to the industrial age image of communication in which goods are carried from the manufacturer to the consumer. What is required is a cybernetic image of information flow in which the possibility of feedback (identification of needs not being presently met) and feed forward (anticipation of future needs) can be built into a model of library and information services. It is ironic that other institutions, not necessarily those involved in information but rather in business and manufacturing, have been able to apply the techniques of modern communication and to reorganize many of their activities along cybernetic principles more readily than the library.

Economic realities, as well as the increased pressure to provide access to the ever-expanding stores of information, will force these new cybernetic techniques upon the library. The industrial age organization of the library is breaking down under the sheer weight of all the information it must handle. Technological fixes for the problem of information overload, such as utilization of computers and the microform formats, will certainly alleviate this condition to some extent but they cannot by themselves cope with the overall problem. {In fact, the very tools to deal with information overload have facilitated the creation of even more information. Each new medium or technology has added to the overall store of information as they have come online. Consider how each of the following media have increased the flow and store of information: the personal computer, the Internet, the Web, email, the various forms of social media, and most recently the Cloud.} Anticipating users' needs, assembling tailor-made information packages, and the like will play an important role in resolving these difficulties. It is not just the new technologies and the services they make possible that will solve the problem of information overload, but also the new ways of organizing the services of the library that these new tools suggest metaphorically. If it is to fulfill its objectives, the library of the cybernetic age will have to do more than just use cybernetic equipment such as the computer;

it will also have to function cybernetically at the organic level. {*Again this is beginning to happen.*}

The processing of information before passing it on to the user is one of the recent trends to decentralize information dissemination. Another factor contributing to this process of decentralization will be the increased and improved communication between libraries. Through cooperation libraries will be able to offer their patrons a range of information that goes far beyond their own particular collection. With some 100 million titles extant in the book format and countless other titles in a myriad of formats, it is impossible for any library, even the largest, to house a significant proportion of the world's "literature." With telecommunications, microforms, photo reproduction, and computers linked together in a network, it should be possible some time in the future for users to access the entire world of literature from their own local library. With the continuing breakthroughs in telecommunications, particularly two-way cable television, it might even be possible in the future to access a large portion of the world's literature from one's own home, school, or office. {*With the Internet some of these developments that we foreshadowed have come to pass, particularly with Project Gutenberg, the efforts of Google to scan the world's libraries, plus the countless activities of librarians and archivists who have scanned so many print-based forms of information.*}

The possibilities are endless. Such developments will drastically alter the nature of the library, but they do not necessarily have to obsolesce elements of the classical library that provide the means of studying the library's physical collection of books and journals. No matter how sophisticated electronic retrieval of information becomes, there will always be those who find it both enjoyable and fruitful to browse through a collection of books and journals.

The form of physical information access, despite its random element or perhaps precisely because of its random element, is still one of the most efficient modes for encountering new ideas, new material, and for making new associations. As we design our information systems for the future we must always remember to build in the opportunity for informal browsing. Neither the electric typewriter nor the computer-composed printing press obsolesced the pencil. Likewise, computers and telecommunication will not obsolesce browsing, unless we allow it.

The car did not obsolesce walking but it certainly made it difficult for the pedestrian, particularly in urban environments. It is only recently that we awoke to the realization that the car had taken over urban life. We are now taking corrective measures to reverse this trend by constructing pedestrian malls and bicycle paths. We have not thrown out the car, we have only made room for the pedestrian and the cyclist. It is not an either/or situation.

The same is true for the electronic versus the manual handling of information. Electronic information handling is in many ways superior to book-bound information handling and likewise the electronic storage of information. It is to be encouraged but not at the expense of the more mundane forms of information access. There is room for both the traditional and electronic forms of data handling. Each has its appropriate applications and, therefore, we should approach our study of the traditional and electronic modes of information not so much in the spirit of "either/or" as in the spirit of "both/and."

When choosing the best media format for information, we should bear in mind that some material is inherently better presented in one medium than another. The photographic reproduction of paintings, the film of a dancer performing, or a recording of a political speech are probably the best means of capturing the essence of these human activities. Sometimes the presentation of material in two formats can be both useful and enriching for comparison and contrast. The transcripts of a political speech along with a recording permit both the careful study of the content as well as understanding of the flavor or tone of the speech. Often when watching a play, one has the desire to read the script in order to savor a favorite passage or to study more deeply the ideas presented in the drama. This is why the "both/and" attitude rather than the "either/or" is essential to media selection.

The challenge facing libraries is to fully exploit the new technologies while at same time preserving the best of the past traditions of the library. Some librarians feel that their profession has shied away from the challenge of utilizing all the media available to them:

> A paradox exists in that while libraries are considered the "storehouse and keepers" of all the world's knowledge, they have not yet forged ahead in making effective use of media and technology. (Chisholm, 1975, p. 3)

Lester Asheim explains this reluctance in terms of habits and traditions, which, he claims, are bound to change with the next generation of librarians:

> Many of the older generation of librarians came to the newer media after we had been firmly attached to the book tradition, and that for many of us the newer media simply do not speak as rich a language. But some of us can understand intellectually, if not emotionally and in practice, that this may be a reflection of our own limitations and not necessarily those of the media themselves. We see a new generation of

library users coming up who are not so deeply wedded to the literary tradition, and understandably we wonder if we can communicate with them. But do not forget that today and tomorrow's librarians are part of this new generation too, sharing with them their highly developed skills in the many new languages that are represented by recordings, tapes, films and multimedia events. We have only to be hospitable to desirable change in library outlook and practice to have it come about; the agents of change are waiting in the wings for their cues. (Asheim, 1975)

{*As Asheim correctly predicted, the next generation of librarians are much more comfortable with electric and digital media, but naturally there still lingers a bias toward physical books, which is appropriate since libraries are the stewards and defenders of the printed book. If not them, then who?*}

Audio-Visual Materials

Margaret Chisholm (1975) finds librarian's resistance to audio-visual formats paradoxical. She argues that the use of audio-visual media and other technologies enhances the basic objectives of the library "to educate the public, to provide information, to provide recreation, to supplement school and college curriculum." Since each individual learns most effectively from different combinations of media, the library can be more effective if it can offer a variety of media. Audio-visual materials such as films permit a larger audience to be reached. They also permit a vaster range of learning experiences to be provided.

The effects of audio-visual materials are often significantly different from those of print material. The effect achieved is not always the one intended, a point made by the former president of Indonesia Sukarno who regarded Hollywood filmmakers

as political radicals and revolutionaries who have greatly hastened political change in the East. What the Orient saw in a Hollywood movie was a world in which all the ordinary people had cars and electric stoves and refrigerators. So the Oriental now regards himself as an ordinary person who has been deprived of the ordinary man's birthright. (McLuhan, 1964, p. 294)

Despite the objection of some bibliophiles, new media and technology are progressively making greater and greater inroads into the operation of the library. This should come as no surprise for, despite the librarians' love of books, other nonbook materials have always been part of the library. {*In fact, digital media are an integral part of today's library at all levels including public, school, and academic libraries.*} "Taking an overall view of libraries rather than a narrow view it is quite clear that they have always collected all media, no matter what type mankind chose to record" (Orr, 1977, p. 79).

The ancient Library at Alexandria, founded around 300 B.C., contained the greatest collection of written material for its time, with nearly half a million volumes. The library also contained a museum in which all types of artifacts and specimens were collected and in which basic scientific research took place. {*The great Library at Alexandria was there to support the Mouseion, where scientific research took place and artifacts and exotic animals were collected. Our modern term* museum *is derived from the name of the Mouseion.*} Even before electric media, modern libraries maintained collections of prints and illustrations. The development of photography greatly increased these collections. Most public libraries carry files of pictures and illustrations for the use of their "readers." Although picture files are definitely a nonprint medium, they do not create the same sort of anxiety as the audio-visual material of the electric genre.

The development of motion picture films, photographic slides, phonographic discs, audio, and videotapes has created a rich panoply of media for the storage of information. These media displaced the book as the sole container for information. The richness of available media creates problems and new challenges for the library:

> We must have, and as educators we must transmit, a far better knowledge than we presently have of the relationship of print, of sound, and of image. We must develop integrated systems that can fruitfully amalgamate all media, understanding the place and power of each within the context of all. (Taylor, 1973, p. 64)

Not only must the information-overloaded library cope with book glut, but it must also cope with media glut. In addition to all the printed editions of Shakespeare's *Hamlet*, the librarian must also consider a phonographic disc version, a film version, a video version, and a tape version. In fact, some libraries even have the facilities to produce the play itself. Such is the dilemma of richness facing today's librarian.

When deciding which media versions of *Hamlet* to choose, the librarian should keep in mind that the medium is the message. Each medium has its own particular message, and each has its own unique contribution to make. One cannot select the most suitable medium for the presentation of *Hamlet*, for instance, without examining the context of such a presentation. What is the nature of the audience? What is the aim of the presentation? Indeed, is there a particular aim? How much time is available? What facilities are available? And so on. Each situation has its own solution, and that solution might not be unique. It is, therefore, essential for the librarians who must decide which acquisition to make to consider carefully the nature of the audience they are planning for, as well as the objectives of the program. There are no absolutes in this area, no rules to follow. Each item requires a new decision. This discussion brings us back to Dean Shera's statement regarding book selection: "The greatest problem that confronts librarianship today is not that of acquisition or accumulation but of selection" (1971, p. 101). Shera also points out:

> Modern society is a duality of action and thought bound together by the communication system. The communication process is also a duality, a duality of system and message, of that which is transmitted as well as the manner, i.e., the medium and environment of its transmission. Therefore the librarian must see his role in communication process as being more than a link in a chain or the intersections in a network. The librarian must concern himself with the knowledge he communicates, its relevance to the individual users, its importance to society, and the environment in which the communication takes place. In short the librarian must know how not only to perform his role, but why the role is to be performed and the extent to which he can fill its demands—he must see librarianship clearly and see it whole. (1969)

Resistance to audio-visual materials has come from librarians like John Ciardi who have a romantic image of the library:

> A library is a quiet storage place and what is stored there is the memory of the human race. It is a place for the soft rustle of pages and the quiet stir of thoughts over the reading table. Ideally there should be a long, slanting fall of light from tall windows as the afternoon goes. If there can be a fluff of elms and maples at the window so much the better. (Ciardi, 1961, p. 24)

This stereotype of the library is breaking down as libraries attempt to integrate the full range of material available to them, as the following policy statement of the Brooklyn Public Library indicates:

> Books have always been and will continue to be a proper concern for the library, but ever greater amounts of information are now being contained in other forms. As research continues in the field of communication, and as the community changes and develops, the library must be a media center, acquiring appropriate materials, regardless of form, and integrating each into its total services. (Bass, 1969, p. 3024)

A-V materials are definitely an important part of most library systems. We have not yet had time to develop the wisdom necessary to fully exploit those new media. Nor have we learned when they can be useful and when they should be avoided. One of the other problems with audio-visual materials is their higher cost compared to more traditional print material. This might only be a function of our present technical capacity, but this is certainly a factor that must be carefully considered given the spiraling costs of education and the continuing revolt of the taxpayers. {*The problem of the higher cost of A-V material has been basically resolved with the Internet with its rich resources of free A-V material.*}

Another criticism that has been leveled at A-V aids is that by replacing the teacher they contribute to the dehumanization of the education system. The same argument can also be made for the book. The book could potentially have replaced the teacher, but this did not occur, particularly at the primary and secondary level. Some arguments can and will be made later in the book that perhaps the best university is a collection of books. The book actually can be looked upon as an aid that helps teachers reach greater numbers of students. A-V equipment can liberate teachers from mundane presentation of factual material so they can spend more time giving their students individual attention. {*A more modern formulation of this idea is that with the Internet and its rich resources the role of the teacher shifts from the deliverer of information to that of a guide or a coach that is captured with the couplet "not a sage on the stage but a guide on the side."*}

There exists a certain prejudice toward audio-visual media because they are usually used as a vehicle for entertainment rather than education, and because they are associated with mass media. {*I cannot resist inserting Marshall's famous one liner on this issue, namely: Anyone who tries to make a distinction between education and entertainment doesn't know the first thing about either.*} A-V material does not have to be used exclusively in the mass media mode, however:

> For those who need convincing, it is possible to identify four salient characteristics of non-print media, which are unique. Non-print materials have the capability of individualizing instruction. While they have most often been used for their mass communication qualities they can be easily adopted for one to one communication. Advances in technology—the audiocassette, the videocassette, and the sound/slide package—provide an individualized playback mode. (Le Clercq, 1975)

{*In fact, a notebook or a tablet linked to the Internet makes an ideal platform for the individual viewing of A-V material.*}

The capacity of nonprint media to function in "an individualized play-back mode" cannot be disputed but we must point out that this property is not unique as the above author claims. The book is also well suited too, for "individualizing instruction," a quality it shares with nonprint media. Advocates of A-V media sometime overstate their case in an attempt to compensate for many librarians' prejudicial attitude toward nonprint media. It is essential, however, to maintain a balanced view and understand the nature and effect of all media. This is one of the aims of this chapter. Let us therefore turn our attention to the effects of individual media and technologies and examine their impact on the library. For a survey of the general effects of a number of the media affecting libraries, the reader is referred to *Understanding Media* by McLuhan (1964) {*and* Understanding New Media: Extending Marshall McLuhan *by Logan (2010a)*} in which detailed examinations of a number of media are made.

As pointed out earlier, libraries have collected A-V materials since the time of the Alexandrian library. The need to supplement the written word with illustrations was recognized from the earliest times. Almost all of the books written before the invention of printing were elaborately illustrated, as Sheviak (1971) points out:

> A Moravian Bishop, John Amos Comenius, examining the educational concepts in the widening curiosity of the Renaissance wrote, "Boyhood is distracted for years with grammar, infinitely prolix, perplexed and obscure. Boys are stuffed with vocabularies without associating words with things or indeed with one another." And so in 1675, he created the "Obis pictus, The World of Sensible Things Drawn; That Is the Nomenclature of All Fundamental Things in the World and Action in Life Reduced to Ocular Demonstration." This has been called the first picture book for children. But wasn't Comenius trying to say something about the education of children beyond pictures in a book? (Sheviak, 1971)

In addition to their picture books, early libraries had collections of illustrations, including prints and drawings. During the nineteenth century, photographs were added to collections of illustrations maintained by libraries.

The first A-V materials to be collected in the twentieth century were phonograph records and motion picture films. Extensive specialized collections of phonograph recordings have been gathered together; the Library of Congress has some 200,000 recordings and the New York Public Library 135,000.

Smaller collections, integrated with the normal library collections of books, exist in almost all communities.

Collections of films are not quite as common as recordings but many public libraries do circulate motion pictures. The collections of the commercial film distributors may also be regarded as film libraries. Special archival collections of films like that of the Motion Picture Academy in Hollywood are also extant.

The A-V collections of libraries are no longer restricted to pictures, films, and recordings. Within the past twenty-five years there has been an explosion of new formats. Of particular interest to libraries has been the cassette or cartridge for audiotapes, videotapes, and filmstrips. These require little or no technical skill on the part of the user and they protect the material from all but wanton destruction. This has permitted a major expansion of A-V services within the library system. In the case of audiocassettes, this has included both the circulation of the cassettes and the cassette players (Egan, 1974). {Internet-based A-V also has the advantage of ease of use as well. As McLuhan once opined, in the electric age products become services. "They send you a package as a direct personal service. This is where we are heading under electronic information conditions. Products increasingly are becoming services" (McLuhan, McLuhan, & Staines, 2003, p. 99).}

Television

Understanding the effects of television is crucial because of the dominant role this medium plays in our information environment. The average child spends many more hours in front of the television set than he does in school learning the three Rs. Exposure to television begins long before the child is capable of literacy. Adults in North America probably spend on the average up to thirty hours a week in front of their television sets. No other medium is used as much or is so universally distributed. More homes have television than telephones. {With digital media there has been a reduction in TV watching but the amount of time spent with screen-based fare has remained more or less the same. A positive aspect of this is that a significant part of digital consumption involves reading, and users of digital media are not merely passive recipients of information but also creators of information.} Television has not heralded the end of reading or the library. It has changed the nature of the reading audience and affected its tastes and desires, but reading still thrives, as do libraries. The challenge of television is not that it will crowd out reading but that it will change the nature of reading.

The earliest studies made when television sets were first being purchased indicated that library use was by and large unaffected by this new medium. "We have found that the number of persons using the library was not reduced by the acquisition of television sets, but the number of books borrowed after set purchase was 20.7% less than the number of books borrowed before set purchase" (Johnson, 1954).

Johnson found that in 40% of the cases with new television set owners the use of the library decreased, but that in 37% of the cases the usage actually increased. In a report prepared at the University of Illinois in 1961 Edwin B. Parker gathered additional evidence to support the notion that electronic media reduced the level of reading but not to the extent of seriously taking people away from reading altogether.

Many investigators have concerned themselves with the effects of radio and television on the use of print media. Lazarsfeld (1940) studied the impact of radio on print media and concluded that "radio has not impaired the reading habits of the population." In a major study in England, Himmelweit, Oppenheim, and Vince (1958) found a slight, but not a significant, reduction in children's book reading as a result of television. A study by Belson (1959) in the United Kingdom, after applying elaborate statistical controls to correct for previously existing differences in reading habits of viewers and nonviewers, concludes that there has been a definite reduction in adult book reading resulting from the viewing of television.

Schramm, Lyle, and Parker's (1961) study of children and television in the United States and Canada demonstrated that television displaced radio and movies more than it displaced print media, and that the print media displacement was mostly comic books and pulp magazines (i.e., print read for fantasy facilitation rather than information-seeking motives). Books or more serious magazines were less affected. E. B. Parker (1961) showed that the relationship between children's use of radio and books had shifted since television became widely available, presumably because of a change in the function of radio after television. A study of the audiences for magazines, books, radio, and movies (conducted before television became widely available) found no correlations were found between all other media pairs. Studies since television have found either no correlation or a negative correlation between commercial television viewing and book reading. Viewers of educational television are much more

likely to be book readers (and to read more books) than nonviewers of education television.

One may therefore conclude that television does not necessarily turn off
readers or discourage library usage.

> Library circulation has continued on an upward path even during the introduction
> of paperback and television. Even though competition from other media resulted in
> lower utilization then would otherwise have been the case, demand for library ser-
> vices has been increasing steadily. (Parker, 1971)

If the quantity of reading is unaffected by television, the same cannot be
said of the quality of reading. The way in which youngsters who have been
constantly exposed to television read has changed. {*A similar claim can be made
for digital media, which favor the reading of shorter texts.*}

> Perhaps the most familiar and pathetic effect of the TV image is the posture of chil-
> dren in the early grades. Since TV children—regardless of eye condition—average
> about six and a half inches from the printed page. Our children are striving to carry
> over to the printed page the all-involving sensory mandate of the TV image. With
> perfect psycho-mimetic skill, they carry out the commands of the TV image. They
> pore, they probe, they slow down and involve themselves in depth … . Suddenly they
> are transformed to the hot print medium with its uniform patterns and fast lineal
> movement. Pointlessly they strive to read print in depth. They bring to print all their
> senses, and print rejects them. Print asks for the isolated and stripped down visual
> faculty, not for the unified sensorium. (McLuhan, 1964, p. 308)

Television has this unique capacity to destroy reading ability. It is, therefore, essential, if one wishes to preserve literacy, that children not be exposed
to too much television {*to which one can add touch screen tablets, which are the
new electronic babysitters in the same way parents use television to occupy their
children. A number of educators have counseled parents not to expose their children
to digital devices before they reach the age of five years.*} Motion pictures, because
of the higher resolution of their picture, do not have this effect, and so they
are more compatible with literacy. One might argue, however, "Why preserve
literacy? Why not convert totally to audio-visual media and allow print to die
its natural death?" Unfortunately, the death of print would probably lead to a
breakdown of our society. The sophisticated technology upon which we have
developed an almost total dependency would break down without literacy.
Alphabetic literacy, as we learned in chapter 2, creates the climate in which
sciences and technology thrives. The loss of literacy would mean the loss of

technology and, subsequently, the loss of civilization. Such is the paradoxical dynamic in which we find ourselves, a double bind. Technology creates the seeds of its own destruction through the creation of a medium like television, which discourages literacy skills.

It is for these reasons that librarians, as the storekeepers of our literary treasure, have a contribution to make in the preservation of our literary and scientific traditions. Paradoxically, television can be used as a way of enticing youngsters to read, through the use of videocassettes and cable television (CATV). Even mass-medium television broadcasting can have a positive effect on reading. The television show *Roots*, for example, has lead to a great deal of reading activity, not just of the book by Alex Haley upon which the show is based, but of other peripheral material dealing with the historic period.

Educational television can be used as another way to stimulate reading. One does not have to rely on the random broadcast of the material over the public broadcasting system such as PBS in the United States or TVO in Ontario, Canada. Instead one can use a special, new kind of library.

"Have You Watched a Book Today?"

Before the advent of electric technology the concept of a library without books would have been a very strange thought indeed. Such an idea is no longer strange. The Public Television Library is, in fact, precisely this kind of library. It serves as a national centralized storage and retrieval system for PTV programming distinct from the real time program offerings of the Public Broadcasting Service interconnected network and thereby permits the delayed distribution of this material to schools, libraries, government agencies and other civic organizations.

The Public Television Library conducted an experiment beginning in 1971 in co-operation with three local public libraries to determine if PTV program in a 3/4 inch videocassette format were suitable for use within the public library context. The result of their study indicates that this medium found a receptive audience both among normal users of the library and also the infrequent users. Over 70% of the occasional library users indicated that they sought out printed material on the subject after they had viewed the videocassette. (*"Have You Watched a Book Today?,"*1975)

In addition to videocassette players, there are a number of other systems that provide flexibility in bringing educational video packages to schools. One of these is the Instructional Television Fixed Service in which four educational video channels are broadcast directly to the schools of a given region consisting of about ten school districts (Ryan, 1971). A similar system can also be operated using cable television to feed the signals into the schools. A third system, Information Retrieval Television, involves the servicing of 130 classrooms of four schools by a central library of 2,500 films and videotapes. The classrooms are linked to the library using Bell Canada's Britannia Switching Center and a twelve-channel cable network. Requests for individual programs are telephoned to the library and transmitted at the requested time (Abbey, 1971). A fourth system involves accessing videotapes and audiotapes from remote locations by dialing signals through a telephone system hooked up to a computer and a transmitting facility. The number of possibilities is endless. In short, one can look increasingly toward a future in which audio- and videotaped material will be available either from centralized collections through remote transmission or directly from a cassette player. {At the time we wrote this section there were no DVDs, Blu-rays, and streaming that are so prevalent today.}

Systems combining videocassette material and printed matter are being produced. One such project involving one of the authors (Logan) is a television series and textbook on environment and health being prepared for the Ontario Education Communication Authority (i.e., TVO) by a transdisciplinary team of educators (Logan & White, 1981). Each member of the team works with a scriptwriter and a director to produce a half-hour program on a particular aspect of health and environment. Using this material they then write a chapter in the textbook that will accompany the television series. This arrangement permits the coordination of the video and printed material. Ways in which mixed media can be most fruitfully exploited have not yet been fully developed. Much research and observation of operational systems will be required before the maximum benefit can be derived from mixed media systems; however, the potential is great.

Community Access Television (CATV) has been slow to develop because of the enormous costs involved in setting up an extensive communication network; but its potentials are enormous.

> The revolutionary potential of interactive cable television makes it the herald of the next major communication innovation, on a par with printing and audiovisual telecommunication systems. The power of this innovation lies in its amalgamation of graphical technology, electromagnetic transport, and the electronic storage of graphic information. The importance of CATV in future planning is heightened by the fact that CATV produces a change in the habits of the people exposed to it. (Vagianos, 1976, p. 151)

Cable television or CATV permits librarians to provide their community with information about library services or by presenting story hours or book reviews to stimulate interest in reading. The library can provide other services for its community including educational programs on specific topics, educational programs for specific groups, lectures, talk shows, interviews, community events, chamber music, adult education, and meetings or conferences. While these latter activities do not relate directly to library functions, if they were provided they could help the library to better integrate its services into the activities of the community. It will also provide librarians with an experience in this medium, which holds great promise for the future, particularly with the advent of two-way interactive cable systems. {*The Internet is, in essence, the two-way cable system we spoke of thirty-five years ago. We had the functionality right but not the hardware and software needed for two-way communication.*} The day is not far away when cable systems will reach a level of sophistication whereby users will be able to request material from their homes and have it sent to them from the library, using tele-facsimile transmission facilities. These facilities already exist and can eventually be integrated into a two-way cable system. {*Instead of interactive cable television the same functionality can be achieved with the Internet where one can find many educational projects.*}

The only potential danger with cable television is that it will become so efficient that people will no longer feel a need to leave the comfort of their homes to learn about the world. Bernard Ostry, Canada's Deputy Minister of Communication, raises this issue:

> What's coming is a Canadian Electronic Highway Network. It's a highway that promises amazing opportunities in education and in one sense the ultimate in freedom. To sit alone in a room with a machine that offers instant access to the whole of the world's information is surely to experience a new dimension in freedom. For some, however, it may also bring a new dimension in alienation. If a little learning is a dangerous thing a bottomless well of information may prove just as dangerous. The solitary mind could drown in it. The global village, it turns out, is a lonely place. Though the mass media have hugely increased the flow of information many over-informed city people feel a cultural emptiness, a spiritual vacuum, a sense of being strangers in their own place. Will the electronic highway give such people a sense of community or will it simply turn them into tuned-in hooked-up hermits? What will the electronic highway do to the feeling of belonging we now derive from schools, offices, conferences, seminars and all the annual gatherings and excuses for domestic travel that the highway may soon appear to render useless? (*Toronto Globe and Mail*, 1978)

{*What is interesting in this comment of Ostry is his use of the metaphor of a highway, which is basically a one-way street for the flow of information from providers to users. What was not anticipated was Web 2.0 and the two-way flow of information between users of the information highway. The users are not only the content as McLuhan once observed but they are also the creators of content. The most successful Web applications like Facebook, YouTube, Wikipedia, Instagram, Flickr, and Twitter do not produce content, they just provide a platform for the publication of different forms of information. Yet some of Ostry's pre-Internet prognostications identify some of the dangers facing some users of today's Internet.—RKL*}

The concerns expressed by Ostry are certainly valid and should be taken into consideration when librarians and educators are planning their communications system. The dangers of the wired city expressed by Ostry could also have been applied with equal concern to the telephone when it was first installed. There was the danger that people would stay at home and not socialize since they could conduct much of their business and make a number of their social contacts using the telephone. The telephone on the whole has not led to an alienating situation where people remain at home all day. It has, in fact, more often than not been an aid in bringing people together. One would be seriously hampered socially in today's society without a telephone. The telephone, in fact, changed the patterns of our socialization. In a similar fashion cable television will probably change our patterns of information gathering, but it has just as great a chance of enhancing social contacts as discouraging them. As people become better informed they often find that the opportunity to share their knowledge and learning with others leads to increased enjoyment of their social contacts. {*The same observations hold for today's Internet.*}

Lilliputian Libraries: The Impact of Microform Technology and Its Potential Uses

The mainstay of any library is the book, which is still one of the best technological artifacts ever created for the storage and retrieval of information.

Microform versus the Book

{*Microforms no longer play the same role they once did in the library. I could have edited out this section but kept it for two reasons. One, I wanted to maintain the record of the original manuscript that McLuhan and I wrote since this is the first time it is being published. Second, I believe it is of historic interest to review the arguments for microforms because they apply with equal force to the digitization of text, which are today's microforms. Readers skimming or skipping this treatment of microforms will not lose the thread of the argument of the book.—RKL}*

> A book is portable, requires no special gadgets to read it with, provides room for marginal notations, is compact, is low-cost, provides high resolution, and can easily be copied and reproduced. Millions of books exist, and are in use. We have developed elaborate systems for handling books or information for them, and have refined and re-refined these systems over hundreds of years and with millions of man-hours of effort. On the other hand, ... (those that advocate microforms cite) difficulties with the book, claiming: 1) it is costly to manufacture, 2) it is bulky for storage or mailing, 3) it is clumsy, and 4) it is a poor device for retrieval. (Teplitz, 1970)

{These arguments for microforms can be and have been made for e-books and other forms of digital text like PDFs.}

It is clear that the time is past when the book can completely dominate as an instrument of information storage. There has been a steady growth of micrographics of all forms. The future of this medium seems bright. *{That future was considerably dimmed by the digital storage of text, especially with the advent of the Cloud.}*

> Microform will become the major medium for new information in reference and research libraries for five reasons:
> 1) Microform can provide humans readable as well as machine-readable records of information.
> 2) Microform allows optical document encoding for automatic retrieval and document handling by machines as an integral part of the recording process.
> 3) Microform, unlike paper documents, can be economically retrieved and handled by machines without human interaction.
> 4) Microform provides the basis for library integrity.
> 5) Microform provides a compact form of information storage. (Otten, 1971)

{Substitute digital text wherever Otten uses the term microform and his 1971 text seems as though it was written today.}

Otten believes in order for microforms to realize these possibilities that progress will have to be made in the following five areas: (1) human engineering of microform systems, (2) standardization, (3) user education, (4) systems planning, and (5) copyright and compensation. *{Otten's points are somewhat applicable to digital text.}*

Microforms are playing a major role in solving storage problems through the microfilming of newspapers and journals. Extensive collections of old newspapers and journals have been microfilmed. This not only increases the storage facilities of those libraries that stocked these serials, but it also makes these items available to many more libraries. Many contemporary newspapers and journals publish microform editions in addition to their hardcopy paper editions, thereby increasing the availability of their publications.

In addition to reducing storage facilities, microfilms have had two major effects on the library. First, they have made material available that a library would not ordinarily stock, and second, they have tended to decentralize the library. These trends will continue in the future. In addition to a greater range of newspapers and journals, microforms have also made rare books available to all libraries. Reprography can also be used to make rare books available, but microfilming is a much better procedure because it is easier to photograph than photocopy. One does not have to push a book flat against the reprography machine. As well as historic rare books, microforms make available out-of-print books, literary manuscripts, and the archival material of governments, institutions, political figures, artists, writers, and other public figures.

Microforms also play an important role in preserving old books that deteriorate with age. Having a collection of rare books on microfilm is a nice insurance policy against their loss due to theft, fire, or flood.

Microforms decentralize the library, since a library can be set up almost anywhere with a set of microfilms and a reader. The potential of the decentralized library will become even greater once the present techniques of laser photography are more developed. It will be possible to store entire world literature on four or five laser-read discs. {*Digital text has the same effects as those described for microforms and at a much lower cost.*}

Microforms have also contributed to the more efficient operation of the library through the use of microfilm catalogs. This catalog has several advantages. First of all it is possible to decentralize the catalog by having a number of cheap duplicate microform catalogs at different locations. This is extremely useful for a library system with a central library and a number of branches, as one finds on the campus of a university or a public library in a metropolitan center. One does not have to go from one branch of the central library only to discover the book one needs are at another branch. {*All of these advantages pertain to online catalogs with the addition that updating the catalog is much easier.*}

Xerox Makes Every Man a Publisher

Reprography has had, and will continue to have, far-reaching effects on the library. As with microform, reprography creates greater accessibility of written material. It too makes rare books and not so rare but out-of-print books available to all libraries. Reprography actually eliminates the category of out-of-print books by decentralizing publishing. It has also created an underground press by providing a relatively inexpensive and readily accessible means of reproduction.

Photocopying facilitates many different tasks in the library. A library system may easily service its remote branches by directly sending them photocopies of material requested by their users that they cannot afford to stock. Because it is easier to carry a Xerox copy of an article rather than the entire journal from which it comes, one is more likely to find a journal available on the shelf. There is also less theft and mutilation of journals, since an inexpensive copy of a desired article may be easily obtained through reprography.

Photocopying makes possible the production of custom-made books for a particular university course. For example, a professor sends a list of readings consisting of excerpts from books and/or journal articles. The library then photocopies these readings to create the custom-made book. Xerox not only enables every man to be a publisher but also an editor.

Reprography is used to simplify a number of library tasks, such as the maintenance of circulation records and the production of overdue notices. By circulating photocopied lists of journals and books to be discarded, libraries are able to exchange materials that might otherwise have been wasted.

Having looked at the many useful and positive aspects of photocopying and micro-forming, let us now consider some of their negative effects on users of the library, the readers, and on authors without whom there would be no library. Barbara Ringer claims that modern society is drowning in an ocean of too much information and that reprography and microforms only add to the problem:

> Wider access to information seems to result in people being less and less informed about more and more. Scholarship and research, once based on reading and note taking, now seems to consist of accumulating filing cabinets full of unread Xerographic copies. (Ringer, 1976)

Not only is the user damaged by this process, but so too is the author:

> Most librarians I know love books and their authors; they consider it their function in life to pass this love on to introduce authors and their works to readers. But by supplanting the publishers function without recognizing and affirmatively protecting the author's fundamental rights (call them copyright or what you will) libraries are destroying the very resource they exist to preserve and nurture. (Ringer, p. 230)

Existing copyright arrangements are totally inadequate in our present cybernetic age of information. Not only do new problems arise with Xerox and microforms but also with the computer, which can store bits of information from one author and combine them with bits from another. Since its existence the library itself has violated copyright by allowing more than one reader to use a book but so has the used bookseller or anyone who has lent a book. Alternatives to our present copyright arrangements are presently under consideration. One suggestion is to reimburse the author for each exposure of his work, whether it is a photocopy, a microform copy, use of a library copy, or purchase of the original book or journal. {*The problems with copyright only increase with digital media because of the ease with which material can be copied and distributed.*}

The Automatic Library

Of all the new technologies introduced into the library none has a greater potential for completely altering the library than the computer. Audio-visual aids provide nonprint alternatives for information, while microforms and reprography dramatically increase the availability of printed information. The computer, however, provides a nonprint alternative to information storage, as well as improving the accessing and retrieval of information because of its ability to convert information into electromagnetic signals that can be easily stored, retrieved, and transmitted. The hardware advances in the storage, retrieval, and transmission of information are increasing the potential usefulness of the computer. In addition to handling information for users, computers are useful for performing various housekeeping activities within the library.

Probably the first major breakthrough in the area of library automation was the development in 1967 by the Library of Congress of Machine-Readable Cataloguing (MARC), a standardized format for machine-readable bibliographic data. This development permitted for the first time a standardized format and marked the beginning of a new era in library automation. By 1975 libraries held at least four million machine-readable records, although the extent of overlap among databases could only be estimated (Martin, 1976, p. 164).

The existence of a common database in the same format encouraged cooperation between libraries:

> The MARC format and distribution service did in fact signal the beginning of a new era of accelerating developments in library automation, but the success of OCLC (the Ohio College Library Centre {now the Online College Library Centre}) and other on-line systems dramatically changed the direction of that development. Instead of each major library subscribing to and maintaining a file of MARC tapes and developing a local system for utilizing them as was initially predicted, it turned out that the emerging pattern is for libraries to utilize on-line terminal access systems and MARC data bases that are centrally maintained by networks or even commercial vendors ... Since it went on-line in 1971, the OCLC system has profoundly changed the nature and direction and quickened the pace of library automation in the U.S. OCLC has been the most significant development since the establishment of the MARC format and distribution service and has achieved a commanding and well deserved lead in the area of cooperative computer based library networks. (De Gennaro, 1976)

Another innovation as a result of the computer and the MARC format will be the likely phasing out, except for very small libraries, of the card catalog. The Library of Congress has announced the closing of its card catalog. A number of universities such as the University of Toronto have already closed their card catalogs and replaced them with a COM microform catalog. One of the advantages of the computer catalog over the card catalog is the ease with which large-scale changes may be made:

> The New York Public Library heralded a new age in authority control when it developed a system capable of making mass changes with one transaction, such as altering all "aeroplane" subject headings to airplane. Mass file modifications of this nature will become commonplace, allowing 1) conformity with current practices of bibliographic descriptions, 2) adherence to current terminology, and 3) reconciliation of bibliographic descriptions among institutions. (Martin, 1976, p. 166)

One of the more successful applications of computer technology has been online bibliographic searches using services such as MEDLINE or Chem. Abstracts. Vendors provide these services to library patrons on a fee-for-service basis. Some of these services now permit the ordering of copies of some of the items retrieved in the bibliographic search, but this particular aspect of the service is expensive.

The automatic retrieval of information has proven to be a much valued and useful service for library clientele. Dr. Paul Crainfield (1967), however, has pointed out one of its potential drawbacks with which we should be acquainted:

> Present day programs of computerized information retrieval overvalue the importance of retrieving facts without either attaching a scale of importance to the material with which they deal or ordering information in any way which corresponds to the order of human thought. The limitations of classification by subject heading become especially apparent when a body of information becomes through new insight pertinent to a new area of thought. That body of information thereby acquires new subject headings: thus one sees that the system of retrieval by subject heading can never serve to aid fundamental discovery. The dangers of the present approach lie in their devaluation of traditional methods. Critical reviews are devalued, personal knowledge of the literature is devalued, and a false impression is created that knowledge is the same thing as retrievable information. This diminishes respect for that sort of creative insight.

The remedy to this situation lies with educators to make sure that their pupils understand the dangers of isolating a figure from its ground. Automatic retrieval of information certainly encourages this. This does not mean online searches should be discouraged, but it does indicate that librarians must be particularly vigilant and warn their patrons of the possible dangers of drawbacks of this service. Here is a perfect example of where understanding the effects of a medium are essential if it is to be a service rather than a disservice to its users.

A major new development in computer technology, the microprocessor or minicomputer, has proven to be a real boon to the library:

> A third significant trend is the development of mini-computer systems capable of handling in an on-line mode a variety of library processes such as circulation, acquisition ordering and accounting, serial control, catalogue access. (De Gennaro, 1976)

A number of minicomputer systems can now be purchased off the shelf and installed immediately in a library. Another advantage of these systems to libraries is that the installation and maintenance of these systems is the responsibility of the vendors.

Workers at the University of Minnesota Bio-Medical Library are trying to develop an integrated system of minicomputers that will provide the whole gamut of library functions. The minicomputers have been designed to interface with the databases of the regional network. If successful the system could provide a complete set of automated services and serve as a model for library automation in the next decade. {*The use of computers in libraries has come a long way since 1979. They are an integral part of almost every function and operation of today's library.*}

Computer Journals

Another important impact of the computer on the library has been the abstracting and indexing of scholarly journals. This is the first step in the ultimate goal of automatic retrieval of all information. Plans have already begun to develop a computer journal. Instead of publishing scholarly journals on paper and then indexing them and reading them into a computer database, one would enter an article, a report, or a new finding directly into the database. Anyone interested in the information could then have it converted into a hardcopy at one's terminal. One could update one's article or report by adding new results, correcting any mistakes, or replacing obsolete sections. Upon reading an article in one's field, one could immediately append comments on, or criticism of the article, that is, instantaneous computer graffiti. Such a system could eliminate the need for refereeing articles. Authors would be inclined to remove their article from the database if the criticism were too harsh. A computer journal would serve more as a dialog than an archive of obsolete results. {*None of these suggestions that are so easy to implement with digital media has been adopted by most journals. However, some aspects of what we predicted have become a reality. A number of Web sites such as arXiv.org, academia.edu, researchgate.net, and many others listed in item 4 Preprint Collections of chapter 7 provide immediate electronic publication of research results as well as a mechanism for a dialog between the authors and their readers. Publication in an accredited journal is used more for evaluation of research for the purposes of academic tenure decisions and promotions than it is for communication.*}

This completes our review of the application of computer technology to library problems. The computer has not yet delivered all that was originally promised for it and in fact might never live up to its initial promise. {*I would amend this last comment to say that as of 2015 the computer has in fact lived up to its promise. One cannot conceive of a library operating without one.*} Despite some of its drawbacks it has already proven to be a useful tool. Progress in its application continues. Its integration into more and more of the library's functions is inevitable.

What do we think about computers we have all too often been asked ... . What we think or like or prefer is quite beside the point. Robert Hutchins is quite right. One of the most important social changes in history is impending. We shall have to develop new social and political institutions to cope with it. We have no doubt that one of these new institutions will be a new kind of library. (Shera, 1971, p. 119)

{*Today's library is certainly a lot different than the library of 1971 but I do not believe that we can claim it is a new kind of library. It has many new and useful services but at its core it is still a place for the storage of physical books and their access and circulation. The brick and mortar library is the only way to provide these services. Its additional digital-based services are best provided in the same location as the storage of the physical books, which still constitutes its unique and central function.*

We now turn in the next two chapters to the ways in which digital media or what we call "post-McLuhan media" have impacted today's library.—RKL}

· 6 ·

LAWS OF THE MEDIA FOR POST-MCLUHAN DIGITAL MEDIA

In this chapter composed at the beginning of 2015, I will update the material in chapters 4 and 5 by examining each of the digital media that Marshall McLuhan never had a chance to experience or observe. I will perform a LOM analysis for each of these post-McLuhan media in chapter 6 and then discuss how they impact the operation and objectives of today's libraries in chapter 7. These digital technologies are changing the ground in which the library operates. This does not mean that the electric mass media we examined in chapters 4 and 5 will no longer have an impact on the library, but only that these media must share the stage with the newer digital media and they will have a smaller effect on the library than the newer digital media.

We begin with a LOM for hybrid technologies since the one characteristic of all the post-McLuhan media we will examine in this chapter is that they are all hybrid technologies. All technologies are hybrids in the sense that they combine simpler components, but digital media are hybrid technologies in two senses. Like all technologies they are composed of simpler components, but what is unique about digital media is that they combine and hybridize functions to a much greater extent that nondigital media. Digital media being hybrids create new functionalities and release new forms of energy, as McLuhan (1964) suggested more than fifty years ago, when he wrote, "The crossing or hybridization of the media release great new forces and energy by fission and fusion" (p. 48).

Hybrid or Convergent Technologies

1. Enhance convenience
2. Obsolesce the clutter of many individual devices
3. Retrieve the Swiss Army knife, and
4. Reverse into clutter

The Personal Computer (The Mainframe Computer)

The items in parentheses are from the LOM in chapter 4 for the mainframe computer so the reader can compare the two LOMs for the personal and mainframe computers.

1. Enhances access to computing (amplifies speed of calculations and retrieval)
2. Obsolesces the mainframe and minicomputer (obsolesces sequence, approximation, perception, the present)
3. Retrieves the personal assistant (retrieves perfect memory—total and exact projections)
4. Reverses into information overload (anarchy via the overlay of bureaucracy and loss of human scale)

The Notebook Computer and the Tablet

1. Enhances mobile access to computing and information retrieval
2. Obsolesces the desktop computer
3. Retrieves the personal assistant who accompanies the users wherever they go, and
4. Reverses into even greater information overload

The Internet

1. Enhances connectivity to information resources and the connectivity to other computer users

2. Obsolesces teletype and fax as well as the specialist as the source of information
3. Retrieves community as in the idea of the Global Village
4. Reverses into information overload, masquerade, and hacking

Wi-Fi

1. Enhances access to the Internet
2. Obsolesces dial-up access to the Internet
3. Retrieves the command center
4. Reverses into constant monitoring

Email and Texting

1. Enhances interpersonal connections
2. Obsolesces telephone calls
3. Retrieves letter writing
4. Reverses into spam

The World Wide Web

1. Enhances two-way communication, access to information, and continuous learning
2. Obsolesces academic journals, newspapers, and paper-based communication in general
3. Retrieves alignment and community
4. Reverses into a platform for games, music, radio, photos, videos, and TV, as well as a platform for a number of negative activities such as cyberbullying, hate messaging, the recruitment of terrorists, and harmful forms of hacking, such as identity theft

The Cloud

1. Enhances centralized storage of large amounts of data
2. Obsolesces the hard drives and external drives of personal computers
3. Retrieves the Library at Alexandria
4. Reverses into information glut

Search Engines

1. Enhance rapid location and retrieval of Web-based information
2. Obsolesce the reference librarian (Note to reference librarians: Please remember obsolescence is never the end of something but rather a new position for it and in this case a new function for the reference librarian. Also as already mentioned, obsolescence "ensures total acceptance and ever-wider use."
3. Retrieve the paper-based index
4. Reverse into the online index and table of contents of the ever-expanding document that is the content of the Web.

Blogs

1. Enhance the exchange of information between the author of the blog and her readers
2. Obsolesce newsletters, physical bulletin boards, and communications sent through the postal system
3. Retrieve communities of interest
4. Reverse into self-promotion

e-books

1. Enhance the accessibility of a book
2. Obsolesce the printed codex book
3. Retrieve the convenience of the original pocket-size paperback book
4. Reverse into self-publishing and print on demand

Social Media

1. Enhance the image of the poster of the social medium content
2. Obsolesce real life and face-to-face interactions
3. Retrieve Narcissus and masquerade
4. Reverse into fake identities

Twitter

1. Enhances immediate communication
2. Obsolesces email, breaking-news bulletins on TV, and newspaper headlines
3. Retrieves the telegram
4. Reverses into the banal and more narcissism

The Multifunction Printer, Photocopier, Scanner, and Fax

1. Enhance the distribution and reproduction of documents
2. Obsolesce mimeograph and carbon paper
3. Retrieve imagery
4. Reverse into "everybody becomes a publisher" (McLuhan & McLuhan, 1988, p. 145)

The Scanner and OCR Software

1. Enhances reproduction, digitization, and distribution of text documents and images
2. Obsolesces the photocopier
3. Retrieves the copyist
4. Reverses into document glut

The Smartphone

1. Enhances the mobile access to information as the Swiss Army knife of telecommunications
2. Obsolesces the cell phone, the land line, access to Wi-Fi
3. Retrieves the Internet and/or friends at any time and any place
4. Reverses into an obsession with the present moment

Wearable Computing

1. Enhances around-the-clock access to information
2. Obsolesces the smartphone and social connection

3. Retrieves the command center
4. Reverses into a cyborg responding to each new piece of information

e-learning

1. Enhances lifelong learning and anytime, anywhere learning
2. Obsolesces the university and other forms of institutional learning
3. Retrieves the teacher or instructor as well as the self-learner
4. Reverses into gamification

Online Card Catalog (The Paper-based Card Catalog)

The items in parentheses are from the LOM in chapter 4 for the paper-based card catalog so the reader can compare the two LOMs for the online and paper-based card catalogs.

1. Enhances access to books and data both within the library and online via the Internet outside the library (Enhances access to books, data)
2. Obsolesces the physical card catalog (Obsolesces the notebook {*the paper-based one*} and memory)
3. Retrieves the library for the user working outside the confines of the library (Retrieves the "hunter," the sleuth)
4. Flips into even more information, given the ease with which data can be retrieved (Flips into excess-information overload-computer)

The online card catalog or more accurately the online catalog plays much the same function as the original card catalog with the following additional services:

• One can search for items without coming to the library, which saves a trip to the library if the item is not there because it has been checked out by another user or it has not been collected. And one can search any library in the world for that matter and hopefully get your hands on the desired item by interlibrary loan.
• One can search on many more subject terms such as a word in a title or the coupling of two or more terms or even a whole sentence using quotation marks. There are more than 2,000 available search engines so if one search engine does not do the job another might (see www.beaucoup.com for a listing of many of these).

- One can identify items that are available electronically such as articles in electronic journals and have them dispatched directly to one's computer.
- One can actually search for articles by title in e-journals that the library has subscribed to and download them onto one's computer, which saves one the trouble of tracking down a hard copy of the journal and reading the article in the library. One can also access e-journals and browse them online instead of reading the journal in the library.
- One can renew their books online, receive notices when books are due for return or renewal, and order books from other libraries through interlibrary loans.

Despite these obvious advantages of the online catalog, and the many others too numerous to name, I still personally miss the card catalog, which at the Robarts Library at the University of Toronto has been retired and placed in storage. What I liked about the paper-based card catalog was browsing through the cards to find items of interest, which is not quite something I am able to duplicate with the online catalog. But browsing through the stacks is still something I can and often do. Once I have the call number of a book on a subject I am researching, as I go to retrieve that volume, I always browse through the books with the same call number, as well as the books in the same neighborhood. This is one of my great pleasures in visiting the library and it often results in my finding some gems that I serendipitously encounter.

Acknowledgment: I want to thank Alexander Kuskis for his many suggestions that enriched this collection of LOMs.

THE IMPACT OF DIGITAL TECHNOLOGY ON THE LIBRARY

When assessing the impact of electric mass media and the mainframe computer on the library in chapter 5, we made it a point to understand how these media affected the ground in which the library operated. I will do the same in assessing the impact of digital media on the library because the figure of the library has not changed radically from the way in which it was first organized. It is still an institution that preserves the culture of its society. The ground of the library operating today in the digital age has changed once again because of the pervasive use of digital media. In chapter 5 McLuhan and I claim that the library "has to a certain degree lost its sense of purpose, direction, and identity precisely because it has lost touch with its ground, the hidden effects of media." I do not believe that is any longer the case today as librarians and libraries have made great strides to incorporate digital media into their operations. That being said there are still issues that need to be addressed. The focus in the era of electric mass media was on information but that focus has now shifted to knowledge in the digital era and as a result the library needs to step up its function as an educational institution in the new digital age, which is perhaps better styled as the knowledge era. For a review of the impact of digital media the reader is referred to my book *Understanding New Media: Extending Marshall McLuhan* (Logan, 2016).

One of the concerns we expressed in chapter 5 many years ago was whether the electric mass media would have a deleterious effect on the preservation of our culture. I believe that is less of a concern because of the way libraries have integrated the use of digital media in their operation. Today, because of the Internet, the Web, and our personal digital devices such as our notebooks, tablets, and smartphones, we are living in the past, present, and future all at once. However, we still need to understand how digital media will affect library operations and the preservation of the tradition of the book and deep reading. I have no fear that we will lose the tradition of the physical book but I do have a concern about the tradition of the deep reading of book-length texts, especially by digital natives. McLuhan expresses a concern for the impact of television on the shortening of the attention span of young television viewers. That is still a concern but television is only one distraction. Today we face the distractions of many screen-based activities such as texting, Twitter, email, and video games, all of which involve some forms of reading but not with book-length texts. I am cognizant that with every new medium, critics arise, predicting a cultural disaster. I do not see an impending disaster on the horizon, but at the same time I believe that teachers and librarians, who are also educators, need to take into account that preservation of our literary traditions will require some adjustments and some understanding of the effects of the many new media that are popping up like mushrooms in today's media ecosystem. We have the additional challenge that the amount of information with which we must cope is increasing exponentially. We must ask, is the tsunami of information that the digital media deliver reducing the attention span of its users in a way even more insidious than television? Are today's readers capable of the deep reading of book-length texts? What is the impact of attention economics on library use? Is the pace of information flow in the library too slow for the users of digital media? These are questions that require careful study by media ecologists, by librarians, educators, communicators, and all those concerned with the preservation of our literary cultural heritage.

In chapter 5 we are concerned that "because of the great variety of media used to transmit information" it will be difficult to isolate the separate effects of each medium. Now with digital media in the mix that complexity is even greater. In this chapter we will survey the way in which digital media impact the library and, for the most part, improve its operation and enrich the services it offers to its patrons.

I would like to begin this study of the impact of digital media on the library with three personal anecdotes from an undergraduate student, a professor of communications, and an academic librarian. The first testimonial comes from one of my students, Melody Ming Liu, who was in the Book and Media Studies program at St. Michael's College at the University of Toronto. She took my McLuhan seminar course and then did a semester of independent study addressing the question of how the dehumanizing effects of digital technology can be avoided. I asked her to write a short essay on the impact of using the library at the U. of Toronto, with a focus on the library's online catalog, as this is one of the aspects of the library's operation that is most affected by digital media. I chose to have a student provide a personal account because I believe the perspective of a student and a digital native would be of interest to my readers. So here is Melody's take on the digitally configured library:

I wish to share my experience with the online card catalog that enhances access to books and data both within the library and online via the Internet. I was born to an age when online catalog were already in use. My knowledge of previous searching method is very limited. However I can comment on the online catalog, which I find very useful because of I am able to search for a particular book or a journal online, which saves me travel time to the library. Usually when I want to rent books, I check online first, and I will go directly to where the books are located in the library. Secondly, there are many books that have electronic sources, which means that I do not need a physical book but I can read its content in its PDF format. One of the most admirable features of online books is that I can search for key words using (CTRL+F) saving me lots of time from reading a whole book to find useful information. Interestingly, many old books have digital holdings as well. For example, Napoleon by H. A. Fisher is a book published in 1916 that through the Internet Archive, I am able to read using the link: http://booksnow2.scholarsportal.info/ ebooks/oca2/32/napoleon00fishuoft/napoleon00fishuoft.pdf.

The second testimonial is from Anne Pym in a private communication via email to me responding to my request of how her use of the library changed as a result of the Internet. Here is Anne's response, which is quite similar to Melody's:

Interesting question! As a student (MEA theology at Dominican School of Philosophy and Theology) and professor of rhetoric and media ecology at California State University, I find your query interesting. As I am presently conducting research for a term paper in a graduate seminar entitled "Trinity," I find my old habits lead me to searching out books and hauling armloads out of the library. Then

I think, but so much more and so much more current is available online—just go to the Web site at DSPT/GTU and I have "tons" of articles at my downloading pleasure. No searches among books/volumes, which may not even be cataloged or may be checked out by some other seeker-of-knowledge. Just sit here in my home library in private comfort seeking for the latest conversation in the form of articles. Download some—those I can read at my leisure—or not. Bookmark them so I can return, again, in my own good time and comfort. And I also have a stack of books on my desk. I can look up subjects in the indexes; pick them up, open and close them at my leisure; and peruse them for hours (even renewing them) without having to use up reams of paper and ink cartridges to copy 30 to 40 page articles. And, it is so much easier to access articles by computer than by searching out the volumes of articles and laboriously copying the desired articles.

The users of the library are not the only ones affected by the digital revolution through which we are passing. Possibly even more affected by digital media than the patrons of the library are the librarians themselves. Here is a testimonial from Dylanne Dearborn, an academic librarian, who runs the Physics Library in my department at the University of Toronto half time and is a research data librarian the other half of her time.

Digital media has obviously influenced and changed the role of academic librarians; however, I think the core concepts behind what librarians have always been responsible for remain. Academic librarians still collect and provide access to materials and provide instruction to users on effective research skills. With the inclusion of the internet in academia and library processes, I think these roles are augmented by the sheer volume of research being generated and material that is available for consumption, as well as by emerging new methods and technologies to conduct and communicate research. Moving to an online format means that there has been an explosion in the volume of information that can be accessed regardless of location, as well as information that can be more meticulously searched under user-dictated parameters.

There have been trends recently for librarians to become involved in what we call the scholarly communication process—which encompasses the creation and dissemination of research. At an institution, research materials can now be stored in digital repositories and this gives librarians the ability to become more ingrained in the research process. For example, my role is related to research data. While librarians have always been involved in the preservation of academic materials (including data), there is a new role stemming from the idea that research data can also be considered an output of research in addition to the traditional forms of publication, such as a journal article or book. There have also been changes in requirements by some funding agencies and journal publishers to make the data behind the research available in a public repository. When mandates or policies change, service and infrastructure is needed to provide researchers with the tools and expertise necessary to meet these requirements. What this means is that we have librarians, such as myself, becoming involved in new services such as training researchers on effective data management as well as designing new technical infrastructure to preserve data or make it available for reuse. Digital media hasn't changed the core of what we do—supporting research—it has just evolved and expanded how we do it.

The Future of the Academic Library

One of the things I learned working with McLuhan was that the best way to predict the future was to understand what is happening today. So in order to talk about the academic library of the future let me describe the one I have used for the past forty years, the University of Toronto Library (UTL) system, ranked by the Association of Research Libraries as one of the top three academic libraries in North America, just behind those of Harvard and Yale.

> The U of T library system comprises 44 individual libraries that hold more than 12 million volumes in 341 languages, millions of electronic resources in various forms and almost 30,000 linear metres of archival material. More than 150,000 new print volumes are acquired each year and its data centre houses more than 200 servers with a storage capacity of 1.5 petabytes. (Wall, 2014)

In addition, the library's servers house 65,410,576 documents as I discovered when an article I was searching for was not found and I received the following message, "Your library's collection of 65,410,576 documents were searched and no results matching your search term(s) were found." Ironically, I eventually found the article on the *Miami Herald* Web site using Google. What I learned from these statistics regarding the holdings of the UTL system is that physical books and digital information are more or less equal partners in UTL's operations.

Another key factor regarding UTL's services is the pride it takes in providing personalized services to its patrons, especially its first-year students as their following announcement proclaims: "To help first-year students navigate the largest research collection in Canada … UTL developed a personal librarian program [that is] … offered to all 7,800 first-year Faculty of Arts & Science students" (Internal University of Toronto memo, April 15, 2015).

From this information from UTL I concluded that the library of the future will consist of three essential components: (1). books, (2). computer-based/ digital information, and (3). librarians offering personalized service and information management to its patrons.

Changes in Library Usage with the Arrival of the Internet

A study by Bravy and Feather (2001) reveals that with the emergence of the Internet there has been a significant reduction in the amount of photocopying, the circulation of books, and the amount of shelving at the Law Library at Georgetown University. Photocopying in the academic year 1998–1999 was reduced by 52% compared to 1993–1994, the year before the Internet went on stream for the general public with the introduction of the Mosaic browser, which later morphed into the Netscape browser, and eventually into Firefox. There were similar reductions over the same period for circulation, which dropped by 44%, and for shelving, which dropped by 52%. A similar decline in book circulation of 54% at the University of California Library System (2005) was reported for the ten-year period of 1991 to 2001.

Although there has been a decline in the use of print materials in libraries as a result of the emergence of the Internet, libraries have found other ways to serve their patrons. Libraries are reinventing themselves. For example, public libraries do not confine themselves to circulating codex-printed books; they also provide for their patrons e-books, audio books, sound recordings, and DVDs of films. They have also fully embraced the digital revolution by providing their patrons with ways to access online forms of information for those without computers or for those with computers but without access to Wi-Fi. Virtually all public libraries have Internet connections. In 1994 only 21% were connected to the Internet but this percentage increased to 80% by 1998, and 99% by 2004. The number of public access Internet workstations rose from 1.9 per public library in 1996 to 10.8 by 2002 (Bertot, 2009). The number of Internet connections and workstations at universities increased at an even faster rate and achieved higher levels of saturation. The pattern of growth and saturation for online catalogs followed a similar pattern to that of Internet connections and workstations. Today's libraries are as much in the computer and Internet business as they are in the book business. They are basically involved in providing their patrons with access to information independent of the medium in which that information is packaged.

Perhaps the most unusual impact of digital technology is the case of the Stratford Ontario campus of the University of Waterloo, which opened its doors on October 16, 2012, proclaiming that it was initiating "a new kind of learning." It describes its new kind of learning in these terms: "This new collaborative education style accelerates knowledge and innovation by bringing together students, leading researchers, businesses and entrepreneurs to advance digital media technology and creative application" ("A New Kind of Learning," n.d.). What is unusual about this campus is that there is no library, only a library service by which "Students/Staff/Faculty/Alumni can place holds/recalls on resources that are housed in the UW [U. of Waterloo] Libraries [some 26 miles away]" ("Stratford Campus Library Services," n.d.). The books are then delivered from Waterloo to the Stratford campus where they can be picked up. Is this a trend for the future? Hopefully not! I would suggest that this campus would be an ideal place for the compact library that we will describe in detail in chapter 9. Another equally unusual university library service arrangement is the fully digital library at Florida Polytechnic University, which opened its doors in August 2014 and does not have any physical books. The students can access 135,000 e-books and, if necessary, they can, like the Stratford campus solution, order physical books from one of Florida's eleven other public universities (Stein, 2014). These are just two examples of bookless libraries; there are others and more to come. But hey, if you have an Internet connection you, too, have, in a certain sense, a bookless library as we suggest very shortly.

Google and Libraries

Google and other search engines provide an alternative to the contribution of reference librarians, giving rise to a love/hate relationship with them as described by William Miller (2009):

> We in libraries have a love/hate relationship with Google ... watching with a mixture of admiration and discomfort as it inexorably displaces our searching tools, and even ourselves to some extent, while on the other hand, it makes our lives easier and in any case is an inevitability we need to accept in a creative way into our own reconceptualized work.

There is still an important role for the reference librarian even with Google and the Internet, as pointed out by a reference librarian in Boston with years of experience:

> When I started out in the '70s, you would walk up to the reference desk and ask a question and I would find an answer. Today it's the opposite. People turn to librarians to help them sift through the 10 million answers they find on the Internet. We're more like navigators. (Seeley, 2014)

Another reference librarian, Rosa Caballero-Li, offered a similar opinion but added the importance of the human touch: "Librarians are 'information specialists,' and can help point patrons to resources that aren't available online. Also, sometimes there's just something about speaking to a human being" ("Before the Internet," 2014).

The Online Virtual Library

The love/hate relationship of librarians with Google has to do with the fact that the Internet is virtually a library, a virtual library (pun intended). We have just completed a survey of how digital media are directly affecting the offerings of libraries. We have seen that for the most part digital media have had a positive impact on libraries. In addition to the direct impact of digital media on the library we must also take into account that the Internet itself functions as a vast virtual library that impacts the brick-and-mortar library and to a certain extent competes with it. The challenge facing today's librarians is how to integrate their collection of books with all the information archived and available online through the Internet. We begin with a LOM analysis of this online virtual library and then go on to describe its components.

1. Enhances access to information and literature
2. Obsolesces the brick and mortar library
3. Retrieves the singer of tales whose tale was customized for his audience
4. Reverses into attention economics

All of the information one can access through the Internet represents a vast virtual library that only came into existence in any significant way in 1994 with the release of the Netscape browser. The existence of this virtual, online mega-library, which we will describe below, is having and will continue to have an important impact on traditional libraries as they form the ground in which these libraries operate.

In interpreting (2) "obsolesces the brick and mortar library" in the above LOM, the reader should remember that obsolescence does not mean the end of something but rather a new position for it and as already indicated obsolescence also "ensures total acceptance and ever-wider use." In other words, the brick and mortar library will endure and persist but its role will change.

Digital media enhance the operations of today's academic and public libraries and increase the depth of information they can make available to their users. Libraries and museums across the globe are able to share resources, thereby enriching each other's holdings. Candela, Castelli, and Pagano (2011) document the history of this development, pointing out that the digitization of scientific papers is impacting the very nature of research because of the universal access that digitized information provides.

At the same time the availability of online information competes with the library in that many of one's information needs can be met with one's computer, tablet, or smartphone connected to the Internet. There are certain advantages that online information has over the print-based collection of the traditional library for the user. First and foremost is the convenience of accessing online information at a time and place of one's choosing. The information is available 24/7. Other users may use the same information at the same time one is accessing it so there is no waiting for another user to finish using that information. The information is easily searched for keywords saving the user the need to search an entire book to find the information they need. This is far superior to the indexing of the traditional book, which does not always exist and when it does exist it is indexed according to what the author believes are the key words, which might differ from what the reader considers the key words to be. The digital format also facilitates grabbing a quote or making notes of what one reads using the process of "cut-and-paste," where allowed, or by taking a screen shot if cutting and pasting is not allowed.

There are also advantages for the library of digitally formatted information. The storage of that information takes up less room. It is also easier to conserve and preserve that information with backup systems such as archiving on the Cloud. This is why the role of the library is changing. Libraries are focusing on things that cannot be duplicated by the online availability of information.

Just to give the reader an idea of how much is available online I will list some of the more prominent sources of Internet-based information that

includes fiction and nonfiction text, images, video, audio, metadata, and information tools. While the reader will probably be familiar with most of these
sources, I believe listing them all in one place is a useful exercise because it
provides an image of the ground in which today's traditional libraries operate.

Among the resources that are listed, many are open access such as search
engines, a number of Google-based tools such as Google Translate; and collections of information such as Google Books, Wikipedia, YouTube, Vimeo,
Instagram, Flickr, Pinterest, Twitter, the Stanford Encyclopedia of Philosophy; preprint and reprint collections like arXiv, Academia.edu, and Research-
Gate; many electronic journals or e-journals; almost all blogs; and almost all
academic and association Web sites. Some resources require a subscription,
as is the case with some online journals, dictionaries, and encyclopedias. We
will designate those services that require a subscription or payment with the
dollar sign ($).

The services that require a subscription are not in competition with traditional libraries but represent an opportunity for a library to serve its patrons
by subscribing to these services and making them available to their clientele
just as they do when they purchase books and allow their patrons access to
those books. Subscribing to these online services just as their subscribing to
print-based journals is an important service that libraries provide and one I
have found to be invaluable. As an interdisciplinary researcher I cannot afford
to subscribe to all the electronic journals of interest to me. My library at the
University of Toronto, however, provides me with access to a wide variety of
electronic and print journals. The electronic journals have the added value
that I can access them on my computer desktop without having to travel to
the physical library.

With this introduction I will now list online information services that
represent the new digital ground in which the traditional library now operates. I have batched services that belong to the same category, beginning with
information tools, reference tools, nonfiction information, literature, and
finally AV materials. This list is far from exhaustive but it is important to
have an understanding of what is available online as open access and what is
available only through subscription.

One can look at all the resources that are available via the Internet as a
vast online library. Within this vast array of resources there are also specialized
libraries or collections. One such example is the Internet Archive (archive.
org), a nonprofit digital library whose stated mission is "universal access to all
knowledge." On its site it describes itself in the following manner:

Most societies place importance on preserving artifacts of their culture and heritage. Without such artifacts, civilization has no memory and no mechanism to learn from its successes and failures. Our culture now produces more and more artifacts in digital form. The Archive's mission is to help preserve those artifacts and create an Internet library for researchers, historians, and scholars.

The Internet Archive provides free public access to a wide variety of digitized information in the form of text such as close to 3 million out-of-copyright books, articles of all sorts, images, videos, audios, music, and Web sites representing more than 10 petabytes (10^{15} bytes or a million gigabytes) of data. The books are available in a variety of formats: PDF, plain text, DAISY, ePub, DjVu, MOBI, and direct to Kindle through the Open Library Web site (openlibrary.org). The Open Library, a division of the Internet Archive, also provides audiobooks for the dyslexic and the blind, which under U.S. federal laws is allowed for use by the disabled. The Open Library, in addition to providing access to public domain books, has the additional goal of creating a Web page for every book that was ever published. The Open Library currently circulates more than 1 million books and has bibliographic records for more than 20 million books.

Most of the books the Internet Archive and the Open Library have archived are due to their extensive book scanning and digitization activities. A large share of their archived material has been collected automatically with Web crawlers and some are the result of uploading of files by the public. Its preservation of public Web sites is through a service called The Wayback Machine, which contains more than 150 billion Web captures. It is a library of Web sites.

I can personally attest to the value of The Way Back Machine. In 1996, just after the release of Netscape, I co-founded a Web development company that we styled as Gutenberg Internet Services Inc. The company was acquired in 2000 and I lost track of the computers that housed our Web site. I foolishly sold the rights to our URL gutenberg.com a year later and thought I had lost access to our original Gutenberg.com Web sites. I actually needed some information on those Web sites for the book I co-authored with Louis Stokes (Logan & Stokes, 2004) titled *Collaborate to Compete: Driving Profitability in the Internet Age*. I wanted to tell the story of how Gutenberg Internet Services designed a knowledge network for Siemens AG that was used worldwide. Thanks to the Way Back Machine I was able to capture my original design at http://web.archive.org/web/19990427193157/http://gutenberg.com/%7Ebubble/index.htm, which I have copied below. Before listing the resources on the vast online library, which is the Internet, I will first make a short detour and describe how a knowledge network operates as a mini-online intranet library.

Knowledge Networks as an Internal Mini-Online Library of an Organization

A knowledge network is another kind of online library in which information pertinent to an organization's operations, including its history, experiences, and lessons learned, are collected, archived, and made easily accessible. I will use the design I created for Siemens circa 1999 as an example. Some of the communication media used with that network design need to be updated but the structure of how the information is presented is still valid.

The Gutenberg Knowledge Network allows the members of an organization to connect with each other to share both their tacit and explicit knowledge. Explicit knowledge is the kind of knowledge that can be documented. It is the kind of information that traditional libraries collect, archive, and disseminate. Tacit knowledge was defined by Michael Polanyi and was incorporated into knowledge management practice by Nonaka and Takeuchi (1995). They define tacit knowledge as "deeply rooted in an individual's actions and experiences" (ibid.), which can only be shared through dialog. The Gutenberg Knowledge Network archives explicit knowledge through the Case Base and Best Practices components in which all the vital data pertinent to the organization is stored. The acquisition of tacit knowledge is facilitated by tools that identify experts through the Competence Pool of individual Web sites of all members of the organization, a Skills Matrix to identify who has a particular skill or expertise, and a database of Coaches and Mentors to identify who can provide guidance when needed.

The Gutenberg Knowledge Network also has an educational component through the Instructional System. Although traditional libraries were not thought of as deliverers of education and training but merely a resource for students and educators, more and more libraries are taking on the educational and training role. Libraries always provided instruction on how to make use of its resources, but with the possibility of courses of study being digitized and made available, online libraries are beginning to offer this new service.

The Gutenberg Knowledge Network - A Learning Environment

The **Gutenberg Knowledge Network** (GKN) is an Intranet based tool and environment that allows any organization to collect and organize its information, knowledge and wisdom in such a way that it can be easily shared by all the members of the community that comprise the enterprise.

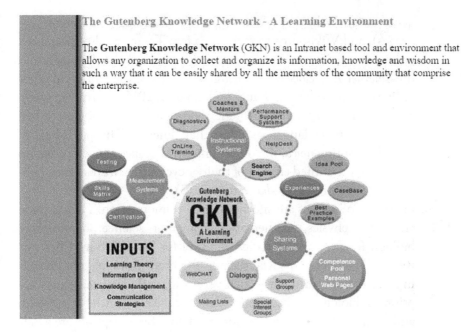

The Components of the Vast Online Library That Is the Internet

As we mentioned above, one may regard the Internet as one vast online library. We turn now to a description of the components of that online library.

1. Search engines in which Google dominates with 1.1 billion unique monthly visitors per month, but there is also Bing, Yahoo Search!, Ask, AOL Search, WOW, WebCrawler, and MyWebSearch, plus a number of others with less that 50 million unique monthly visitors per month.

2. Online dictionaries exist in open access formats in all the written languages of the world. In English there is dictionary.com and also by subscription the complete edition of the Oxford English Dictionary ($). Another interesting online dictionary is Google Translate that allows one to translate among 71 different languages from Afrikaans to Zulu.

3. Online encyclopedias, such as Wikipedia, are available in more than 200 different languages. The Wiki Foundation produces other open access Web sites including Wikiquotes (there are also many other

quote sites), Wikibooks, Wiktionary (available in 71 different languages), and Wikisource to mention a few. There are also specialized online encyclopedias like the *Stanford Encyclopedia of Philosophy* and the *Internet Encyclopedia of Philosophy*. A list of sixty-five different online encyclopedias was found on January 1, 2015, at http://en.wikip edia.org/wiki/List_of_Internet_encyclopedias. Most of these are free and many are in languages other than English. The publishers of *Encyclopedia Britannica*, the oldest English-language encyclopedia, no longer have a printed edition of their encyclopedia; instead they publish the *Online Encyclopedia Britannica* ($).

4. Preprint Collections are another source of information. They include arXiv for physics, mathematics, computer science, quantitative biology, finance, and statistics; bioRxiv for biology; Social Science Research Network for social science and humanities; Nature Precedings for biology, medicine, chemistry, and earth science; PeerJ Preprints for biology, medicine, and health sciences; Philica for any field; and Sciencepaper Online also for any field. These preprints are available for free and used by their contributors to circulate their research findings.

5. Online Journals are another source of information available over the Internet. There are open access journals and those that require a subscription. It is with the latter category of journals that libraries have an important role to play, which is subscribing to those journals that cater to the needs of their patrons.

6. Online Literature, Nonfiction, and Textbooks are an important component of the virtual library. There are a number of online sources with free access to their holdings including: Google Books (having scanned 30 million books Google provides free access as follows: the full book for books out of copyright and partial view of books depending on the instructions of the publisher holding the book's copyright); Project Gutenberg that offers more than 47,000 free e-books; LibriVox (providing approximately 7,000 audiobooks); and Wikibooks (specializing in open-access textbooks). Then of course there are purveyors of e-books, which no more compete with libraries than do bookstores.

7. Blogs are self-published sources of information that deal with the special interests of their authors whether that interest is academic, a social or political cause, the activities of an association or a hobby.

Blogs can be and often are a high quality source of information depending on the blogger. Because the readers of this book are probably interested in the scholarship of Marshall McLuhan, I will refer my readers to Alex Kuskis's excellent blog, the McLuhan Galaxy, which can be found at https://mcluhangalaxy.wordpress.com/. Unlike many shallow personal opinion sites it is packed with reliable information about Marshall McLuhan and McLuhan studies.

8. University and Academic Association Web sites are another source of quite reliable information. University Web sites list their faculty with information about their research. Frequently the professors post on their page downloadable copies of their research papers as PDF or doc files. In addition there are two Web sites, academia.edu and research gate.net, that feature the published and preprint research papers of individual scholars and allows researchers to communicate with each other.

9. The Web Sites of Businesses, NGOs, and Associations are another rich source of information.

10. Audio-Visual Web Sites provide a rich source of images, videos, and audios, many of which are open access. Examples include YouTube, Flickr, Photobucket, Shutterstock ($), Snapfish, Instagram, Pinterest, iTunes ($), and the Way Back Machine (an archive of past Web sites).

11. Social media sites can be a rich source of information and includes listservs of various organizations, Facebook, Tumblr, LinkedIn, Google Groups, and other social media sites.

· 8 ·

BOOK GLUT, INFORMATION OVERLOAD, AND PATTERN RECOGNITION

Perhaps the greatest challenge facing the library today is the growth of the information that it must collect, organize, and make available for circulation:

> It is a curious paradox that the information revolution ... so far has really failed to reproduce the information, which is necessary to evaluate it. We may perhaps drink deeper of this particular spring before we can even know what kind of water it is. (Boulding, 1967)

The growth of the amount of printed matter has been exponential. The total number of books produced doubles approximately every ten years. Libraries have literally been unable to accommodate this exponential growth because of a lack of shelf space. Daniel Gore and Claudia Schorrig's documentation reveals that building programs at North American universities between 1967 and 1974 have added enough shelf space for 163 million volumes. During this eight-year period, however, these universities actually added 166 million volumes, which represents a 3 million volume short fall (Gore, 1975). The exponential growth of the literature has grown in all fields, including library science for which there were more than 5,000 journals as of 1971 (West, 1971). {And the growth of printed matter has only accelerated since those figures were first reported and then there is the exponential growth of online information as well.}

The problem of too many books is not just the lack of space. There is also the more serious problem of information overload. When the library user is overwhelmed by too many books and too much information, the usefulness of the library breaks down, as was the case with the youngster who asked for a book on airplanes: "This tells me more about airplanes than I wanted to know" (Glover, 1974, p. 31).

The concept of information overload is not a new concept. We read in Ecclesiastes 1:2: "Vanity of vanities, saith Koheleth; Vanity of vanities, all is vanity. ... For in much wisdom is much grief; and he that increaseth his knowledge increaseth his sorrow." A century after Gutenberg's invention of the printing press, Luther wrote: "The multitude of books is a great evil."

The problem of information overflow or book glut does not result alone from the sheer number of volumes created by the printing press but also from specialists. The printing press, by stepping up the use of the alphabet, created specialism, which, in turn, led to an information explosion. One of the impacts of the phonetic alphabet on the Greeks was that their learning became specialized. The printing press enhanced this process even more. The effects of specialism are to fragment knowledge into isolated and specialized compartments. This fragmentation automatically multiplies the amount of information and knowledge with which one must deal. Now fields emerge, and new categories are created:

> There is increased evidence that we are being bogged down today as specialization extends. The investigator is staggered by the findings and conclusions of thousands of other workers—conclusions which he cannot find time to grasp, much less remember, as they appear. Yet specialization becomes increasingly necessary for progress, and the effort to bridge between disciplines is correspondingly superficial ... professionally our methods of transmitting and reviewing the results of research are generations old and by now totally inadequate for their purposes. (Bush, 1945)

The problem of information overload became acute with the emergence of electric media. The specialist living in the mechanical age was not really aware of information overload precisely because of his specialism. The awareness of information overload is a result of the effects of our new electric {and digital} media, which creates pattern recognition through information speed-up. As information and knowledge in a specialized field increased beyond the capacity of an individual, the field fragmented further into more specialized areas. This mechanism of subdividing and narrowing the areas of knowledge one feels responsible for, allowed the specialist to cope with the information explosion.

Actually if one does not feel the compulsion to know the details of every field of study and is content to read the review articles in the fields that are not central to their research then the so-called information overload disappears on the personal level. One can acquaint oneself with review articles if one is content to know the general state of a field of study and not worry about the details. {*One does not even have to worry about reading a bunch of review articles any more because with Wikipedia one can quickly access the general state of a field of knowledge with a few clicks of one's keyboard and mouse.*}

The fragmentation and explosion of knowledge practiced by the specialist are the products of the mechanical age of industrialization and mass production. This is no longer possible with electric {*and digital*} media. Our world is imploding. Our electric technology extends our nervous system so that we reach out and touch everything. We are involved in everything, and our response time is instantaneous. The world is imploding, and holistic ways of viewing nature are emerging. Fragmentation and specialization are no longer possible, and as a result, we feel unable to cope with all the information and knowledge that we have created. We can no longer push down into our subconscious all the details that we once considered extraneous. At the speed of light all knowledge surfaces and one experiences information overload. It is not the printing press that creates the overload, it is the telegraph, the telephone, the radio, the television, the computer, {*digital media*}, and others, and the new information environments they create.

Limits to Clutter

Even though we are becoming aware of the negative effects of information overload, the proliferation of knowledge and information seems to increase at an ever-faster pace. The range of our experience is continually increasing. So many new facts are discovered each day that even if we were to perfect our theoretical understanding of phenomenon and hence reduce our description of these phenomenon, knowledge would still continue to explode. Each day brings new events in the affairs of man, which become the grist for historical, political, and social analysis. Artists, poets, novelists, and musicians are continually creating new works of art, many of which we will want to preserve and store in our libraries. The creation of material to be preserved is never-ending. Modern technology only accelerates the information overload by permitting the cheap production of printed matter for specialized audiences. Reprography {*and especially digital media and the Internet*} make every man a publisher. The number of specialized journals and books for specialized audiences continues to multiply. Modern technology also creates new materials for the library to collect, such as films, phonograph discs, audiotapes, and videotapes.

There are limits, however, to the amount of material a library can safely and efficiently store before it begins to break down. The aim of the library presumably is to store information, which will be readily available and useful to its patrons. If the library clutters its shelves with deadwood by indiscriminately storing all available material, it will no longer serve the function for which it was originally organized. Librarians are therefore searching for new ways to be more selective about what they collect.

Librarians feel compelled, however, to save all of the material that comes their way as the following remark of Senator Major R. Owens (1976), former community coordinator of the Brooklyn Public Library, suggests: "All information is potentially significant and a comprehensive, inclusive system which gives equal attention to all of the information being generated represents the ideal." Although Owens recognizes we are light years away from such an ideal it is still a dangerous one because there isn't the possibility that this ideal can be realized, and if we are not to be bogged down by irrelevant information we must begin to move in exactly the opposite direction. The statement, though expressed as an ideal, reflects the bias of librarians to maintain complete collections, not unlike the collectors of other objects. The goal of almost all collectors, whether they collect stamps or butterflies, coins or arrowheads, is to have a complete collection. This is a luxury librarians can no longer afford even as an ideal.

> The great problem that confronts librarianship today is not that of acquisition or accumulation, but of selection. Book selection is the area of the librarian's greatest responsibility and the most severe test of his professional skill; yet, ironically, it is also the scene of his greatest failure. Such few inquiries as have been made into book selection practices suggest that most institutions have no real policy but place their faith in numbers and the law of averages—the sheep and the goats, the live branches and the dead, are gathered in alike; some lambs are overlooked and some few kids are deliberately excluded, but no one really bothers much about what the herd looks like or makes the effort to prune the tree. (Shera, 1971, pp. 101–102)

If the medium is the message and the library is a medium, what is the message of the library? Too often the message is quantity, not quality—trivia, not discernment:

> It is worth recalling that information is not wisdom; and that a civilization based on different philosophical premises might well regard our increasing obsession with information as neurotic and even, perhaps, rather pathetic. (J. S. Parker, 1974)

The aim of library science is to collect and preserve human knowledge. Science is not just knowledge, but, rather, it is also systematized and organized knowledge. Library science, by the same token, is not merely the accumulation of knowledge but, rather, its organization into a format that makes it readily accessible and useful. An essential feature of any system of information is the elimination of noise or extraneous and useless information. A science textbook does not describe all the failures, half-baked theories, and irrelevant experiments. Thomas Kuhn points out that scientists destroy the historical sense of their field in this manner. Librarians do not have to follow suit. Material of historical interest, but not of current interest, does not have to be destroyed. It can be deposited in archives, perhaps microform {or digitized} archives, to save space. It should not be allowed to be mixed with material of current interest, however, and thereby diluting the usefulness of the library's collection.

One suggestion for cleaning up some of the deadwood on our shelves deserves mention, even though it is only a partial solution. Trueswell (1968) discovered, logically enough, that the probability of a book circulating is related to the last time it circulated. He found that books that have not circulated for seven years only make up 1% of those books that circulate on any given day. This population of books, however, comprises about 30% of most collections. Therefore, removing 30% of the books from a collection will only reduce the availability by 1%, which is not very high. Books that are very popular and circulate a great deal are not available 50% of the time (on average).

Babel—Babble

Today's librarian is caught in the dilemma between completeness and usefulness. The surrealist author and former director of the National Library of Argentina, Jorge Luis Borges, describes the ultimate complete library in a short story titled "The Library of Babel":

A librarian of genius [discovered] the fundamental law of the Library. This thinker observed that all the books, no matter how diverse they might be, are made up of the same elements: the space, the period, the comma, the twenty-two letters of the alphabet. He alleged a fact, which travelers have confirmed: in the vast Library there are no two identical books. From these two incontrovertible premises he deduced that the Library is total and that its shelves register all possible combinations of the twenty-odd orthographical symbols (a number which, though extremely vast, is not infinite): in other words, all that it is given to express, in all languages. Everything: the minute history of the future, autobiographies of the archangels, the faithful cata-logue of the Library, ... the true story of your death, the translation of every book in all languages, the interpolations of every book in all books. ... When it was proclaimed that the Library contained all books, the first impression was one of extravagant hap-piness. All men felt themselves masters of an intact and secret treasure. There was no personal or world problem whose eloquent solution did not exist in some hexagon. ... The universe was justified, the universe suddenly usurped the unlimited dimension of hope. ... As was natural, this inordinate hope was followed by an excessive depres-sion. The certitude that some shelf in some hexagon held precious books and that these precious books were inaccessible, seemed almost intolerable. (1998)

Today's library is not quite as bad (or complete) as Borges's "Library of Babel"; however, it presents some of the same problems. Patrons are frequently unable to find the material they need, or what they want is in such high demand that it is unavailable.

Part of the failure is due to scale. Today's library is lacking the human scale appropriate to a human institution. We will deal with this issue in chapters 9 and 10. Another aspect of the failure of the library to accommodate the needs of its patrons is the way information is organized. Today's reader needs a guide to the literature. We believe that the compact library to be discussed in the next chapter will enable the user to cope with today's ever-increasing information overload.

· 9 ·

THE COMPACT LIBRARY AND
HUMAN SCALE

{Editorial note: Some of the early parts of this chapter were drafted by McLuhan before we received the commission to write this book. The language at times is McLuhan's literary style as opposed to his more expository style and is frequently written in the first person. I take responsibility for the editing of this chapter but wish to state for the record that the credit for what you find of value should be attributed to McLuhan alone.—RKL}

What today's reader, faced with book glut and information overload, requires is not access to all information but, rather, guidance to that information. There is not enough time to read all the information that is generated anyway. This is why not only must the librarian be selective but also the reader, the user of the library. Therein lies the motivation to the construction of what we call "the compact library," which would serve as an up-to-date guide to the literature. The information explosion can only be remedied by finding new ways of putting together the bits of information created by the analyses of specialists. Holistic patterns and guides are the only way of dealing with the overload, and not ever-more efficient ways of collecting, storing, and accessing information. Otherwise we will never distinguish the forest from the trees.

What is called for is basically a right hemisphere approach. A collection that succinctly provides the ground for learning, a framework upon which one can attach one's reading. This approach is antithetical to the goal-oriented left hemisphere–dominated thinker who is basically interested in only the facts, and rarely their context. For such a user, nothing is more ideal than a complete collection with an automated searching system that provides immediate access to the information required at hand, and nothing else—in short, a system that minimizes contact with other information not required for immediate use. In contrast, for the right hemisphere user, any and all books are useful. Read in depth, it doesn't matter which books you read, since almost any book will lead your interest to all the others anyway. The expert in depth produces a holistic approach and flips into our age of "electronic" integration of all knowledge.

Signatures of all things I am here to read.—James Joyce, *Ulysses*

The world exists to end in a book.—Mallarme, letter to Henri Cazalis

At electric speeds the hieroglyphs of the page of Nature become readily intelligible and the Book in the World becomes a kind of Orphic hymn of revelation.—McLuhan, 1970

As an undergraduate at the University of Cambridge, I (McLuhan) encountered a library in the English Department that had immense advantages. I never have seen one like it since. It consisted of no more than 1,500 or 2,000 books. These books, however, were chosen from many fields of history and aesthetics, philosophy, anthropology, mathematics, and the sciences in general. The one criterion, which determined the presence of any book in this collection, was its immediate and top relevance for twentieth-century awareness. The shelf-browser could tell at a glance exactly which poets, novelists, critics, painters, and which of their individual writings were indispensable for knowing "where it's at."

Where It's At (It = The Environment)

This remarkable phrase "where it's at" may be the only one in any language to express the idea of both corporate consensus and sensory focus—a kind of "consensuality" of persons, places, and things in a single instant of awareness. This phrase, invented by young rock musicians to indicate areas of relevance and aliveness in the present time, is, of course, an acoustic, resonant expression, quite alien to anything like "clock time." Nothing could be further away from "where it's at" than the "time of day" or the "time of year." The English language has gone without even a corporate word for the French *on*. Now we have this phrase, which is enormously more sophisticated in its aesthetic range and sensitivity.

The library of which I spoke existed in a corner of the English Faculty Library at Cambridge, but it enabled hundreds of students to share all the relevant poets, painters, critics, musicians, and scientists of that time as the basis for an ongoing dialog. Would it not be possible to have similar libraries created by other departments in the university? Could not the History Department indicate those areas of anthropology and sociology that were indispensable to the most advanced historical studies of the hour? Could not the Department of Philosophy pool its awareness of many fields in order to create a composite image of all the relevant speculation and discovery of our time? Only now have I begun to realize that this unique library represented the meeting of both a written and oral tradition at an ancient university. It is this figure-ground pattern of the written and the oral that completes the meaning of the book and the library. Newman was perhaps the only person of his day to give full recognition to the indispensability of the oral tradition in perfecting the written and printed forms of communication:

> I protest to you, gentlemen, that if I had to choose between a so-called university which dispensed with residence and tutorial superintendence, and gave its degrees to any person who passed an examination in a wide range of subjects, and a University which had no professors or examinations at all, but merely brought a number of young men together for three or four years, and then sent them away, as the University of Oxford is said to have done some sixty years since, if I were asked which of these two methods was the better discipline of the intellect, —mind, I do not say which is morally the better, for it is plain that compulsory study must be a good and idleness an intolerable mischief,—but if I must determine which of the two courses was the more successful in training, moulding, enlarging the mind, which sent out men the more fitted for their social duties, which produced better public men, men of the world, men whose names would descend to posterity, I have no hesitation in giving the preference to that University which did nothing over that which exacted of its members an acquaintance with every science under the sun. (1933, p. 122)

It was probably the omission of the oral dimension that made the famous Five Foot Book Shelf—later known as *The Harvard Classics* (1906), developed by Dr. Charles Eliot, president of Harvard University—and Mortimer Adler and Robert Hutchins' Great Books of the University of Chicago so inadequate and so lacking in contemporary relevance. It was Newman who spent years struggling to introduce the tutorial system at Oxford (Culler, 1955) that saw that the mercenary cram coaches, who helped undergraduates get ready for their examinations, really had recovered a grip on the oral tradition, which had faded from the Oxford and Cambridge lecture scenes. He succeeded in getting these mercenary cram coaches appointed as tutors at Oxford. Since then they have represented the very highest levels of the educational process. For the young student making his first contact with the full range of contemporary awareness, it is indispensable to know the authors and creators in all fields that the conversation among his teachers have approved as the basic nutrient to perception and impulse for ardent spirits.

Consensuality or Dialog in the World of Books?

To look at the finest library in the world or to browse in the finest bookstore in a great city is not to enjoy any of the advantages that accrue from the existence of such a small collection of books chosen by an oral consensus of many top minds. In fact, without a milieu of eager and incessant dialog, such a collection of books is unthinkable. It was a poet of our time who said: "The job of the teacher is to save the student's time." There are very few students who have not wasted many years for lack of contact with teachers in touch with all the relevant creative activities of their own time. It is the first business of the city itself to create a heightened human awareness, and then the business of the university, as the perfection of the city in microcosm, to give the direct polish and luster to the social dialog that perfects the growth of corporate intelligence. A library, which is a mere collection of classified items, however comprehensive, can never even approach the resonant model of this small choice of concentrated oral wisdom and insight.

No More Monopolies of Knowledge

The specialist is the last person in the world who could contrive or even contribute to such a library of inclusive contemporaneity. The specialist lives in a world of small talk and gossip. It is only when he crosses the boundaries of his own field into another field that dialog begins. If a man like C. P. Snow had had any competence in the world of Picasso, Joyce, or Siegfried Giedion, there would have been none of the naïve "hang-ups" he presents in his book *The Two Cultures and Scientific Revolution* (1959). There would have been no difficulty whatever in relating all of the existing cultures of our time. The electric age presents no difficulties in interrelating all of the cultural processes of our time. In the electric age there can be no more monopolies of knowledge, and scientists and artists for the past century have accepted the esprit de l'X-ray. Since Baudelaire, the poets and painters have recognized the Faradays and the Claude Bernards as participating in a common quest with themselves.

The Muddle Crass and the "Bestseller List"

Having mentioned the compact library of the Cambridge English school, it might be well to consider its counterpart, the bestseller list. I do not mention the bestseller list in disdain, since I am fully aware that whereas a good book tells you where it's at, a bad book is an invaluable guide to the panic, fears, and responses of countless millions of somnambulists. In the age of operations research, we have discovered how invaluable a commodity ignorance can be, and also how irrelevant and misleading the expert can be. One of the outrageous features of great contemporary art, from Flaubert and Joyce to Pound and Eliot, has been the freedom with which very high-brow artists have exploited and incorporated the dregs of popular art. Ragtime and jazz found their way into vers libre and into the most esoteric rhythms of T. S. Eliot. The most vulgar American jazz of the 1920s inspired painters and architects in Paris.

The nature of the bestsellers is changing under the new pressures of mass marketing. Because the wide distribution of a book is required to make it a bestseller, the role of book promoters and jobbers is crucial in determining which books will make it. Without the big advance to insure the widest distribution, a book can no longer make it as a bestseller.

Slanging the Doors of Perception

The bestseller lists, which are still eagerly scanned, represent not "where it's at," but a kind of a dream of "galloping poltergeists"—a nostalgic profile of remote romantic agonies. An enormously popular book like *The Godfather* (1969), by Mario Puzo, has great sociological significance like M. Ostrogorski's *Democracy and the Party System in the United States: A Study in Extra-constitutional*

Government. *The Godfather* is in reality a documentary about the rise of a new oral culture in electronic America. America, the only country ever founded on the printed word, has now reverted to the preliterate form of human awareness and organization, first under the impact of radio and then of TV. Any form of nonliterate or nonlegal power structure necessarily has the character of the gang or the tribe. In a literate society, oral culture is always a threat to the establishment, as much as slang is a threat to the schoolteacher of English grammar. Like any other affliction it can, if understood, become a positive resource. Slang is not incorrect English. It is an untiring probe of the frontiers of a changing corporate awareness. The cat's whiskers and the cat's meow were first felt and heard in the age of the crystal set. No more delicate probe was ever advanced than the cat's whisker as it explored the declivities of the galena crystal.

A Bad Book Is the Life Blood of a Vampire Spirit

To the knowledgeable literary historian, bad books are an even more fruitful guide to the state of the human psyche than the highest forms of art. It is one of the oddities of literary historians that they eschew the investigation of public taste. When Q. D. Leavis wrote *Fiction and the Reading Public* (1965), there were fierce outcries of pain among the literati in general. The rigor with which she swept the literature of good taste into the dustbin, created a kind of pandemonium among those for whom the reading of books is a relaxing and entertaining activity. In his own day, Shakespeare was widely regarded by the university wits as an ignoramus, as having an untutored mind of yokel propensity and vulgar taste. John Milton and Dr. Johnson confirmed this estimate. The modern Shakespearean cult emerged with the Rousseau and Wordsworth glorification of the spontaneous and the untaught genius as preferable to the learned and cultivated one. Cornielle was held in disfavor by the academics for *Le Cid*, which nevertheless enjoyed great success with the public.

It could be argued that the *Forsythe Saga*, as presented by the BBC on TV, represents a higher level of sensibility and artistic achievement than the prose of John Galsworthy. We are all familiar with the fact that a popular movie like *Gone with the Wind* may increase book sales, but there have been few studies of the effects of the movie or the TV form on the novel or the arts. About the effect of industry on the university as a knowledge factory, however, there is no need for doubt. The voice of Thomas Carlyle resounds with the nineteenth-century enthusiasm for hardware and massiveness when he says: "The true university of these days is a collection of books" ("The Hero as a Man of Letters: Johnson, Rousseau, Burns").

The scientist Thomas Huxley is just as certain as Carlyle about the role of studies in the mass production of learning:

> Those who take honours in Nature's university, who learn the laws, which govern men and things and obey them, are the really great and successful men in this world. The great mass of mankind are the "Poll," who pick up just enough to get through without much discredit. Those who won't learn at all are plucked; and then you can't come up again. Nature's pluck means extermination. ...
>
> That man, I think, has had a liberal education, who has been so trained in youth that his body is the ready servant of his will, and does with case and pleasure all the work that, as a mechanism, it is capable of; whose intellect is a clear, cold, logic engine, with all its parts of equal strength, and in smooth working order; ready, like a steam engine, to be turned to any kind of work, and spin the gossamers as well as forge the anchors of the mind; whose mind is stored with a knowledge of the great and fundamental truths of Nature and of the laws of her operations; one who, no stunted ascetic, is full of life and fire, but whose passions are trained to come to heel by a vigorous will, the servant of a tender conscience; who has learned to love all beauty, whether of nature of art, to hate all vileness, and to respect others as himself.
>
> Such a one, and no other, I conceive, has had a liberal education; for he is, as completely as a man can be, in harmony with Nature. He will make the best of her, and she of him. They will get on together rarely; she as his ever beneficent mother; he as her mouthpiece, her conscious self, her minister and interpreter. (Huxley, 1920)

Libraries have performed many functions, past, present, and future. The opening lines of Eliot's *Four Quartets* (1945) have relevance here as an indicator of the dimension of contemporaneity conferred on all ages by means of recorded learning:

> Time present and time past
> Are both perhaps present in time future,
> And time future contained in time past.

Richard de Bury memorably recorded the joys of simultaneous access to the riches of the totality of human wisdom in the fourteenth century:

> "That the Treasure of Wisdom Lieth Especially in Books"
> The desirable treasure of wisdom and knowledge, which all men covet by an instinct of nature, infinitely surpasses all the riches of the world. In respect to this, precious stones are cheap; in comparison, silver is clay, and gold but paltry sand. In its splen-

dour, both sun and moon darken to the sight; in its admirable sweetness honey and manna grow bitter to the taste.

O Excellency of wisdom that wasteth not with time
Ever-flourishing virtue that
Purgeth all venom from its possessor
O heavenly gift of the Divine bounty
Descending from the Father of Lights to bear
Up the rational spirit even unto heaven
Thou art the heavenly food of the mind, and
They who eat thee shall hunger again, and
They who drink thee shall thirst again.
Thou art a melody bringing joy to the soul
Of him that is wary, and he who hears thee
Shall in no wise be confounded. Thou art
The mistress and the ruler of morals, and
He who acts after thy laws shall do no sin.
By thee, kings reign and princes decree
Justice. By thee, laying aside the rudeness
Of nature, polishing their thought and speech,
And plucking out by the roots the thorns of
Vice, they attain the heights of honour, becoming
Fathers of their country and companions of
Princes, who, but for thee, had beaten their
Spears into pruning hooks and ploughshares or,
Haply, with the prodigal son had now been feeding Swine. (1948, p. 7. {now available at sunsite.berkeley.edu/philobiblon})

That great treasures of wisdom lie in our libraries unused cannot be denied. What is required is the equivalent of the pirate's map that shows where the treasure is hidden. This is the role of the compact library like the 2,000-volume collection at the University of Cambridge referred to earlier. This type of collection would contain an update of all the fields of human intellectual endeavor so that the user can immediately discover what books should be consulted in this field of interest. The existence of this type of collection would turn all our libraries into self-help institutions where an individual could pursue his studies independently. Providing tutorial service could further enhance this independent study program. This would allow greater depth of the independent study program and create a creative mix of written and oral education.

The library has usually played the subsidiary role of a resource center for traditional educational institutions such as secondary schools, universities, vocational schools, among others. With a compact library and a tutoring program, the library becomes an alternative education facility, not unlike a number of the free schools organized in the past decade to service the large number of dropouts from our conventional school system.

Young students who grow up in today's electrically configured world cannot operate in the fragmented, specialized environments created by our conventional schools. The students desire integrated patterns of information in which the relation and relevance of each part to all the others is explicit. The compact library provides precisely the type of pattern recognition that combats the fragmentation due to information overload. A compact collection also provides the active participation in the learning process that the school dropout so earnestly seeks and desires.

Information overload is due to the runaway of the left side of the brain, which focuses on the fragmented and specialized. The holistic, pattern-recognizing facility of the right side of the brain was pushed down by print and permitted the takeover of the left brain. With the speedup of electric communication, patterns re-emerge and the right brain reasserts itself, creating the need for the compact library. The left brain perceives **figure** while the right brain provides the **ground** without which the figure is meaningless. The compact library provides the ground in which the meaning of the book as figure would emerge. Because the ground is continually changing so are the meanings of books and, therefore, the update of the compact library is essential or else one loses the sense of where it's at. The story of the elderly woman who took a sexy novel out of the branch library instead of her usual history book illustrates the figure-ground relation. When the elderly woman was told, "I thought you only read history," she replied to the librarian, "At my age, honey, this is history."

The figure-ground library, the compact library, is a radical form of education. The great books idea never worked precisely because it presented figures without grounds. Even great books out of context lose their meaning. The compact library does not allow one to lose touch. It allows the reader to be selective and this, as we learned earlier, is the only defense against book glut and information overload.

The compact library can, in addition to serving as a guide to large libraries, function independently. Because it is compact and relatively cheap, it can help decentralize library function by providing a large number of outlets within convenient reach of its potential users. This is an important asset in view of the studies that revealed convenience is more important to the user than depth of collection (Dougherty & Blomquist, 1974, pp. 64–65).

Each compact library does not have to be identical. Some elements would remain universal, but some elements would vary according to geography and user interests. The compact library could contain a guide to the legal system of its users, which naturally varies from locale to locale.

Human Scale in the Library

The compact library can do much to reduce the complexity of today's literature to the point where it achieves a human scale and, once again, becomes accessible to a wide audience. But the compact library cannot do the entire job. The institution of the library must find other ways of achieving human scale. The tendency for the library, whether it is a university research library or an urban public library system, has been growth. Size can sometimes have negative survival values, as the experience of the dinosaur taught us. Because of the pressure to maintain an up-to-date collection in an era of book glut, books tend to push people out of the library. Other pressure, such as management techniques in the name of efficiency, tends to emphasize book consumption rather than human growth.

Perhaps the way ahead for the modern library lies in the past. While the Bait Al-Kutub library of medieval Baghdad might not be the model for today's library, there are still valuable lessons to be learned from its operation:

> The great Bait Al-Kutub—the House of books built by a caliph of medieval Bagdad was a wonder of its day. Scholars composed rhapsodies concerning its elegance and the treasures it contained. But a large portion of its floor area was taken up with sleeping rooms for its patrons, and a major function of its staff was to feed the scholars who thronged to study the books, and a considerable item in its budget was for the purchase of paper and ink for the copying of manuscripts … . The building, which housed the House of Books would scarcely be considered an efficient library structure today. (Randall, 1946, p. 323)

The aspect of the Bait Al-Kutub, which makes it different from today's library, is the excessive effort that was made to make the library convenient for its users. While the luxuries of the Bait Al-Kutub are no longer necessary, convenience still plays a major role in the functioning of a library, as a recent study of library use by university professors reveals. Dougherty and Blomquist (1974) found that ease of access was more important in determining a faculty member's use of a particular library than the actual depth of the library's collection:

> The library use pattern of Syracuse University faculty did not appear to be influenced by the percentage of relevant documents housed in any one specific location. The distance of a Syracuse University researcher's office from the libraries he used was a more positive predictor of his expectation rate than was the richness or lack thereof, of holdings in the libraries used. (pp. 64–65)

These results are consistent with earlier studies of both academic and public libraries, which revealed that the ease of use and convenience of access to a library collection influences its users more than the depth of its collection unless the user operating in the left hemisphere mode is searching for a specific title.

> Slater (1963) found that the distance from a researcher's office to the library he typically frequents influences his use of that library. Likewise, Ennis (1965) stated that, with public library users, availability affects what is read. Bereleon (1949) reported … that a survey based on a national sample revealed that one-half of the public library's adult users lived within a mile of the public library. Allen (1968) and Rosenberg (1967) found that the information channels are selected on the basis of convenience rather than on the amount of information those channels are expected to provide. (Dougherty & Blomquist, p. 2)

These studies reveal that mundane things such as ease of access are important in promoting the use of the library. Another absolutely essential feature that promotes the use of the library and the exchange of information is the quality of human contact, as was revealed by recent studies of library use by academic researchers:

> Voigt (1959), Harrison (1964) and Flowers (1965) all stressed the importance of personal contacts to scientists in their information request. Hanson estimated from his studies that personal contacts satisfied between 25 and 50 percent of a researcher's information needs. (Dougherty & Blomquist, p. 2)

What holds true for university professors holds equally true for the nonacademic users of the public library. One-to-one conversations are still often the most efficient way of accessing information. More sophisticated technologies tend to push out simpler technologies, even in situations where the simpler technology is more appropriate. The automobile is a great convenience, but it often discourages the use of the foot, even in situations where walking would be more convenient than driving. The same is true of writing versus speech. A well-organized cataloging system is certainly a valuable asset to a library, but it cannot replace individual help on a person-to-person basis.

Ellsworth Mason describes the operation of a very simple library with a 3,000-volume collection, and no classification system operated by a single, aging librarian for youngsters in an impoverished Latin American neighborhood:

> That little lady knew every book in the place, and what is more, stocked books that these youngsters wanted to read. Her circulation was high, and she constantly scrounged the right kind of books to replace the old ones and refresh her stock. She knew those youngsters backward and forward, what they could do and what was new to them and was able to keep them reading actively. This, I take, is the central purpose of any library. (Mason, 1972)

He then goes on to analyze what is the root of the public library's problem:

> The public library is suffering all the ills of contemporary society—over-marginalized, over-crowded, inconvenient, directionless, and unable to get rid of its trash. We tend to substitute organization for personal effort, to keep our chain of command straight rather than our humanity straight. We confuse computers, and other machines, with libraries, which they are not. We confuse buildings with libraries. We confuse book collections with libraries, and even book collections are not libraries. (Mason, 1972)

At the beginning of this book we mentioned that every extension of man affects the entire psychic and social complex and, hence, all the other extensions of man. The techniques of management science are no exception. This extension of man has had profound effects on the library, as was alluded just above.

In order to apply their techniques, the management scientist attempts to quantify the objectives of the library:

> Under the assumption that the basic objective of libraries is to maximize exposure to documents (direct or indirect, in the library or outside the library, in the short run and in the long run), we proposed several measures of library performance based upon document exposure. These are exposure counts, item-use-days, and exposure. (Hamburg, Clelland, Brimmer, Ramist, &Whitfield, 1978)

Their definition brings to mind the gag about the speed-readers: "I read Tolstoi's *War and Peace* in 4 and a half minutes. It was about Russia, wasn't it?" This joke helps to illustrate the superficiality of their definition, which distorts the aims of the library.

Quantitative measures that fail to take into account the quality of the information exchanged denigrate our social values. What is to distinguish between the effectiveness of a well-used library and a pornographic bookshop? The development of quantitative measure by the management science boys is a typical example of consideration of a **figure** in the absence of its **ground**.

Hamburg and colleagues admit that maximizing document exposure is not the objective of all libraries. For those libraries whose clientele are basically interested in reading and are using the library to gather information, the object might be to minimize document exposure time. The authors, in this case, "suggested performance measures such as the proportion of users satisfied and documents retrieved." While showing some sensitivity to the gross simplification of their assumptions, the management science advocates, nevertheless, base their entire approach on rather limited premises. What we, as users of a library, want cannot be measured. There are times when one just wants the information as fast as possible. There are times one would like to have comfortable surroundings in which to browse and encounter new information as one tracks down a particular item. One of the pleasures of looking up a word in the dictionary is all the other words you encounter on the way. If someone designed an interactive terminal that provides an entry each time we spelled out a word, we would lose a great deal. {*Well this has, in fact, happened since we wrote those words in 1979. That pleasure is gone but replaced by others since every time we Google something we invariably get sidetracked as we encounter interesting and unexpected nuggets of information.*}

If the aim of the library is to promote and enhance those human qualities that separate us from animals and machines, then we cannot foresee numerating or codifying the objectives of the library. The mere attempt to do so destroys something. To the management science crowd who ask us to define our goals for the library so they can help us make better decisions, one could reply: "My goal for the library is that it provides the kind of inspiration and creativity that no management scientist could measure or evaluate." Any library that focuses its attentions on goals that can be measured has lost sight of its most important mission, the preservation of our human heritage.

Those that advocate the quantitative approach to management science will no doubt feel maligned by our somewhat moralistic attack on their techniques. They will protest that it is not their intention to neither emphasize the quantitative nor detract from the humanistic aims of the library. Although these technocrats have the best of intentions, they are extremely naïve about the effects of their technology, as is the case with all innovators of new technology. Ford did not foresee correctly the effects of the automobile. He thought the auto would bring city people to the countryside where they could enjoy nature. He could not foresee that the automobile would destroy nature, and cities as well. Efficiency experts are equally blind to the effects of their technology. They do not see how it destroys human scale. Perhaps they should set as an objective for their activity the reinstatement of human scale in the activities of mankind. Perhaps if they considered each of their schemes in light of these criteria, they would be able to make a more solid contribution. Systematization, by itself, is not contra-productive but one must assess carefully the effects of each system one initiates, and understand the cost of the efficiency it purchases.

· 1 0 ·

THE PUBLIC LIBRARY: PAST, PRESENT, AND FUTURE TRENDS

The public library is a recent social phenomenon not more than 150 years old {*when we wrote the first draft of the book but now not more than 185 years old*}. Because the political, technological, and social conditions that created the public library have changed so dramatically since its origin, the aims and purposes of the public library have undergone constant study and scrutiny.

Today is no exception. There is great ferment among librarians as to the directions in which the public library should move. Before examining these issues, let us review the origin of the public library. Before the eighteenth century, libraries were organized strictly for the scholarly. This changed as a result of the new image of humankind that arose with the scientific revolution. D. W. Davies (1974) notes popular libraries

> are to a considerable extent, but not wholly, the consequence of the idea of the perfectability of mankind which was put about in the world by Rene Descartes and Francis Bacon, and which got entirely out of hand with William Godwin and Jeremy Bentham. (p. 2)

The first popular libraries actually grew out of the commercial subscription libraries organized for the middle class in the eighteenth century. The standards of these lending libraries were not very high, as the following remark of Coleridge reveals:

> For as to the devotees of the circulating libraries, I dare not compliment their pass-time, or rather kill-time with the name of reading. ... We should, therefore, transfer this species of amusement ... from the genus reading, to that comprehensive class characterized by the power of reconciling the two contrary yet co-existing propensities of human nature, namely indulgence in sloth and hatred of vacancy. (as cited by Davies, 1974)

Toward the end of the eighteenth century, libraries for the working class were organized in England and North America. The eighteenth century also saw, no doubt due to the influence of the Enlightenment, the organization of athenaeums, literary societies, philosophical societies, and scientific societies. The purpose of these societies was to disseminate information rather than provide a society for the discovery of new information. This role was played by the royal societies and national academies that were organized strictly for scholars. The athenaeums and the like were organized strictly for the education of the middle class. Similar societies, called "lyceums" and "Mechanics" institutes, were organized for the working class. Both these types of societies featured, in addition to a library and newspaper reading room, such cultural activities as gymnasiums, chess, concerts, lectures, demonstrations, classes, and exhibits. These uplift societies were, more or less, private clubs supported by their members but sometimes subsidized by philanthropists and do-gooders.

These institutions fulfilled the educational need of their time by preparing or training workers for the new mass-production environment. Literacy, a luxury for rural existence, was a necessary skill for those who wanted to prosper or even survive in the new industrial setting. The generosity of the philanthropists who supported these institutions—like those of modern-day industrialists who support universities—was tinged with a lot of self-interest since their enterprises required literate workers, as not all factory work could be carried out by unskilled workers. Someone had to organize activities even at the intermediate level and others had to tend to the machinery, both of which activities required a certain level of literacy and understanding of the new mechanical world order.

In the nineteenth century the notion of a public library supported by a local tax base grew in popularity. These first libraries were frequently dependent on the generosity of philanthropic up-lifters, such as Andrew Carnegie, to provide the initial capital to house the library and to begin the collection:

The modern public library was born of the identification of noblesse oblige with economic status: capitalism idealized in a sentimental Victorian liberalism and personified as Lady Bountiful dispensing books to improve the intellectual status of the electorate. (Shera, 1971, p. 23)

The motivation of those who founded the modern public library was not always above reproach:

It is ... commonly believed that the origins of the public library movement testifies to the power of popular democracy in this country, yet everyone knows that historically only a very small portion of the eligible users have ever crossed the threshold of a public library. According to (Michael) Harris, public libraries were founded by upper-class men, who were contemptuous and distrustful of the masses and wanted to furnish means of popular education to preserve social order in a changing world. They were run by similarly motivated, authoritarian, inflexible, middle-class librarians whose inability to reach the masses eventually demoralized them, made their work "increasingly aimless and bureaucratic," produced an "obsession with detail and technique" and sunk public librarianship into "mindlessness." (Dain, 1975, p. 261)

At first, the tax-supported libraries focused solely on the collection and dissemination of books. As it became apparent that there was not a tremendous demand by the public, the libraries switched over to an operation similar to the athenaeum and private up-lift societies:

When it became obvious that there was no great passion for up-lift on the part of the public, the third concept of the public libraries developed, the idea of the library as social service and recreation center. ... Because public libraries were established and flourished in the era of uplift, the activities of lyceum, mechanics' institutes, settlement houses, ragged schools and commercial entertainment became part of the tradition of public libraries, and they have been carried over, almost without change, to present-day public libraries. Excursions, visits to the poor, festivals for ethnic groups, games, lectures, the distribution of literature from house to house in poverty areas, education for those that dropped out of the education system, conscious efforts to live among and understand the poor and under-privileged, reading sessions, clubs within the organization, the rendition of miscellaneous social services, are all part of the good works of libraries conceived as social, and entertainment centers. (Davies, p. 106)

At the present time, the words of Marshall McLuhan, "Everything is information," are often quoted. It follows that since libraries are traditionally interested in information, the modern social library is interested in everything.

"Today," one enthusiastic librarian declared, "we are in pursuit of the total population and hoping to capture a large segment, because there is truly something for everyone." The social library is particularly in pursuit of those who have no interest in books. (Davies, 1974, p. 106)

The social library is not a universally accepted view of the library. There are those who hold that the social functions of the library are best carried out by other agencies, and that the library should concentrate on what it can do best, namely, provide books for those who are interested in reading:

If libraries confined themselves to books and reading it would certainly be true that their public would be narrower, as would their field of endeavour but it is difficult to see why such a change would not be for the better. Symphony orchestras do not attempt to interest all of the people or even to reach all of those interested in music, but the importance of symphony musicians and the respect accorded them are not diminished by their consciously limiting their field of endeavour. ...

The suggestion made here is that librarians take a new direction, that they become interested in and confine themselves to the concept of libraries as places for books and reading. By so doing they have little to lose other than those who are not interested in books anyway. What they have to gain is the friendship and confidence of bookish people; and the respect, which the modern world has for the specialist and the expert. (Davies, p. 125)

Davies makes persuasive arguments. If all is information and the library is vested with the responsibility of providing information service to the community, then why should the library limit itself to the book? On the other hand, if the library spreads itself too thin, it runs the danger of duplicating services and hence losing its opportunity to make a real contribution. Certainly the library was originally organized to specialize in books, but a number of things have changed since then. Perhaps a review of those changes would provide some insight that could help us resolve this controversy and apparent conflict.

When the public libraries were first being organized, print was the only means for mass distribution of information. There was no television or radio, only newspapers and books. Books were expensive. There were no cheap paperback editions. The library, as a consequence, was the principle means for the distribution of information. The library also served an important role in the recreational life of a community in the days before movies, radio, and TV. Times have changed and the library no longer has a monopolistic hold over information and recreation. In fact, the library is hard pressed to compete with mass media in these areas. {*And now it must also compete with the Internet, which is a great source of both information and recreation.*} It is for this reason that a number of librarians have been looking for new roles for the library to play in our overentertained and information-overloaded society.

{*As for the Internet not all members of the general public can afford computers and Internet access. As a result the public library provides an essential service by providing this service for those who cannot afford it on their own. The July 8, 2014,* New York Times *reported how some users make use of the library's Internet access after the library closes: "Joey Cabrera stands for part of most evenings on the doorstep of the Clason's Point Library ... in the Bronx. There, he taps into the Wi-Fi that seeps out of the library after it closes. He checks in on Tumblr, Snapchat, Facebook —'the usual stuff,' he said." The article goes on to report that the New York public library system is experimenting with a program where patrons can check out a device that they can plug into the wall at home and provide them and four other users with a Wi-Fi connection. For the moment the library has received a grant to allow a trial program to take place. This could likely be a future trend for the public library, as many households cannot afford the annual fee of $1,000 for household Wi-Fi. I believe that this is likely to become a future trend for public libraries. Access to information is a right that should belong to all citizens in a democracy, as does the use of the streets and sidewalks of a city and access to potable water. We should also mention that many cafes and restaurants offer free Wi-Fi as a way to attract customers.—RKL*}

Information and Referral Service

One of the principal roles of information and referral service is to help members of the community to cope with the glut of information required to survive in our modern complex society. As society becomes more complex and more specialized information services become available, as interconnection becomes more feasible technically; there is likely to become unnecessary demand for referral and switching services so the individuals can use the library as a one-stop information service with confidence of being able to appropriate when the desired information is not available locally. (Parker, 1971)

Public libraries have begun to inaugurate a number of information and referral services to meet information needs within the community. When public libraries were first organized more than a hundred years ago, the most essential service they provided was information about the world outside their community. Providing information about what was happening within the community would have been totally redundant. People were well informed about local happenings. Society was not complex and, therefore, there was not all that much local information. There weren't that many social services to which people could be referred. Today, paradoxically, the situation is reversed. People seem to know more about the outside world than they do about their own community. Before electricity, most of the information that a person encountered was generated locally. With the coming of the telegraph, more and more information came from the outside, until today, with radio and television, the majority of the information we receive is generated outside our community. Hollywood and New York City dominate the nonprint media. {*With the proliferation of TV channels with cable television there are now many more channels for local news.*} The public library, therefore, has an important role to play in the dissemination of community information. There are those that would insist that not only should the library disseminate community information, but it should also help to generate community information:

> We are living in the middle of a myth, the myth of an information explosion. Rather, there is a mass communications explosion, a plethora of media to transport broad-based information from area to area. But, there is still a dearth of local community information in any given area. This information, possibly the most vital of all, is usually not available in any of these mass communication formats, and therefore cannot be supplied on an individual demand by the public library or any other agency in the community. The traditional library only supplies the passive use of mass-produced resources: periodicals, books, records, et al., and these resources do not facilitate the dissemination of community information. The library, if it is to be a community information resource, has to change from its old staid role to an active one; creating information, giving a voice to the community, and helping it learn about itself. If the informational needs of the community are not being filled by traditional libraries, then what has to be created is a library geared toward local production of community information resources, helping people understand the dynamics of their community. (Peyser, 1973)

The information and referral services being offered by urban public libraries involve the active participation of the library staff in a quasi-advocacy role in obtaining information for their users. These new services are defined as follows:

> Information and referral is the active process of linking a person with a need or problem with a service, which will meet the need or solve the problem. The link between the person and the service is made up of information. It is because the success or failure of the information link depends on communication involving specific individuals

in specific problem situations, that we emphasize that information and referral is a process and not a product. (Croneberger & Luck, 1975)

The goal of the modern public librarian, like that of her nineteenth-century predecessors, is that of social uplift. The nineteenth-century approach was much more passive, based on the erroneous notion that the mere presence of "proper" books in a library's collection would automatically improve "the public morals, mental health, civic virtue and intellectual growth." Today's librarian takes a much more active role in

helping a person get information or services which he cannot get for himself. Then by definition, information and referral is advocacy, which may require varying levels interpretation and intervention. We think this kind of advocacy is needed, appreciated and safe. (Croneberger & Luck, 1975)

While, in some sense, this type of service represents a departure, it is still within the mainstream of traditional library services, as the following statement of philosophy for the TIP information and referral service of Detroit indicates:

1. information and referral service is simply a broadening and a deepening of the library's traditional function;
2. as in every aspect of service, the public librarian serves as an ombudsman or expediter, not as advocate;
3. the necessity of follow-up is emphasized as a strength unique to the TIP service and to make sure that the patron has actually received the help he or she needs. (*Library Journal*, 1975, p. 1283)

The head of TIP's program in Detroit's Chaney Branch elaborated on this statement:

The Library is not designed, by definition or purpose, for direct social action. ... Our genius, if you will, is in locating, indexing, arranging, and making accessible information about the community and its resources, in a free atmosphere, so that such information can be applied to problems. (ibid.)

Information and referral services have been organized in a number of American cities, including Atlanta, Baltimore, Cleveland, Detroit, Houston, and New York. These programs can no longer be described as experimental. They are part and parcel of today's public library.

In addition to the active role librarians have accepted in their information and referral services, they have also given careful thought to the other social responsibilities they should assume as librarians. A major part of this thrust has centered on the activities of the task forces of the Social Responsibilities Round Table (SRRT) of the American Library Association:

> Their activities range from providing access to materials (Alternatives in Print, Government Documents, Sex Media), to working with minorities and other oppressed persons (Chicanos, Migrant Workers, Prison Libraries, Service to the Poor), to working toward improving the profession (Recruitment of Minorities, Student Affiliates). … Topics and activities are varied—resulting from, and responding to, need. They all should result in action and improvement. Task forces have been responsible for some tremendous forward movement in the profession. Many have resulted in permanent programs and even some effective committee action. The number of those involved in each task force have ranged from a half dozen to well over 100. (Marshall & Emerick, 1972)

There are also task forces on Gay Liberation and Women's Liberation, as well as the Clearinghouse for Reference and Acquisition Information.

· 11 ·

THE LIBRARY AND EDUCATION

Left is left and right is right. And never the twain shall meet?—paraphrasing Rudyard Kipling

The educational needs of the world are changing. We live in a complex world of high technology and intractable social problems. At one and the same time we must confront the effects of exploding population, diminishing resources, information glut, and overspecialization. We face dangers of imminent famine, a poisoned environment, runaway inflation, economic decline, large-scale unemployment, structural poverty, pervasive alienation and malaise, political breakdown, nuclear proliferation, and political terrorism {*and global warming*}.

We live in the era of information explosion. We are flooded by a plethora of data, yet seem unable to use our knowledge and understanding to come to terms with the difficulties facing us. This, we believe, can to a great extent be attributed to the effects of our communication systems and to the way they bias our thought processes.

The solution to any one problem exacerbates one or more of the others. Solving the problems of a dwindling energy supply often entails a worsening of environmental degradation through increased pollution or nuclear proliferation. Combating inflation carries the price of increased unemployment;

creating jobs often leads to increased inflation. Our society and technological environment has grown so complex that we find ourselves victims of a double bind where each solution creates additional problems.

It has become obvious to students of this seamless web that a simultaneous attack from many angles is required. Linear sequential attempts at finding a solution have failed. What is needed is an approach to the world, which is characterized by intuitive, ecological patterns of thought (right brain). At the same time, analytical, scientific thought processes (characteristic of the left brain) will also be essential because of the technical nature of many aspects of our contemporary world.

The thought patterns of these two hemispheres of the brain are complementary, inclusive rather than exclusive. Man evolved in such a manner that this division aided his survival. It has been surmised that the brain more easily performs multiple tasks if these activities are separated in the brain, hence, the division of functions between the two hemispheres. The corpus callosum indicates that coordination of left and right activities is built into the structure of the brain.

Given this biological fact, one might ask why is it that most individuals and cultures seem to favor one hemisphere at the expense of the other. An explanation for this may be discovered by studying the biases in our thinking processes that result from our communication patterns. In order to discover how we can have the better of two worlds—the left world of analysis and the right world of synthesis—we must learn to understand how the media of communication affect our thought patterns.

Left-brain activities came to dominate the other hemisphere as disjunctive, lineal, rational thought processes inspired by reading invaded all aspects of man's economical, social, and intellectual activities. Dominance of the left hemisphere began with the use of the phonetic alphabet and the invention of Euclidean space in the first millennium B.C. This dominance was reinforced in the Western world by centuries of manuscript culture, culminating with Gutenberg and the development of movable type. The patterned or lineal typography provided a social environment, which enormously intensified left-hemisphere dominance. This lineal pattern of the left hemisphere underwent a dramatic reversal with the arrival of the telegraph and the instantaneous transmission of information. The transition from written or printed communication to simultaneous electric information media represents a major reversal of form and the return to oral culture.

The impact of this revolution in communication, based largely on electricity, has transformed every element of modern society. Each new medium or technology is an extension of man that affects his entire psyche and social complex. At the speed of light, the sender is sent. Under the conditions of this speedup of information, new patterns of decision making and organization emerged. The right hemisphere began to reassert itself over the long-dominant left. In these circumstances Freudian psychology came into existence by resurrecting the therapy of the word, an ancient Semitic tribal healing technique, described in *The Therapy of the Word in Classical Antiquity* (Entralgo, 1970). Anthropology turned its attention to oral cultures. Sociology begins to examine the patterns of man's social interactions.

The ecological and environmental patterns that emerged with the speedup of information are essential for attaching the global problems referred to earlier. This interdisciplinary approach is a welcome relief to the intense specialism that prevailed when print was the major medium of communication. Electric media, however, will not provide a panacea and automatic solution to our problems.

An unfortunate side effect of electric media is that they reduce the attention span and, hence, discourage reading and the development of other analytic skills associated with the left brain. This is particularly true of the effect of television on the reading patterns of young people. Television, using the eye as an ear, in the words of Tony Schwartz (1974), changes the sense ratio of the child's psyche, making reading difficult. Youngsters do not develop the fine motor coordination of the eye required for reading when they watch too much television. The increasing decline of reading skills since the advent of television has been documented in articles typically titled "Why Can't Johnny Read?" Educators have also been asking other questions, such as "Why can't Johnny write?" or "Why can't Johnny add and subtract?" These queries reflect a decline among our youth of the analytic skills associated with the left hemisphere.

Television cannot be used to teach reading. *Sesame Street* is a blind alley, a contradiction. Television, via rear projection, destroys the faculties necessary for the utilization of the left hemisphere. The real world becomes fantasy, and Disney World and science fiction become the real world. "The only emperor is the emperor of ice cream" (Wallace Stevens, 1923). Every service environment creates a disservice environment.

We are caught in a double bind. Electronic media are a mixed blessing. They encourage ecological patterns of thought and help us recognize the nature of our global village, but they discourage the development of reading and its concomitant analytic skills. Put the other way, reading is a mixed blessing. With too much print we are blinded by specialism and are unable to see the patterns crucial to our survival. However, if we allow our reading skills to deteriorate, we lose our capacity for analytic thought and, consequently, our control over our complex technological machinery. How, then, shall we survive on an overpopulated and underresourced planet?

The unique challenge facing educators, communicators, information scientists, and librarians in this era of mixed media is to discover a synthesis of the two basic modes of communication, the electric and the literate, so that the better of these two ways of handling and transmitting information can be utilized. There exists a dynamic tension between these two ways of knowing that can be very creative. We must find the societal and instructional equivalent to the corpus callosum, so that the left-brain- and right-brain-inspired activities of mankind can be coordinated and blended to dialog creatively. Only thus can we hope to deal successfully with the critical problems facing us in the near future.

Librarians have a unique contribution to make toward the resolution of this dilemma. By nature librarians are generalists. They must be acquainted with all aspects of man's knowledge. Yet librarians have a discipline, a structured approach to their profession that combines left-brain analytic skills with a right-brain capacity for patterning.

As a major dispenser of both print and nonprint material, the library has an important role to play in this process. Historically the library played an essential role in all aspects of literacy, including storage, circulation, and the actual production of literary material. The library also provided instruction in the arts of writing and reading.

The Library as Publisher and Promoter of Education

As a publisher, the library has a fair record of achievement. In the beginning it was as much a publisher as a collector and custodian of books.

Attached as it was to a religious temple, it became part of the system that educated the chosen few in the twins of literacy, reading and writing, and having taught writing, it then retained the scribes to produce texts: "Every sanctuary possessed its library and school, 'The House of the Tablet' or 'The House of the Seal' in which temple archives and liturgical texts were preserved, and the young were instructed in the art of writing" (Orr, 1977, p. 185).

Libraries through the ages have been associated with learning. The Alexandrian Library is a famed example. During medieval times learning and the library were closely associated with each other in the monasteries. Later universities, each of which was associated with a library, replaced these centers of education. During the Industrial Age, when specialism took over as a way of organizing learned activities, librarians wandered somewhat away from their tradition of being closely associated with education. This was not true in all cases. Universities still maintained their libraries, but librarians tended to be less involved in academic matters and concentrated more on maintaining their collections rather than using them. In all fairness to librarians, the rapid rise in the number of books made the maintenance and preservation of a collection a full-time concern, with less leisure time available for educational duties. In short, the librarian specialized, like other professionals of the time. Under the conditions of instantaneous electric information, this trend is reversing, and librarians are once again integrating their activities with other aspects of scholarship. {*This reversal is even more the case with digital media.*}

> The time was when a library was very like a museum, and a librarian was a mouser in musty books, and visitors looked with curious eyes at ancient tomes and manuscripts. A library is a school and the librarian is in the highest sense a teacher, and the visitor is a reader among the books as a workman among his tools. (Dewey, 1876)

Training the Reader

The most useful contribution librarians can make as teachers is teaching their users the art of reading, how to read a book, how to use a library. These skills could be taught in night classes for adults, afterschool programs for school children, and in morning programs for preschoolers. Deciphering alphabetic codes is only one form of reading. Printed books are only one form of books {*especially with the arrival of e-books, e-journals, and the plethora of digital texts, images, and video on the Internet.*} Librarians could teach other information-gathering skills as well. Learning how to decipher the millions of messages that bombard us daily is essential.

It is also essential to teach library users the skills of how to search out and find information that is not obviously available. This means more than just learning how to find information not in books or on tapes or slides or film; it includes learning how to find out what organization or individual might have valuable information or access to such information. {*It also includes how to make use of the Internet and the integration of the library's resources with those of the Internet.*} Library users should also be taught when certain information does not exist and must be created through research or synthesis of existing information. Patterns in education are changing in order to respond to the increased flux of new information and the rapid turnover of ideas that characterize our modern times:

> The changeability of the environment and the enormous growing mass of knowledge are leading to a shift in emphasis away from attempting to learn what is known in anticipation of its possible later value, toward learning the means of finding out what one has to know when the need arises. (Adelson, 1972) {*Just in time, information is now easily accessed with the Internet.*}

> If we go along with Adelson then we must recognize that it is becoming ever more important to be able to locate what it is you need to know than it is to gather data into the mind for possible future use. (Shields, 1978)

{*A new role for librarians is providing formal instruction of how patrons can best use the Internet to compliment the library's resources.*}

The role of the librarian in meeting these new educational needs is obvious. The information explosion has brought the skills of the librarian into greater-than-ever demand. However, since others will also aggressively seek to fill these needs, the library profession cannot afford to sit back waiting for the public to turn in its direction. Librarians must learn both to market their skills and to provide leadership in the information field. This is very important because librarians, as opposed to information scientists and systems managers, bring with them a longstanding humanistic tradition with a built-in notion of individualized service. The dehumanization of society arising from the information explosion is a major challenge to be faced in the future. Librarians have a large contribution to make in fostering a new spirit of education, one suited for the Age of Information.

Librarians are not yet meeting this challenge:

> Educators generally acknowledge as fact the idea that progress in every sector of American society depends today more upon ready access to information resources including all types of media than upon any other single factor, but this idea seems a more urgent concern to non-library professional and technical specialists working in communication and information service field than it does to librarians. (Stone, 1975, p. 262)

Some patrons will seek information for personal enrichment; some will want to put it to practical use in business, or in sharing it with others to raise public consciousness of community or global problems. Some needs will be satisfied by existing information; some will require a synthesis from various sources to create new information.

At the same time that the library encourages alphabetic reading skills, it must guard against the narrow specialism that the medium of alphabetic writing promotes. The use of a mixture of media in an integrated fashion provides a natural defense against the excesses of tunnel vision. In addition, pattern recognition and ecological thinking can be positively encouraged by creating packages of information that provide overviews of particular subjects or topics.

Along with the figure of the book or other media packages, libraries should also provide the informational ground or context in which a particular book can be read. This is particularly true of historical material. A novel by Charles Dickens can come further alive as the reader is acquainted with the social and political conditions that prevailed at the time of writing.

The library can also play a role in the development of our perception of communication media. This can be very useful, given the large percentage of time people spend absorbing information of one kind or another.

Education

All our mental processes depend upon perception. Inadequate perceiving results in poor thinking, inadequate feeling, diminished interest and enjoyment of life. Systematic training should be an essential element in all education. (A. Huxley, "Education on the Nonverbal Level," 1962)

The domination of our educational processes through domination of our perception is best exemplified by the effect of the book on the nature of education.

The "book" has profoundly influenced education ever since printing was invented, and those subjects, which are most easily propagated by the book have tended to prosper. The new media {especially digital media} service other subjects which have a high experience quality such as music, drama, art and craft, bringing the best experience to everyone with the kind of immediacy which some people gain from a book. This may very well produce a new evaluation of several disciplines, within the curriculum and an alteration of the balance between them. (Hyer, 1975)

The incorporation of media other than the book has led to changes in our educational system. Less emphasis is being placed on dissemination of information directly by the teacher. The teacher plays more of an advisory role directing or guiding students to appropriate sources of information. More emphasis is being placed on independent studies. Computer-assisted learning is another example of the trend toward individual study as opposed to class-room work. The city becomes a learning resource replacing the classroom as the focus of the educational process. The librarian's role flips from the private to the corporate role. She becomes a navigator or guide enabling users to have access to information and directing them to their goals. In such a climate the librarian has a much more substantial role to play in the educational process and a new role at that! "For years we librarians have celebrated our support of the classroom. But if the classroom is soon to become secondary what then will we support?" (Shores, 1968).

The answer to the question posed by Shores is obvious—the student. With the shift of emphasis and responsibility from the teacher to the student, librarians must redefine their role vis-à-vis the educational process. Shores calls for:

> a new dimension in academic librarianship. It is more important than ever that our profession abandon its auxiliary complex, its supportive role, its devotion to manage-ment and housekeeping and assume educational leadership. ... The only question is how many of us are willing to library teach rather than to library manage? (ibid.)

Librarians have a long tradition of dealing with individual needs and therefore should have no trouble fitting into the new scheme of things.

The immediate impact of technology is on the individual rather than on the system as a whole. The educational system must therefore come to the aid of individuals to give them an understanding of what they are experiencing. As a result, one can expect to see a more prominent role for libraries and information and media centers within educational institutions. "More school districts will mandate 'team teaching' approaches. Such approaches require that there be established at the 'heart' of each school some kind of Instruc-tional Material Centre" (Stone, 1975).

We are already seeing emerging alternatives to the university with a large physical plant and attendant escalating operating costs. Classrooms have become expendable in the case of "open college" courses presented on radio and television. The open college idea is, however, still wedded to hardware in the sense that it depends upon existing institutions and edited supplements via mail, bookkeeping, and accreditation with all the fragmentation of sub-jects that implies.

In the age of electric information, the "knowledge industries," which include broadcasting and advertising, are themselves dependent upon a great deal of academic training. Back in 1946, Clark and Sloan (1960), two Colum-bia University economists, did a study of "classrooms in the factories." They discovered that the budget for teaching a wide range of subjects on company time greatly exceeded the community budget for secondary and university education. Since that time such training programs have greatly increased in number and in scope, with the result that many employees who switch over to academic work might well be entitled to a year or more of academic credits upon entering the university.

A generation ago Harold Innis saw the need to get rid of subjects from uni-versity curriculum. He favored instead the holistic approach, which implies that wherever you begin to study, you will simply extend the range and depth of that study to the point of understanding. All forms of packaging of knowl-edge and credits belong to the quantitative approach to knowledge, which we have long pursued as a reflex of our industrial consumer society.

In the electric age we return to the world of software information and to the pursuit of wisdom rather than the training of skills. Training of skills, like acquiring the ability to read books and speak languages, naturally belongs to the pre-university level of specialized technical schools. Wisdom has always been associated with direct oral instruction. Television, though oral, has the disadvantage of being an "inner trip," with the effects fading rapidly. Atten-tion and retention are brief in this medium, making it unsuited to education. Radio is more adequate, but it too is a group with all the disadvantages of the tribal identity pattern.

{Media Literacy, Information Literacy, and the Use of Digital Media for Educational Purposes

In the intervening years since we wrote this chapter on the library and education, two new developments have arisen that are now worthy of inclusion. One is the rise of media literacy and the other is the proliferation of online courses.

Media literacy has been defined as "the ability to access, analyze, evaluate and create messages in a wide variety of forms" (Thoman & Jolls, 2005). Libraries are playing a key role in media literacy education. Given that libraries are no longer just storehouses of books but, also institutions that facilitate the access to information, providing their patrons with media literacy skills is now a central part of their mission. In addition to media literacy, some librarians are advocating information literacy, the ability to find the information one wants to access. Alan Turner (2015) believes there is an important connection between lifelong learning and information literacy:

> Librarians epitomize lifelong learning, they want their users to be able to do it for themselves, and no longer preside over knowledge. Libraries are the antithesis of corporations who try and control access to information. ... All literacies involve media in McLuhan's sense of the word and all of the mediums contain information, placing information literacy at the pinnacle of learning.

Another role for public libraries has emerged with digital media, namely, their offerings of online continuing education courses. Public libraries have had a rich tradition of providing instructor-led courses for children, young adults, and adults. Now with the emergence of online courses, libraries are able to expand their educational service in a cost-effective manner by making use of online courses. Some libraries are even considering becoming involved in the massive open online courses (MOOC) movement. For example, "the University of Wisconsin–Madison (UWM) is offering a new four-week massive open online course (MOOC) on Changing Weather and Climate in the Great Lakes ... the university, in coordination with Wisconsin Library Services (WiLS), is partnering with 21 public libraries across the state" (Lee, 2015). Another way public libraries could participate in the MOOC movement is by organizing local study groups within the library for those taking the same MOOC course.

In addition to MOOCs for the public, there are those that are organized for librarians, such as a free one presented by the iSchool at the University of Toronto titled "Library Advocacy Unshushed: Values, Evidence, Action." ("iSchool Brings Library," 2013). San José State University (SJSU) School of Information is also offering MOOCs freely available to the public and of special interest to librarians.— RKL}

· 1 2 ·

FUTURE OF THE BOOK

Much confusion about the figure of the book, past, present, and future, results from the new ground that environs both book and reader today. The printed book is a definitive package that can encode ancient times and be sent to remote destinations. More than electronic information, it submits to the whims of the user. It can be read and reread in large or small portions, but it always recalls the user to patterns of precision and sequential attention. Unlike the user of the telephone and other electric media, the user of the book retains his physical body and identity. Unlike radio and phonograph, the book does not provide an environment of resonating information that merges with social scenes and dialog. As the levels of sound and video images envelop the user, he "turns off" in order to retain his identity. The first video age presents the example of a generation of literate people who, in various ways, have turned off or gone numb. In contrast, the merely tribal man, or preliterate, would seem to feel no threat to his personal life from the new electronic surround.

The book can be sent anywhere, as a gift or as a component of a service environment. With electric media, it is, paradoxically, the sender who is sent. This flip, or chiasmus of form and function, occurs at the level of instant speed and is characteristic of telephone and radio and video alike. When the ground or surround of a service assumes this instant character, the figure or the user is transformed and becomes discarnate, losing his relation to natural law. As a component in a service environment of readers and reading public, the book does not have its meaning alone. The book in the preliterate world appears as a magical form of uniform and echoing symbols. Margaret Mead once told one of us (McLuhan) that the natives on the Admiralty Islands were astonished to discover that the symbols in the various copies of her book *Coming of Age in Samoa* were identical. They cried, pointing to the pages, "Same! Same! Same!" Mr. Eliot captured the same feature of the printed word when Madame Sosotris, famous clairvoyant in *The Waste Land* (1922), tells a client, "Tell Dear Mrs. Equitone I bring the horoscope myself." Sometimes affected speech has the character mimicking the printed word by maintaining an artificial monotone as though the individual were uttering printed prose.

To the literate world the book serves a myriad of roles, ornamental and recreational and utilitarian. What is to be the new nature and form of the book against the new electronic {*and digital*} surround? What will be the effect of the microdot library {*as well as e-books*} on books past, present, and future? When millions of volumes can be compressed in a matchbox space, it is not the book merely but also the library that becomes portable. {*This is a reality today with e-readers and with smartphones connected to the Internet and, hence, Google Books.*}

There are many ways in which the book and literate values are, of course, threatened by the mere fact of the electric service environment. The extreme distraction presented by the acoustic, cinematic {*and digital*} rivals of the book brings decreasing opportunities for attentive and uninterrupted reading. Beginning with the typewriter, and then the mimeograph, the nature of the book underwent immense change of pattern and use. The typewriter changed the forms of English expression by opening up once more the oral world to the writer of books. Whether it was Henry James dictating interminable sentences to Theodora Basanquet, or the semi-literate executive giving abrupt letters to a secretary who can spell and compose grammatically, the new services of typing and mimeographing transformed the uses and the character of the printed word {*and digital media are now doing still another transformation of the printed word*}. In tracing some of the effects of the printed word on liturgy, James F. White points to a result of the mimeograph:

> A further development considerably affected Protestant worship though not men-
> tioned in any liturgical textbooks. In 1884 a Chicago businessman, A. B. Dick, solved
> a business need for rapid duplication by inventing a process for stencil duplication. It

proved so efficient that he marketed it under the name of "Mimeograph." Gutenberg made it possible to put prayer books in the hands of people; Dick made prayer books obsolete ... Dick gave each minister his own printing press and a new possibility of printing only what was needed on any specific occasion. (White, 1971, p. 28)

It would seem clear from this passage that the advantage of always studying any figure in relation to its ground is that unexpected and unheeded features of both are revealed. It is in Ray Bradbury's "fantasy" fiction *Fahrenheit 451* (1953) that the world ahead is shown to fear the book as the cause of dissension and diversity of opinion and attitude. As such, the book is the enemy of unanimity and happiness; therefore, it must be destroyed. To save the book from the furious firemen and the incinerator, numerous individuals volunteer to memorize separate works as a means of perpetuating them to a life beyond the flames. Today, there arises the possibility of direct "brain-printing" of books and data so that the individual can be equipped instantly with all he need ever know. Such a bypassing of all reading raises many questions about the function of books. {*The idea of "brain-printing" that we suggested had an air of science fiction to it but now it is within the realm of the possible with wearable computing pioneered by University of Toronto Professor Steve Mann and now freely available on the market as Google Glass. Today one can wear a library if one so chooses.*}

The future of the book raises the question of whether men can ever program their corporate social lives, in accordance with any civilized pattern, by any other means than that of the printed book. There is no question that people can associate in large numbers without books or training in literary perception. At present even computers depend on literate people for their programing. The entire use of yes-no bit programing derives from the alphabetic modes of Western civilization. But many people look to the computer to bypass present forms of human action and limitation. Yet, even the written and printed word, it might be argued, has helped us to surpass ordinary human scale in the matter of the scope of the reading public.

Eric Havelock's *Preface to Plato* and *Empire and Communication* by Harold Innis have shown us how Western man has shaped himself by the phonetic alphabet and the printing press. Paradoxically, the very individuality achieved by these means has inhibited the study of the effects of technology in the Western world. Having fostered a high degree of private self-awareness by literacy, Western man, unlike Oriental man, has shunned the study of technological impact on his psyche. A recent development in Western literary criticism titled "reception aesthetics" seems to point toward the study of effects on reading publics. A new book has recently appeared. But no Western philosopher has evolved an epistemology of experience or looked into the relation between social and psychic change in regard to man's own artifacts. So, it is inevitable that Western man should be excluded from awareness of the side effects of his own actions by the principal effects, namely the development of his own private psyche. That prime product of our own phonetic literacy is the shaping awareness of individual interiority and privacy. Before our time, any approach to a study of this interior life had been avoided by Western man. Since the fifth century B.C., neither Plato nor Aristotle nor any subsequent investigator has studied the creation of Western individuality by the action of phonetic literacy. Likewise, consideration of any outer technology on the inner life of man has been ignored until the electric age.

But today the electronic effects are so pervasive that they cannot be neglected. Scholars such as Eric Havelock and Harold Innis have looked into the matter and found the personal transformations by phonetic technology to be quite demonstrable. Writing, printing, and broadcasting constitute new service environments that transform entire populations. And whereas private Western man shuns and deplores the invasion of his privacy by the historian or by the psychologist, the tribal or corporate man feels no such reluctance in studying the psychic and social effects of technology. Oriental societies have always been eager to know the effects of any technical innovation on their psychic lives, if only in order to suppress such innovation. Western man prefers to say, "Full speed ahead and damn the torpedoes!"

The future of the book is inclusive. The book is not moving toward an Omega point so much as rehearsing and reenacting all the roles it has ever played; new graphics and new printing processes invite the simultaneous use of a great diversity of effects. Poesie concrete (concrete or shape poetry) has inspired many new uses of older printing methods and has called for the invention of new print and paper surfaces. Photo printing permits the imposition of letters on and through many materials. Print can be moved through liquids and impressed upon fabrics, or it can be broadcast by TV and printed out in the home or study or office. {And now it can be presented on many different digital devices and the display can be either standard backlit screen or an electronic paper screen that works with reflected light.} Thus, the current range of book production varies from the cultivation of the art of the illumination of manuscripts and the revival of hand presses, to the full restoration of ancient manuscripts by papyrologists and photographic reproduction. The age of electric technology is the obverse of industrial and mechanical procedures in being primarily concerned with process rather than product, with effects rather than "content."

In the present age of ecology, it is not easy to write of the future of the book apart from the effects of the book, for ecology is concerned with anticipating effects with causes. In order to program any situation, it is necessary to know exactly what components are congruous and which ones are incongruous with the intended effect. The printed book has a very different meaning and effect even for a TV audience and a radio audience. It certainly has a very different effect in the Orient from its effect in the West.

Recent studies of the twin hemispheres of the brain point to the effect of phonetic literacy in developing the left hemisphere to the neglect of the right hemisphere. The third world has had an age-old stress on the use of the right hemisphere, with its simultaneous and holistic and intuitive patterns. The left hemisphere, on the other hand, is the area of the lineal, the syntactical, and the sequential, which we associate with verbal expression. With the advent of the printed word, the intense stress on the visual continuum of Euclidean space encountered the reverse pattern of the Einsteinian revolution. It flips from the visual continuum to the space-time discontinuum. The Orient may decide to adopt not only our mechanical technology (including Newtonian mechanics) but also may switch its education establishment to phonetic literacy and left-hemisphere culture. This they are tempted to do in the interests of taking over our "hardware" and our physical power.

Meantime, the West has moved steadily toward the East with its fascination with the occult and the intuitive. This fascination has restored the primacy of the spoken word in broadcasting and it has also undermined the ground of the printed word.

Until now, our print culture has been the primary means of developing detachment and civilized objectivity in a world of profound sensuous involvement. It also has been the principal means of developing habits of private initiative and private goals and objectives in the electric age.

The book has always been the vortex of many arts and technologies, including speech and mime and pictorial elaboration. At first, the printed book seemed to have obsolesced much of the richness of manuscript culture. This led to many book buyers in the fifteenth century taking the precaution of having their new printed books copied out by hand at the scriptorium. Who knew how well this new-fangled paper would wear? The durability of vellum was long established. Again, the printed or mass-produced book discouraged reading aloud, and reading aloud had been the practice of many centuries. Swift, silent scanning is a very different experience from manuscript perusal with its acoustic invitation to savor words and phrases in many leveled resonances. Silent reading has had many consequences for readers and writers alike, and it is a phase of print technology that may be disappearing. {*There are no signs of the diminution of silent reading. Audio books are used by some who enjoy listening to a book being read to them while they engage in another activity, such as driving their car.*}

Gutenberg had, in effect, made every man a reader. Today, Xerox and other forms of reprography tend to make every man a publisher. This massive reversal has for one of its consequences elitism. The nature of the mass production of uniform volumes certainly did not foster elites, but addicts. Paradoxically, when there are many readers, the author can wield great private power, whereas small reading elites may exert large corporate power.

Today Xerox has brought about many reversals in the relation of publics to writers, and these changes help us to see not only the past and present but also the future of the book. For example, Xerox extends the function of the typewriter almost to the point where the personal memo is moved into the public domain, as with the Pentagon Papers. When notes for briefing individuals or committees are first typed and then Xeroxed, it is as if a private manuscript were given to the general reader. The typewriter plus photocopies thus, unexpectedly, retrieves many of the features of confidential handwritten records. Committee dialog depends very much on such Xerox service, but the very public character of the service is difficult to restrict. It is important to consider the impact of Xerox, because it illustrates how profoundly one technology can alter traditional patterns between writing and speaking.

To study the **figures** of the book, with an eye on its changing **ground**, is to notice how many new forms the book has assumed in our time. In all patterns, when the ground changes, the figure is altered by the new interface. When the cinema, and gramophone, and radio, and TV become new environmental services, the traditional book began to be written and read by a different kind of public. If Gutenberg created a reader with new perception and new goals, the electric age of radio and video has restored a public with many of the oral habits of the pre-Gutenberg time.

Had anyone asked about the future of the book in the fifth century B.C., when Plato was beginning his war against the poetic establishment and its rigorously trained rhapsodes, there would have been as much confusion and uncertainty as now. The time when the Book of Nature would appear as an extension of the glorified art of the scribe lay ahead. For Plotinus the stars are "Like letters forever being written in the sky, or like letters written once and for all and forever moving." Concerning the seer, Plotinus says that his art is "to read the written characters of Nature, which reveal order and law." Yet, strangely, in ancient Greece, "there is hardly any idea of the sacredness of the book, as there is no privileged priestly caste of scribes" (Curtius, 1953, p. 304).

Reading and writing were assigned to slaves in ancient Greece, and it was the Romans who promoted the book to a place of dignity. But essentially, "It was through Christianity that the book received its highest consecration. ... Not only at its first appearance but also through its entire early period Christianity kept producing new sacred writings" (Curtius, p. 310).

It was the elucidation of these writings that called forth encyclopedic programs of learning and scholarship, which drew as freely on the page of Nature as on the sacra pagina of Revelation.

Throughout the Middle Ages, the trope of the Book of Nature dominated science. The business of the scientist was to establish the text and its interpretation by intensive contemplation, even as Adam had done in the Garden where his work had been the naming of creatures. Unexpectedly, the massive and ancient trope of the Book of Creatures ended with printing. It became old cliché. What would a sage have said in the early Gutenberg time if asked to predict the future of the book? How would Erasmus or Cervantes have answered this question just at a time when the printed book was opening new vistas of reputation and influence to writers? A century later, Francis Quarles (1592–1644) could still play with the idea of the Book of Nature in a merely decorative way: "The world's a book in folio, printed all with God's great works in letters capital: Each creature is a page; and each effect a fair character, void of all defect" (Curtius, p. 323).

Shakespeare had still found vitality in the trope of the Book of Nature as in As You Like It, where the banished Duke finds the voices of nature: "And this our life exempt from public haunt, Finds tongues in trees, books in the running brooks, Sermons in stones, and good in everything" (2.1.62–66).

It was Mallarme, the symbolist, who proclaimed, "The world exists to end in a book." His perception complements and also reverses the ancient and medieval tropes of the Book of Nature by assuming that in both the Industrial and Electric Ages Nature is superseded by art. Thus, the future of the book is nothing less than to be the means of surpassing Nature itself. The material world, as it were, is to be etherealized and encapsulated in a book whose characters will possess all the formulas for knowledge and re-creation of Being. Such was the ambition of James Joyce, whose *Finnegans Wake* is a symbolist Summa involving all creatures whatever. Joyce embraces both art and artifact in his encyclopedia of creatures, encompassing his task by means of language alone.

Taking the book in the more mundane sense of a printed package, it can have as many incarnations as it can find new techniques to wed. We have already alluded to the power of Xerox to transform the reader into publisher. Indeed, a prominent American publisher, William Jovanovich, has written about the subject of how reader and writer and publisher switch roles today:

> William Saroyan wrote me from Paris: "I seem to have the notion that anything anybody writes has got to be published—so that the writer can begin to feel better, I suppose … " I replied: "Your idea that anybody who writes should be able to be published may, in fact, come true. Xerography is a process that can make this possible, but whether it will make people feel better I cannot surmise, unless they happen to be Xerox shareholders. Certainly, if publishing becomes universal, and if it is regarded as a kind of civil right, or a kind of public requital, then our concept of literary property must change. Everything will be published and it will belong to everybody—power to the people. There is nothing illogical in your idea. If everyone finds a publisher, he will then find a reader, maybe just one reader—the publisher himself. Of course, writers want lots of readers, but this desire will be less and less fulfiled as there are more and more writers. Quantity declines as specialization declines. Eventually, every man will become at once a writer, publisher, librarian and critic—the literary professions will disappear as a single man undertakes all the literary roles." (1971, p. 249)

In the light of this new publishing technology, it is less surprising to hear the alarm in the voice of Jean-Paul Sartre who has already anticipated the Jovanovich report in *What Is Literature?*

> From this point of view, the situation of the writer has never been so paradoxical. It seems to be made up of the most contradictory characteristics. On the asset side, brilliant appearances, vast possibilities; on the whole, an enviable way of life. On the debit side, only this: that literature is dying. Not that talent or good will is lacking, but it has no longer anything to do in contemporary society. At the very moment that we are discovering the importance of praxis, at the moment that we are beginning to have some notion of what a total literature might be, our public collapses and disappears. We no longer know—literally—for whom to write. (1950, p. 241)

{An Update: The Future of the Book in the Digital Age

E-books

The purpose of this section is to supplement our treatment of the future of the book circa 1979 by taking into account the way in which the book has been transformed by the emergence of digital media, with a particular focus on the e-book (short for electronic book), the e-reader (short for electronic book reader), and the way books can be previewed, reviewed, and purchased on the Internet. Google Books and Amazon and other online bookstores are examples of Internet-based developments that have altered the book by transforming the ground in which the figure of the book operates.

The most dramatic development in the evolution of the book since 1979 was the emergence of the e-book. The history of the e-book can be traced back to the days of mainframes as early as 1971 and with the Sony Data Discman in 1992, which could read e-books stored on CDs. The e-book phenomenon really took off with the emergence of the Internet and the release in 1999 of the universal e-book format Open eBook, which morphed in today's open format EPUB, first released in September 2007. Starting with the release of EPUB, e-book sales as a percentage of total book sales steadily increased until it hit the 20% level in 2013 where it has remained. At first e-book enthusiasts claimed that the printed book would soon become obsolete but that does not appear to be in the cards. As reported in the New York Times March 7, 2014, print is very much alive:

> While e-books are gaining popularity, print is still king. In 2012, 28 percent of adults nationwide read an e-book, according to the Pew Research Center, while 69 percent read a print book. Only 4 percent of readers are "e-book only," the center reported. ...

> The Santa Rosa branch library in Tucson went all digital in 2002, but a few years later, it brought back books. A lot of content was not available digitally, and patrons wanted print. (Seeley, 2014)

E-books have many advantages, such as being more mobile so that one can easily carry a library in a compact portable digital device, and they are easy to search. But these advantages do not outweigh the fact that printed books are easier to read, especially for deep reading, which is why university students overwhelmingly prefer printed codex textbooks over digital ones. They also prefer printed books for recreational reading as reported in the Washington Post, February 21, 2015, in an article titled "Why Digital Natives Prefer Reading in Print. Yes, You Read That Right" (Rosenwald, 2015). The codex book is easy to flip through. The e-book represents a step backward in terms of scrolling. One of the advantages of the codex book over its predecessor was page flipping versus scrolling, but with e-books we are back to scrolling and all the disadvantages of that format. It is hard to see the structure of a book when it is formatted as an e-book whereas with a codex print book the structure of the book is immediately evident once one thumbs through it to see what it is about. In fact as I updated this book, I had to make hard copies of the book in order to see where to add new material. Given this experience I would assert that to truly appreciate a book and understand the structure of the ideas presented, it is necessary to read it in the codex print format, especially if it is a nonfiction book.

Socializing the Book

Both the e-book and the printed book are very much here to stay. In fact a number of publishers publish their books in both formats and, given the unique advantages of each of these formats, they often bundle them together so that the purchaser of the printed codex book also gets a free copy of the e-book version. I, together with my colleagues at OCAD (Ontario College of Art and Design) University, Greg Van Alstyne, Peter Jones, and Garry Ing, have created a new format for the book under a new publishing house we created, which we call DEMO Publishing. We published my book What Is Information?—Propagating Organization in the Biosphere, the Symbolosphere, the Technosphere and the Econosphere (2014) as a combined printed book and e-book like many other publishers. But we also created a Web site that houses the e-book that is available for free that includes a facility for readers of the book to leave comments to which the author and other readers can respond, as would be the case with a blog. The Web site, therefore, creates a social dimension to the book. A book is more than just a manuscript that is printed in a codex format or digitized as an e-book. It is also the impact of the book on its readers, which the Web site that we created is designed to capture.

SmartBooks

Another dimension to the book that we have not yet realized but which we have proposed is the idea of a SmartBook, in which the e-version of the book is coupled on the Web site to a recommender engine. This engine is an AI software that can capture the interests of a reader so that the recommender engine can point to those pages in the book that are of particular interest to the reader (Logan, 2010b). This would be a useful feature for nonfiction books, saving readers time if they do not wish to read the entire book. The power of such a system would be realized not with a single SmartBook but with a library of SmartBooks because of the time it would save researchers.

I invite the reader to check out our Web site at demopublishing.com to see how socializing the book works. You will also find a free copy of What Is Information? there for your reading enjoyment. You may also choose to leave a comment about the book once you have begun reading it.

e-books and Libraries

The lending of e-books is allowed by the DRM (digital rights management) built into commercial e-books whereby the lender loses access to the e-book during the time the book is being lent out. A recent survey (Frederiksen et al., 2011) revealed that 92% of libraries have begun lending out e-books and that 27% of those libraries are involved in interlibrary loans of e-books. According to Geoffrey Fowler, writing in the Wall Street Journal, public libraries provide a fairly good selection of e-book titles compared with subscription services like Kindle Unlimited, Scribd, and Oyster that cost about $10 a month. The only drawback is that one often has to wait a while for a particular book one wants to read to become available (Fowler, 2014)—RKL}.

· 1 3 ·

LIBRARY FUTURES: SUMMING UP

This chapter is divided into two parts. Part 1 is basically the original summing up chapter that McLuhan and I wrote circa 1979 just before he suffered the stroke that ended his career as an academic. I have inserted in between {curly brackets} my 2015 insertions, bringing up to date some of what we wrote in 1979. In part 2 I will make some additional suggestions summing up where I think the future of the library is headed from today's 2015 perspective.

Part 1: The Future of the Library from a 1979 Perspective

We are living in a time of rapid change. Many institutions are changing, including the library. People are worried about their jobs, their work, their roles in society. They feel threatened by change. The future is no longer anticipated with hope. It has new meanings associated with decay and demise. For many librarians to discuss the future of the library is to discuss its end as the following passage from Lester Asheim's writing indicates:

> When in 1955 the Graduate Library School held a conference entitled The Future of the Book, which suggested that the format should be seen as a means and not as

an end itself, it became necessary to add an "Afterword" to the proceedings volume, to refute a widely disseminated report that the Graduate Library School has assumed the imminent and inevitable demise of the book which would soon be replaced by movies, television, and mechanical devices, and that, indeed, we welcomed this over-throw of the tyranny of print. ... But for a librarian to even hit upon a title like "the Future of the Book" was threat enough to the traditionally book-oriented to trigger a violent reaction. (1975)

{*I would interject here to suggest that in fact most of today's librarians are opti-mistic about the future of the library. With so much information to cope with these days their skills and expertise are in even greater demand.*}

For those readers who are library oriented let us reassure you that we have no intention of writing an obituary for the library. This venerable institution will survive in one form or another. That is not to say, however, it will survive automatically without adjusting to the enormous amount of change that sur-rounds it.

Therefore, let us consider the library, an old figure in a new ground. As mentioned earlier, the organization of the library has not changed much since its inception. The communication surround and information environment of the library, its ground, on the other hand, has changed significantly. This dramatic change requires us to rethink and redefine the notion of the library. What is it? What is it becoming? What will it become? A cultural storehouse? Culture carrier and communicator? A passive institution or an active one? An educator? An auxiliary or backup system to education? A library that caters to left-brain needs and the interests of analytic specialists, or one that caters to right-brain needs, a center for information ecology, which helps its users develop an overview of man's knowledge? {*In fact, most libraries carry out both of these functions today.*}

We must answer these questions in terms of what we want the library to do. In terms of what role we want it to play within our society. There are a number of possibilities or futures to choose from. There is no single correct choice that can be arrived at in a rational analytic manner. The choices will have to be made in terms of our values. There is not just one future for the library, there are many. They co-exist, fulfilling different needs. Each individ-ual institution will have to decide its own future. What follows are some ideas and thoughts that might aid that process.

The future is not a place in time that we have to await passively. The future is ours to plan and create. Getting ready for the future is not merely a question of extending present trends and then preparing for them. The future can be determined by designing it or inventing it. The power of self-fulfilling prophecy cannot be ignored. If we think in terms of a strong dynamic role for the library, then that will come to pass.

There are two ways we can go about planning and designing the libraries of the future. One is to start with the presently available resources of the library, including its store of information, its organization, and its technical tools. And then try to plan the best way these resources can be used to accomplish one's information objectives.

A second approach is to consider the ideal organization of the library and its relation to society that incorporates all of one's objectives. One then assesses one's present resources and plans a path of development between the realities of today and one's dream for tomorrow. The first approach is more conservative and likely to succeed. The second approach, however, provides an ideal or a goal to guide one's planning. Both approaches are useful and, therefore, should be employed. {*This action plan is still valid despite all of the changes brought about by digital media.*}

Librarians are aware of the need to carefully consider the future of the library. At the Issues and Answers program at the 1977 annual meeting of the American Library Association the following conclusions emerged:

> The theme, which recurred with the most frequency, was that of the need for more planning in the library world. Most people felt that libraries engage primarily in crisis service. There is no anticipation of problems on the horizon nor, obviously, of strategies to deal with them. It was the impression of the participants that librarians and their administrators tend to view each crisis as an isolated problem. Libraries, they felt, have traditionally been, and continue to be, reactive rather than proactive in the matter of deciding their future. (Boisse & Stoffle, 1978)

Rank-and-file librarians are also aware of the lack of futures planning and technological assessment by their administrative superiors as evidenced by

> their strong criticism leveled at library administrators for inadequate planning with respect to technological applications in their institutions. A great number of comments stated that administrators appear to rush headlong into technological applications with little analysis or evaluation of its impact on the quality of service. Some individuals perceived a piecemeal approach to computerization rather than a well thought-out, planned, comprehensive, structured approach. (Boisse & Stoffle)

Other questions and issues raised at the forum included the following:

Libraries should be examining their goals and realigning their priorities. If libraries do not themselves examine the library's role in society, its future will be shaped by others. Do costs associated with technology cause some services to be sacrificed in order to raise money to implement technological advances? (Boisse & Stoffle)

These are extremely cogent questions that cannot be simply answered in the short term. They are the kind of issues one must live with in order to provide any insights. But they are certainly key issues.

One of the hopes of those responsible for planning the future of various institutions is that the solutions to the social problems caused by new technology can be solved technologically. It is presumed that we are passing through a rough period of transition in which the problems that plague us now will automatically disappear once our technology reaches a new plateau of sophistication. This myth is slowly being exposed for the sham that it is in a number of areas of human endeavors, including library and information science.

Western society has been conditioned to believe that scientific innovation, through its handmaiden applied technology, could overcome any societal problem. Our present pattern of industrial and social development has been centered on the notion of pushing back technological limits until they reach theoretical boundaries. In recent times it has become clear that we have reached the point of diminishing returns with this approach. There are many reasons. ... The present information arena (again as will be demonstrated later) is fragmented and has achieved only modest success in adapting existing technology to its needs. The future of the information world is in the present and consists of a logical extension of elements already well established. (Vagianos, 1976)

In order to design the library of the future we must have a clear notion of our goals as well as a realistic appraisal of the social, informational, and technological environments in which the library will operate. Perhaps most essential is the fact that we are moving into an age in which information is becoming the prime concern of mankind, the key to survival in a complicated environment. We have become totally dependent on sophisticated technology. Short of disaster we could never return to a simple nontechnological-, noninformation-oriented way of life.

During the Paleolithic era all of man's time was taken up by the physical activity of hunting and gathering food. During the Neolithic age the major share of man's time still involved the physical activities required to assure a steady supply of food. It was during this period, however, that the production of food became reliable enough to permit the rise of a leisure class that was able to pursue learning. It was during this period that writing and science developed, laying the foundation for the industrial age and the future age of information.

The industrial age began with the scientific revolution and the large-scale systematic application and exploitation of technology. The invention of the printing press stepped up the level of information. The development, innovation, and service of the rapidly growing and industrial machine created a greater demand for information services. The percentage of man's time spent in the information and service sector was still small compared with the agricultural and the industrial sectors, but its growth was steady.

The harnessing of electricity and the development of electric technologies signaled the end of the industrial age and the beginning of the post-industrial age of information, automation, and cybernetics. Electronic media created a greater demand for information for programing. {*Digital media have ratcheted up the demand for information for programing even more. This quantitative change in the amount of information available has created a qualitative change in which attention economics must be taken into consideration.*}

These sophisticated technologies require more learning and education to install and maintain. {*Once those sophisticated technologies are installed, however, the users of those systems will require less direct assistance from librarians and will be able to perform many reference tasks on their own. As McLuhan once observed: "As technology advances, it reverses the characteristics of every situation again and again. The age of automation is going to be the age of 'do it yourself." Users will be able to track down information on their own but, as we mentioned earlier, they will require instruction on how to best make use of the new digital tools that will be made available to them.—RKL*}

With the increased leisure brought about by automation, the service, entertainment, and education sectors will flourish. The limits to growth and the depletion of natural resources will lead to a greater emphasis on information-based services:

> Industries designed to satisfy physical needs will reach a saturation point as a point of diminishing returns while new industries will expand more rapidly. ... Replacing the unattainable hard goods such as cars, motorboats, and deep freezers will be a wider variety of soft goods, individually satisfying services, new forms of entertainment, and objects that are artistically and intellectually stimulating. ... How-to-do-it classes, budget magazines, mail order specialties and book clubs are a few examples of growth industries. (Owens, 1976, p. 20)

As we move from the age of production to the age of information, those who control the means of production will no longer control society as Karl Marx suggested in the nineteenth century. Instead those that control the flow of information as well as its storage will be in a position of power. Librarians have not traditionally thought of themselves as power brokers and therefore might not be able to take advantage of their new position. Unless they assert themselves and take on a more aggressive stance than they have in the past, their roles will be usurped by others, namely commercial information handlers. This has already begun to happen. Many entrepreneurs are performing services for fees using the resources collected by libraries over the years.

In order to maintain preeminence in the field of information, librarians will have to develop new ways to remain viable in a climate of increasing commercial competition. One of the positive signs of vitality is the cooperation that has been developing among libraries through the techniques of networking:

> Informal co-operation among libraries of all kinds is a long-standing practice, but in recent years additional, more formal ventures have come into being. The National Committee on Libraries and Information Science recommends national networking as the most effective means of disseminating information to all areas of society. (Jones, 1976)

{*The practice of networking made a quantum leap forward with the emergence of the Internet and the World Wide Web starting in 1994.*}

The motivating factor for the increased cooperation between libraries is the increased pressure on individual libraries to collect, organize, store, and provide easy access to a body of information, which is growing exponentially in magnitude and more complex in nature. Individual institutions are no longer able to be self-contained, and this will become progressively truer with time. The only solution for libraries will be cooperative pooling of resources, that is, collection rationalization as described by Logsdon (1970), "We have no choice in my judgment but to develop the network concept of collection building and library service. Each institution will become increasingly dependent on this network for total library service."

Libraries have cooperated in the past through the sharing of resources facilitated by interlibrary loans in which materials were exchanged through the mail or by messenger service. Another method of sharing materials has been cooperative arrangements in which photocopied material is sent from one library to another. In some instances information has been exchanged through fax transmissions. Another area of cooperation has been the sharing of online computer facilities. As communications become more sophisticated, the level of cooperation and the extent of the networks will increase. John Corbin (1976) created the following scenario to describe the developments that are likely to take place in library cooperation and networking in the period 1995 to 2015:

> The "typical" library network participant of the era 1995–2015 will physically or outwardly seem unchanged from today. Its collection still will be composed mainly of books and documents, and its reading rooms will remain as havens of solitude, study, and social contacts. Missing will be visible evidence of the indexes and catalogs to its collections, many ready reference books, and most technical services operations.

> The indexes and catalogs to the library's own collections will be machine-stored and tucked away in a closet or blocks or miles away in some central computer. Access to the indexes will be by visual display terminals scattered around the library, in other public buildings, and in some private dwellings. Users will be able to search the indexes thoroughly and easily, through controlling computers. The same terminals can be used, on a more limited basis due probably to incomplete development and insufficient funds even in this era, to locate and retrieve some textual materials (short facts of a ready reference nature). Files of general bibliographic citations and abstracts located in national and regional data banks will also be available routinely, through the same terminals. The library's technical services will be limited to small staffs for ordering, receiving, and physical processing. Data required in these functions will be centralized into one or more national or regional centers and distributed to the library through computer terminals. One or more minicomputers will be used to control and coordinate the various activities located within and without the library.

> The library will interface or connect with different networks at different times to obtain different services. It might be "plugged" permanently into a small number of networks, such as those for general interlibrary loans and technical services, but into a variety of others for specialized data bases and location of esoteric or little-used materials only as needed. The library will serve primarily as an outlet for face-to-face public services and as a switching center or broker between users and information located near or far away. (pp. 204–205)

Corbin does not see a very dramatic change in the physical appearance of the library as a result of networking. Stone, on the other hand, envisions a fundamental reshaping of both the idea and the physical manifestation of the library.

> For librarians, all of this means that the future is calling for new institutions no longer concerned with supplying specific media but rather with providing access to recorded

knowledge and communication services generally: recorded knowledge that may be distributed on demand by light beam pulses or via microwave technology drawn from data banks stored in electronic memories or new microforms and which may be searched out, retrieved, transmitted, and/or reproduced as required. Acceptance of this or any similar view of the future requires a substantial personal reorientation on the part of many librarians and calls for a willingness to acknowledge the need for professional evolution—if not revolution—across the board in libraries, library schools, and within the library profession at large. In the future, the competence of those performing the library function will no longer be measured in terms of specific media backgrounds as such but in terms of subject mastery and communications expertise. Needed to manage library services in the future will be several new classes of personnel including specialists in communications analysis, production, packaging, and evaluation; systems designers and analysts; and dynamic distributive program administrators. All must be thoroughly familiar with ways in which the various forms of recorded knowledge can be acquired, stored, retrieved, distributed, and used with maximum effectiveness. (1967, pp. 182–183)

{*Both Corbin and Stone were not far off in their description of today's libraries. The physical appearance of the library has not changed in terms of the storage of books, and they still operate out of most of the same buildings that were extant when Corbin and Stone wrote their future scenarios. What has changed is the proliferation of computers and terminals that can be found in almost every corner of today's library.—RKL*}

Stone believes that the new approach to librarianship in which the "library function" is more important than the "physical institution" will, nevertheless, have a profound effect on how the library is physically organized:

The point is that in the future it will probably be less and less necessary to have all the pieces of a library program in one place so long as the program parts can be linked together in networks and the resources of each part deployed to support an over-all system. The library of the future is not wisely conceived as a place at all, but rather as a far-flung network composed of units of various sizes and types, each of which may perform similar as well as different functions, but all of which will be linked together electro-mechanically.

Future Scenarios of the Library

It is absolutely essential for those who wish to plan or design the libraries of the future to have in their possession a rich and diverse set of images of possible library futures. We have in the course of this project encountered a number of images, some of which we would like to share with our readers in their original but somewhat abridged form.

We begin with three scenarios collected by F. Leimkuhler and A. Neville (1968) in their article "The Uncertain Future of the Library." The first scheme is that of a Dartmouth mathematician, John Kenney, who proposed that the user would sit at a console connected to a central library computer and enter into a dialog to access the information being sought.

J. C. R. Licklider (1965), in his book *Libraries of the Future*, proposed a system in which information rather than documents would be stored in a national computer and the output of the system would be

> not mere reproductions or translations of particular inputs; they are suggestions, answers to questions, and made-to-order summaries of the kind that a good human assistant might prepare if he had a larger and more accurate memory and could process information faster. ... In organizing knowledge, just as in acquiring knowledge, it would seem desirable to bring to bear upon the task the whole corpus, all at one time or at any rate larger parts of it that fall within the bounds of any one man's understanding. This seems to call for direct interactions among various parts of the body of knowledge, and thus to support the requirement ... for an active or directly processible store. (p. 25)

Licklider's proposal was actually a more elaborate development of Vannevar Bush's (1945) suggestion of the Memex, which was based on information stored in a readily accessible microform format.

Most images of the future of the library draw heavily upon recent breakthroughs in technology. The scenario that Ellsworth Mason creates is a refreshing exception to this trend. It emphasizes human scale and incorporates the idea of networking:

> We are going to have to do away with the idea of a great, fixed-location central library with large collections, and reading rooms, and with fixed branches, and begin to think more of a central warehouse for the collection, a storage and issuing point, and fluidly moving, constantly changing, much smaller branch libraries, whose central function will be to get readers interested, and serve as substations for the central warehouse that will have become a pumping station. ...
>
> Service will involve infinite production of photocopied materials—the photocopier is the only revolutionary machine in the entire range of technology; everything else is a chimera. ...

Service will involve a great range of book purchase on demand, for immediate processing and issuing. And let us talk about processing, which will now become part of the service system. It should be simple and as completely designed to be humanly acceptable as possible. I suggest that for a whole range of public libraries, the use of classification is minimal, and its use will decline further under a system of central storage libraries with little access by the users. It has been completely useless for the bulk of the collection at the New York Public Library for a long time. This sacred cow, I think will succumb to common sense in the future and classification will become a location symbol. Technical processes too will become humanized as time goes on. (1972)

{*If one substitutes for "infinite production of photocopied materials" digital copies of materials represented by e-books and e-journals, then Mason's predictions for the future of libraries from his 1972 vantage point seem to have worked out more or less as he predicted.*}

Other librarians in addition to Mason have become critical of the high technology image of the library, which only serves the interests of a very specialized segment of society as this missive from Teague and Carroll (1973) demonstrates:

Information scientists, like other specialists, overrate their own importance. They see the world as an importunate mass of users, frustrated daily in their search for "answers," turning eagerly and even despairingly to the information scientists for the "documents" which will satisfy their quest. They predict dire consequences, if their advice is not heeded. Information is a flood, an explosion, and lately a pollution, and only with the information scientist at the controls will the world survive.

In actual fact, most people have very little need for information, or at any rate for the stock that the information scientist keeps in his store. Besides a few research scientists and academics (numbering in the U.S. some 300,000 or 0.15% of the population), how many people would have any use at all for a retrospective literature search or a current awareness service, at least as they are presently constituted? Are most people, in their daily existence, looking for documents? For answers? Do they really have any questions? Once upon a time, a fair amount of knowledge was essential to survival. One needed to know how to fish, hunt, grow crops, build a house, make candles, milk a cow, and ride a horse. This was information one had to retain for life. Nowadays, few skills beyond the ability to drive a car and dial a telephone are regularly required.

The information scientist must learn to identify the true information needs of our total society, not just those of a small, inbred group. He must learn to cope with dynamic rather than static information needs.

What we are talking about is getting information to the people, and remember, information is power. So this is "where it's at." But with a difference. We are not out to propagandize, pander, palliate, or titillate. We see it as the function of the information scientist/specialist to tell it "like it is" and the name of the game is involvement. Finding out what the members of the community served want to know, acquiring that information, and marshalling our skills in information science to structure and display it in the manner most useful and acceptable to our community.

In order to serve the public's information needs better, Evelyn Geller suggests that perhaps the role of the librarian has been too passive and that a more active role of the librarian as a journalist is called upon in order to present information to people in such a way as to arouse their interest and curiosity.

> To me, the public library's main function today is to extend the concept of journalism to its services: find out what the important issues are, issues to highlight, to display, upon which to spend valuable research time, upon which to run film programs, and to build the collection about. This requires a decision like that of the newspaper or television station on what the library is to cover in depth. (1971)

Our image of the library continues to change as our technological capacity to handle information has improved. The notion of the library as an information utility grew out of the development and the integration of the computer, television, CATV, telephone, and fiber optics {and now digital media}.

> In a society, which has ready access to communication and information, services such as those envisioned, one's perspective will have to change radically regarding future "librarial" planning and development. Advantages will be seen in conceiving of "Information Access," as a national public resource or utility, to be provided. ... It's probably true that less room will be found for the librarian "jack-of-all-trades" and clearly future staffing requirements will call for more use of highly specialized knowledge and skills in performance of management functions, production research, technical design, etc. But very basic roles remain. The author's concept of these may be expressed simply: Continuing surveillance of knowledge production, appraisal of its worth and relevance in terms of given purposes, interpretation of user inquiry and demand. (Stone, 1975)

Our Suggestions for the Future of the Library

We have presented the ideas and images of a number of librarians, indicating possible future directions for the library. We would like to add to this collection some of the images and notions that came to mind during the years we worked on this project. We do not pretend to be experts. We are not librarians, only users. Nor do we suggest that our conjectures necessarily provide solutions to the problems facing libraries. We present our ideas as probes for further thought, or hypotheses for further testing.

If there is any coherence to our suggestions, it is that each of our proposals is an attempt to return human scale to the institution of the library. This is perhaps the most important objective for any institution in our modern world. It is only by understanding the dehumanizing effects of modern technology that the librarian stands a chance of performing the most important tasks of the library, which are the preservation of human culture and the facilitation of communication between people over space and time.

Turning on Readers

One of the primary objectives of the library should be to encourage and cultivate the love of books, particularly among the young who so easily fall prey to television, which destroys their capacity to read. {*Digital media is another culprit. Although there is a fair amount of reading with digital media they do not encourage the reading of book-length texts but rather much shorter amounts of text as in tweets, text messages, blogs, and social media entries.*} This is a job that calls for close cooperation between schools and the public library. Students should be encouraged to build their own libraries. The advantages of a home library should be explained, as well as the ways and means of creating such a library. Children should also be encouraged to create their own books. They can even be taught how to make their own paper and set type. {*They can also be taught to create e-books, which they can easily share with friends, classmates, and family.*}

Children's story hours help teach youngsters the enjoyment of books. The material chosen should be such that children can relate it to their own environment and experiences. Sylvia Ashton-Warner found that teaching Maori children how to read was extremely difficult until she had them make their own books containing material relevant to their own surroundings.

Encouraging and cultivating the love of books and other information services should not be restricted to children only but should include the whole community. The library program should enhance community access to information. In-house instruction on how to use a library, particularly the catalog and reference material, is essential.

Programs of instruction to improve reading skills or to provide literacy training for functional illiterates sometimes have been included as a function of libraries. ... As new media for storage and retrieval come into increasingly common use, instruction in the use of such media may become more needed, particularly if schools do not teach it [as they do for print]. (Parker, 1971)

Librarians can also leave the library to give talks to groups or counsel individuals on the various resources and services of the library. They can prepare newsletters, brochures, and community radio and television announcements {blogs and Web sites} promoting the library in general, or specific items within the collection that will draw people to the library.

Mediacy, Nonprint Media

While the primary aim of the library should be to encourage reading and to develop the reading skills of its users, attention should also be given to nonprint media. Users do not have to be encouraged to use these media, but they could be provided with guidance for the intelligent use of audio-visual media such as radio, television, cinema, {and the Internet}. Students in school are given direction in the appreciation of literary works. While this program could be improved and strengthened, at least it exists. There is very little instruction given in the appreciation of nonprint media, even though most young people spend more time with electric media {and nontextual digital media} than they do reading. Because little skill is required to operate nonprint media, and virtually no skill is required to "read" it, these media have been totally ignored. This is another area where the library, functioning as a media center, should cooperate with the schools. There now exists a textbook, *City as Classroom: Understanding Language and Media* (McLuhan, Hutchon, & McLuhan, 1977), especially designed for young people, which introduces them to the understanding of various media and could be used to facilitate this type of program.

Broadcasting and Illustrating Books

Schools are not the only place where reading can be encouraged. Libraries should seriously consider broadcasting, radio, and television production {and the Internet}, which promote and foster reading and, hence, their own facilities. Book reviews, discussions, dramatizations, and the like can be used to encourage the electronic media audience to change consumption patterns. Other techniques for directing readers might include illustrated catalogs of books, which help the reader to visualize what is to be read. Comic books of the "classics" genre should not be ignored. They can provide an entrée into reading for some readers. One of the reasons for the popularity of magazines is their illustration. The demise of picture magazines like *Life* and *Look* and the survival of the *Atlantic Monthly*, *Time*, and *MacLean's* attests to the fact that people are still willing to read, but format is very important.

In the electric {*and digital*} age, oral traditions are resurfacing and therefore they should be used to stimulate reading rather than being allowed to compete with it unnecessarily. Film and video presentations of dramatic material inspired by novels can be used creatively to encourage the reading of the original material. A discussion that compares a film version of a novel and the novel itself can infuse the printed word with greater life for the young reader. Such a discussion can also be used to understand the difference between these two media.

Oral Histories

Many libraries have successfully incorporated the oral tradition into their program by organizing an oral history of their community or region. This activity is not only intrinsically valuable but it also stimulates the further study of local history and other topics.

Idea Depots—Street Libraries

The trend to involve the community more in the operation of the library should be greatly enhanced. Suggestions for handling books should be solicited from the community. There is more than one solution to a problem, and the user sometimes has a greater insight than the professional library administrator. Street libraries, which create ready access, should be found everywhere people congregate. They could be located in shopping plazas and along business streets. These tiny branches could contain a reference section like the compact library we suggest in chapter 9. These mini-branches could also contain a microform {*or rather a computer-based*} catalog and some mechanism for ordering material and having it delivered, perhaps through the mail or by courier. Why not a delivery system? Liquor stores provide such a service. It's only a question of priority—books or booze!

Etobicoke, a section of Toronto, already has a delivery service for senior citizens and shut-ins. It also has a book mobile, which visits shopping centers.

Declassifying the Library

Libraries cannot afford to accept all the books donated to them because of the cost of accession. In view of this fact, it is obvious that, where possible, the library should declassify its collection, particularly for its recreational nonresearch collections. Broad general classifications by subjects such as mysteries, Slavic literature, science fiction, sports, historic novels, politics, travel, and so forth are sufficient for the purpose of a general interest reading library.

As for classification in research libraries, more activity is called for. Instead of relying on elaborate classification schemes and technical aids such as computer-based catalogs and the like, there should be properly trained informationists to help the user. An informationist would be trained in the techniques of library and information science as well as in a general area of specialization. Such individuals would be familiar with a particular literature and understand how it relates to research. Informationists would also work on preparing review articles and creating collections of relevant articles in their field. They would be the ideal people to create the compact library we discussed in chapter 9. But, most important, they would be able to provide face-to-face assistance to those in search of esoteric bits of information necessary for their research.

Part 2: The Future of the Library from a 2015 Perspective—The Future Is Already Here

I will first summarize the many recommendations from part 1 written in 1979 that are still valid today. I will then update our recommendations from part 1 by making use of the old McLuhan trick for making predictions: "Every thing that I predict about the future has already happened." I will therefore describe the future of the library by describing a number of current library projects that I believe represent the best way forward for the libraries of today and the libraries of tomorrow. And finally I will conclude with my final thoughts about the future of the library.

The 1979 Recommendations Still Valid Today

Much has happened since McLuhan and I wrote our concluding remarks, but much of what we wrote I am ready to stand by today. For example, we said that we had no intention to write an obituary for the library. As it happens the library is stronger today than it ever was and it plays a key role in today's information environment. We wrote that the library would thrive though accommodation to the new technologies coming on stream. That has largely happened but the job is not yet complete. We have not quite digested all the technological innovations that we have been treated to today, and the pace of innovation has not slackened, so there will be future developments that will continue to challenge the library.

In 1979 we talked of the challenges to libraries due to the fact that we live in the information age. That is even truer today, and in fact we might add that we not only live in an information age but we are also progressively living in a knowledge age as well. Information is a collection of data or facts that have been made more valuable because the data and facts have been contextualized. But knowledge is the ability to use that information to achieve one's objectives. Libraries today are playing a more active role in the transmission of knowledge and are no longer content to be just a storehouse or archive of information. The library's role as an educational institution is growing.

One of the trends in the digital age is DIY (do it yourself) and this applies to lifelong learning as well. Libraries are taking over the educational role where the schools have left off once their students have graduated. This will be a large growth area for libraries as is beginning to happen with their role in online continuing education. We will return to this topic when we discuss MOOCs and libraries below.

One of the major themes of the 1979 version of our manuscript was the value of compact libraries to provide context in an information-rich environment. The notion of a compact library is still a solid idea and even more necessary given that the information overload we have to deal with continues to grow.

In a certain sense the access to information on the Internet guided by search engines operates much like a compact library. Wikipedia is actually an example of a compact library in that one can find background information on virtually any topic of interest. Some educators and scholars dismiss Wikipedia as being inaccurate and inappropriate. Studies have revealed that

Wikipedia is every bit as accurate as the expert created *Encyclopedia Britannica* (EB) (Wolchover, 2011; Reliability of Wikipedia, n.d.). What the Internet with search engines and Wikipedia do not provide, however, is context, but coupled with a compact library of appropriately selected books, one would have an ideal combination of a guide to all of human knowledge and in particular a guide to the library's collection of physical books.

Today's Leading Edge Library Initiatives that Portend the Future of the Library

The library has undergone enormous change since the first edition of this book was written in 1979. I have collected some images of the future of the library that are happening in certain leading-edge libraries today and certainly portend the trends of the libraries of the future.

I will make use of McLuhan's insight that the best way to predict the future is to understand what is happening today. As he once said, "We live in post-history in the sense that all pasts that ever were are now present to our consciousness and that all the futures that will be are here now." So here are my predictions of the future of the library based on the following interesting initiatives that are in play today. You will note that in each of these scenarios the emphasis is on greater participation of the patrons of the library than was the case for the libraries of circa 1979, an increased educational role for the library, and, of course, a much greater deployment of digital technology.

Before launching into my description of the "brave new world" of librarianship I want to share the thoughts of Anthony Verdesca Jr., an academic reference librarian and very much a traditionalist, who kindly provided me with some assistance in researching material for this update of *The Future of the Library*. Here is an excerpt from his email response to my request for comments on this last section of the book. He wrote:

> Please understand if you perceive any harshness in my tone, it's certainly not directed to you; it's my fellow librarians! I have heard for a number of years now about how technology is doing this and that for today's library … . While digitization has produced marvels in library efficiency, it must not undermine reading—sustained reading of complex, long-form texts … . That librarians would "no longer be content to be just a storehouse" flies in the face of what libraries have been for centuries. … There is great value in a large collection of print based books. Digital collections should only supplement the print collections.

Although I am an advocate of all the changes in library practices I am about to report on, I believe that Anthony's remarks are still relevant. There is room for both visions of the library to coexist and great value in both of these visions. There is no need to sacrifice one for the other.

Making Labs

In addition to providing patrons with access to computer work stations and Wi-Fi connections, a number of academic and public libraries also have initiated making labs where patrons can access various kinds of digital technology to make their own information packages or digital tools. A few libraries are even allowing their patrons to access wearable technology like Google Glass. These operations include the Fab Lab at the MIT Media Lab (fab.cba.mit.edu) with more than 300 affiliates on every continent in the world (fablabinternational.blogspot.ca); Maker Space by the iSchool at Syracuse University (infospace.ischool.syr.edu/2011/12/01/a-makerspace-takes-over-a-local-library); and the Critical Making Lab at the iSchool at the University of Toronto (criticalmaking.com). Other universities with making labs include Drexel University, Lawrence Technological University, University of Illinois in Champaign-Urbana, and University of Victoria in British Columbia.

Some of these labs based in universities have also developed programs and workshops in public libraries close to their campuses. Other labs are strictly for their students, but in either case a making lab is a technology library in the sense that they collect technologies instead of books for their patrons' use in research and/or the production of new tools. A number of public libraries have also organized making labs that operate in one or two of the branches of their library system. Susan Down of the Innisfil Public Library in Ontario developed the Innisfil ideaLab, which is a hacker lab that combines traditional library materials and digital maker tools (www.innisfil.library.on.ca/idealab). The Toronto Public Library operates "digital learning workspaces with free access to technology and training at two of its branch libraries" ("Digital Innovation Hubs, n.d.). Other public libraries with similar programs include the Kitchener Ontario Public Library's Digital Media Lab (www.kpl.org/about/media_lab.html) and the Chicago Public Library's Maker Lab in its Harold Washington branch (www.chipublib.org/maker-lab). Some labs like the Make IT Lab (www.makeitlabs.com)

in Nashua, New Hampshire, is not associated with a library, but like a library it is supported by the community's tax base.

Nate Hill, a librarian in the Chattanooga Public Library, runs a maker lab on the fourth floor of his library. His vision statement captures the spirit of making labs:

> **Our Vision:** The 4th floor is a public laboratory and educational facility with a focus on information, design, technology, and the applied arts. The more than 12,000 sq.-foot space hosts equipment, expertise, programs, events, and meetings that work within this scope. While traditional library spaces support the consumption of knowledge by offering access to media, the 4th floor is unique because it supports the production, connection, and sharing of knowledge by offering access to tools and instruction.

In addition to all of the making labs we have listed, there are literally hundreds of similar operations that operate as hacker spaces. The Web site https://wiki.hackerspaces.org/List_of_Hacker_Spaces lists 1,892 existing or planned hacker spaces as of March 27, 2015, when I visited the site.

Many public libraries are offering their patrons access to 3D printing. Some libraries have installed Espresso Book Machines that allow a user to create their own book or print an out-of-copyright book (www.ondemand books.com). Another technology impacting libraries is the smartphone. The opportunities this technology offers libraries is explored by Jason Griffey (2010) in his book *Mobile Technologies and Libraries*.

Aarhus, Denmark Mediaspace: A "Place of Relation"

Here in their own words is a description of the library services in Aarhus, Denmark (http://www.urbanmediaspace.dk/en/mediaspace/background):

> In 2001, Aarhus City Council decided to build a Mediaspace, which can meet future needs within use of media.

> Mediaspace must be an open space for learning and experience, rethinking the physical frames for the library and provide free and equal access to knowledge sharing and knowledge distribution. ... Apart from developing and expanding The Main Library, Mediaspace will also house Citizens' Services—which in one service point brings together the public services which most citizens have a need for. Thereby, Mediaspace ensures the best possible service for citizens through joint service points, cooperation on development of digital self-services, and knowledge sharing on citizens' needs.

From transaction to relation—Concurrently with the development within media, the role of the library too has changed. Today, the library is not merely a frame for circulation of media—a "place of transaction". The library is—and will to an even greater extent in future be—a place, which supports learning. It is not merely a place where we borrow media; we also experience media and enter into new relations with each other and the world. In other words, the library has changed into a "place of relation".

British Columbia's Public Libraries

Ken Roberts (2012), in his report *Facing the Future: A Vision Document for British Columbia's Public Libraries*, calls for greater community involvement in library spaces similar to the developments in the Aarhus Mediaspace and identifies the need for libraries of the future to expand the physical space in which they operate:

> There is a growing realization that physical libraries are becoming even more important community spaces, places where people gather, share and learn from each other. Print collections will occupy less physical space but, if anything, libraries will find that the competing demands for both quiet study space and for noisy public space will mean that, if anything, library buildings may need to become larger and more flexible. (p. 3)

Miami-Dade Public Library System

As reported in the September 29, 2014, *Miami Herald* in an article with the headline "Miami Dade Libraries Need to End 'Bookish' Attitude, Panel Says," it was reported that the panel convened to discuss the future of the public library urged "a remake of the library's core identity—away from a quiet place for reading into more of an amenity-rich community center, with enough offerings to attract people uninterested in free books or computer time." Among the initiatives suggested were increased creative and educational services, making labs, programs to teach preschoolers reading skills, and even services to help start-up entrepreneurs.

Helsinki's Library 10

The Helsinki public library system created a unique specialized library focused on music production, performance, and appreciation, as well as IT. Library 10 is located in central Helsinki near the railroad station in the old post office building. It is extremely popular with 4,000 visitors every day (Korpela, 2005). Sixty percent of its visitors are young males, a demographic that does not usually visit a library. The library contains a lot of musical instruments and various digital tools. It does not house books but offers its patrons the opportunity to request books from the other branches of the Helsinki Library System, which are delivered to the Library 10 location for the convenience of its patrons. While short on books Library 10 has an extensive collection of "34,000 music recordings plus DVDs, videos, musical literature and sheet music" (Korpela). The library provides headsets, scanners, DVD players, and other electronic equipment for use in its premises.

> Library assistants are on hand to help anyone in need of assistance with IT and will show patrons how to use the programs or databases. These assistant librarians have time to help because customers themselves handle their own borrowing and returning procedures by using the self-service facilities.

> "Our staff do not sit behind a service counter. If a customer asks for help, say, in searching for a particular publication, the library assistant will sit next to the person and search the databases with them. Two pairs of eyes are better than one. At the same time, we are gently instructing customers on how to use equipment and how to search for material," says Kari Lämsä. (Korpela)

Academic Libraries and Their Integration with Various Digital Tools

Almost all academic libraries and many public libraries allow their patrons to access their digital holdings via the Internet. Academic libraries also allow their users to archive the electronic holdings that they have accessed in order to have handy access to these files. For example, at my library at the University of Toronto (U of T), one can create an account called My.Library to archive both library resources and files pulled off of the World Wide Web. The library's server is basically serving as a Cloud for its students and faculty.

My library at the U of T and many other academic libraries subscribe to BrowZine, which is a free downloadable app that delivers to one's smartphone or tablet thousands of articles from open access journals and from the journals that one's academic library subscribes to. The articles in BrowZine are organized by subject. One can then read those articles offline or archive them on the desktop with Web programs such as Refworks, Zotero, or Mendeley that also allow users to network and collaborate with other users to share research articles and data.

Mobile Apps and the Library

Many libraries, both academic and public, now have mobile apps that allow patrons to access library services and digital holdings directly from their mobile device.

Library 2.0

Library 2.0 is both a concept and an online organization (http://www.library20.com) with more than 20,000 members who embrace the notion of Library 2.0. Like Web 2.0 and Business 2.0 the idea is that rather than being passive recipients of information, the users of libraries should play an active role in how their libraries are organized and what services they provide. One of the key elements of Library 2.0 is the delivery of as many services as possible via the Web and naturally the use of the Web to enable patrons to provide feedback and suggestions for improving library services. Those who embrace the notion of Library 2.0 have organized the online community www.library20.com that holds online continuing education activities, an online annual conference, and a platform for members to communicate with each other.

Open Source Journals

A number of organizations have emerged in recent years that promote the open dissemination of research articles, research data, and educational resources. This section describes a few of these organizations that are impacting the operation of academic libraries.

The Scholarly Publishing and Academic Resources Coalition (SPARC)

SPARC, an international alliance of academic and research libraries, is very much in the spirit of Library 2.0. Its specific goal is to

> create a more open system of scholarly communication ... SPARC believes that faster and wider sharing of the outputs of the scholarly research process increases the impact of research, fuels the advancement of knowledge, and increases the return on research investments. SPARC focuses on taking action in collaboration with stakeholders—including authors, publishers, and libraries—to build on the unprecedented

opportunities created by the networked digital environment to advance the conduct of scholarship. (www.sparc.arl.org/issues)

SPARC advocates the open access of (1) scholarly and research articles, (2) digital data that can be reused by other research groups, and (3) educational resources. SPARC has 200 member libraries in the United States and Canada. Its sister organizations are SPARC Europe (sparceurope.org), with 96 member libraries in 23 countries, and SPARC Japan, an initiative of Japan's National Institute of Informatics (www.nii.ac.jp/sparc/en/).

Public Knowledge Project (PKP)

The Public Knowledge Project (https://pkp.sfu.ca/) is another initiative that promotes the open access of research results through its development of its two open-source softwares: Open Journal Systems and Open Conference Systems. It has approximately 5,000 users worldwide and has been translated into twenty-five languages.

> The Public Knowledge Project was established in 1998 by John Willinsky at the University of British Columbia. Since that time PKP has expanded and evolved into an international and virtual operation with two institutional anchors at Stanford University and Simon Fraser University Library. John Willinsky, PKP's founder and director, is based at Stanford and oversees the general direction of PKP and leads its research activities. Since 2005, the SFU Library has served as the administrative and operational home for PKP and is responsible for software development and support, PKP Publishing Services, and other administrative activities. PKP also has three major development partners—Ontario Council of University Libraries, the University of British Columbia Libraries and the University of Pittsburg Libraries—who provide significant financial and in-kind support.

Ontario Library Research Cloud

The Ontario Library Research Cloud (OLRC) involves the collaboration of eleven Ontario university libraries that are building

> a high capacity, geographically distributed storage and computing network using proven and scalable open source cloud technologies. The OLRC will be designed to house large volumes of digital content to allow for cost effective and sustainable long-term preservation and to support data and text mining using innovative research tools. (Marks, 2015)

The motivation for this project is to create a cost-effective and sustainable way of storing the vast amounts of digital content that has already been created, is being created today, and will be created well into the future. The physical storage of information is no longer viable. The Robarts Library at the University of Toronto, a mammoth structure built in 1973, can no longer hold its entire collection. Books that are not actively circulating are held in storage at the very northern end of the city and delivered by request when needed as I discovered when I recently wanted to refer back to Dougherty and Blomquist (1974), a book that McLuhan and I consulted back in 1978.

Digital Libraries

Digital Public Library of America and Europeana

In chapter 7, I (RKL) discussed the notion that the Internet functions as a virtual online library and I provided some examples of Web sites like Google Books, Wikipedia, academia.edu, arXiv, YouTube, Flickr, and archive.org that comprise this informal digital library. One can access the contents of this informal virtual online library by making use of a search engine. Other than that, there is no organization of this vast collection of information. Two initiatives, one in the United States, Digital Public Library of America (DPLA), and another in Europe, Europeana, have emerged in recent years that are attempting to create a structured digital library that would provide free access to the public of cultural riches that are not copyright protected.

The DPLA started in 2010 at the Harvard University Berkman Center for Internet and Society and was launched in 2013. It provides a union catalog for the holdings for public domain and openly licensed content held by the nation's archives, libraries, museums, and other cultural heritage institutions such as the Library of Congress, the Internet Archive, and the Hathi Trust. The Hathi Trust contains books scanned by Google for its Google Books project from the university libraries of Harvard, Michigan, Oxford, and Stanford and the New York Public Library.

Europeana.eu is a similar project drawing on the collections of European archives, libraries, and museums with a similar goal of DPLA. The idea for the creation of this European digital library was first suggested by French president Chirac in a 2005 letter to the president of the European Commission, Manuel Durao Barrosco, that was countersigned by the premiers of Germany, Italy, Poland, Spain, and Hungary.

Europeana and the DPLA recently agreed to share resources to insure the interoperability of their metadata:

> The Search DPLA and Europeana app lets users do side-by-side searches of Europeana and the DPLA, providing quick and easy access to both libraries' vast resources. By default, users are shown each object's title, author, format, date, and link, along with a thumbnail; additional metadata about each object is available by clicking a drop-down arrow. (Domìnguez)

Norway's Digital National Library

Norway National Library wants to make all of the public information generated by their country's publishers and broadcasters to be available online according to Jingru Hoivik in an article titled "Global Village: Mobile Access to Library Resources":

> The National Library of Norway is now in the process of digitizing all its collections in order to establish a Digital National Library. These efforts play a key role in the country's digital library strategy. The library goes beyond print: it preserves digital signals as well. Data from four national radio and TV channels are transferred directly to the library every night. The library's goal is to become an outstanding multimedia knowledge center among Europe's modern national libraries. By now, more than 100,000 digital books have been made accessible through its website. Every week about 1,000 additional volumes are digitized.

Wikipedia Library Project

Another initiative to better integrate the online world of information and traditional libraries is the Wikipedia Library Project in which "Wikipedia seeks libraries who are willing to host a Wikipedia editor and give that editor access to their library materials in order to enhance the article citation process on Wikipedia" (www.oclc.org/research/events/2014/02-25.html).

Funding Problems Facing Libraries

Whatever the cost of our libraries, the price is cheap compared to that of an ignorant nation.—Walter Cronkite

So far in my 2015 review of libraries I have cited a number of exciting and promising developments for the future of the library. I would be remiss if I did not review some of the problems and challenges facing today's libraries. Perhaps the most serious problem is the steady decline in the funding of public libraries. Amien Essif (2015), in an article titled "The Internet Can't Replace Libraries: Why They Matter More Than Ever in the Age of Google," indicates that in the United States, "Federal funding for libraries is down nearly 40 percent since 2000. Our democracy may never wholly recover." This decline of financial support is counterintuitive given the overwhelming support of libraries by the public. In a Gallup Poll "over 90 percent of Americans feel that libraries are a vital part of their communities. Compare this to 53 percent for the police, 27 percent for public schools, and just 7 percent for [the U.S.] Congress." According to Palfrey (2015), "Too many mayors, and town managers, forced to make hard budget choices are slashing library budgets to save other essential services" (p. 5).

A similar situation pertains in Canada where library attendance is up. "In Canada, library use has increased slightly year after year, according to statistics from the Canadian Urban Libraries Council. From 2008 to 2013, the CULC tracked an 18-per-cent increase in library use, which includes the population served, attendance at programs and the number of programs offered" (Tabor, 2014). Despite this public support there has been unfortunately an "unprecedented number of cuts to library programs" (www.accessola.org/web/OLAWEB/Home/SearchResults.aspx?q=unprecedented%20cuts x).

Off-site Storage of Physical Books and the Problems Associated with This Practice

At the same time that financial support of libraries is on a downward trend, the job that libraries need to perform is becoming increasingly more challenging just in terms of the amount of information they are called upon to steward. "Humans are producing such quantities of data—2.5 quintillion bytes of data daily, to be precise—and on such a steep curve, that 90 percent of all existing data is less than two years old" (Essif, 2015). The number of books that libraries are expected to collect and hold is growing exponentially with the consequence that libraries are running out of shelf space in their facilities. The solution to this has been the off-site storage of books that are not actively circulating. Part of the motivation for this was to make room for Internet-based and social activities at the library.

This solution has had some dire consequences in some libraries most notably at the New York Public Library (NYPL) as reported by Scott Sherman (2015) in an article titled "The New York Public Library Wars: What Went Wrong at One of the World's Eminent Research Institutions?" The management at the NYPL took the draconian step at its iconic main library at Fifth Avenue and Forty-second Street in which "three million books in the stacks were to be sent to an off-site storage facility near Princeton, N.J." (Sherman). The trustees thought they could save money by not using such expensive real estate in midtown Manhattan to store books. A number of champions of the traditional way in which the library operated were incensed and fought to retain the stacks, which were slated to be destroyed. They succeeded in obtaining a cease and desist order for the destruction of the stacks, which as of this writing sit basically empty. The conflict between the traditionalists and the NYPL management remains unresolved at the time of this writing, a very sad situation indeed.

One of the space-saving moves by libraries is to subscribe to online information services such as JSTOR and ProQuest, which extract a subscription fee from the library. The problem with this solution is that subscription fees have been steadily increasing while at the same time financial support of libraries has been decreasing. With the old system of paper-based information once a library bought a book or subscribed to a journal they owned it and there were no ongoing costs for that material other than housing and managing it.

Public Libraries and the MOOC (Massive Open Online Course)

Let me end on a more positive note. Public libraries are playing an interesting role in the support of online courses known as MOOCs (Massive Open Online Course). Many libraries across North America are offering continuing education Gale Courses (http://solutions.cengage.com/GaleCourses/), which are free to their patrons. Libraries offering these courses describe their program in the following way: "Gale Courses offers a wide range of highly interactive, instructor led courses that you can take entirely online. As a library cardholder in good standing, you are entitled to these courses at no cost. Courses run for six weeks and new sessions begin every month." Gale offers courses for the following topics: Accounting and Finance; Business; College Readiness; Computer Applications; Design and Composition; Health Care and Medical; Language and Arts; Law and Legal; Personal Development; Teaching and Education; Technology; and Writing and Publishing.

An example of the partnership of a public library with a MOOC is the New York Public Library program that is supporting its patrons taking a MOOC by University of Pennsylvania professor Al Fireis titled Modern and Contemporary American Poetry. The library is making a special effort to provide its patrons with the readings for the course and they are providing a space where the students in the New York area can meet and discuss their course with each other. The New York Public Library program began in the fall of 2014 and is destined to be the harbinger of more partnerships with MOOCs and public libraries for courses where enrollment in a local area warrants such an effort.

Final Remarks

Today's library is about accessing information, not just books but all forms of media. It is also a place where people can access different kinds of information media and, hence, can create information as well as consume it; not just the creation of print-based information but also the creation of videos, audios, apps, storytelling platforms, and music, as well as the integration of digital forms of information with traditional books. It is also a place where people can do more than just access information. It is also a place where people can learn new skills and gain new knowledge so as to put the information they access at the library to the good use of achieving their educational, professional, and personal goals. In short it is a place where people can enrich their lives and the lives of others.

The users of today's libraries are not just the patrons of the library who enter the libraries' physical space. They are also includes all those who make use of the library's online services. While it is true that the number of users who actually visit the libraries' physical space has declined somewhat with the emergence of the Internet, the actual number of patron visits has increased when one takes into account the patrons who have been serviced online. The library is a collector of information of ink on paper, online text, and a variety of other media. It has become also, in many instances, a cultural center, a social center, and a learning center, a place where all kinds of things associated with information can and do take place. The library as an institution has undergone a great deal of change in recent years and as it is still evolving, its future is yet to be fully determined.

REFERENCES

Abbey, A. S. (1971, February). Information retrieval television. *Audiovisual Instruction*, 44–45.

Adelson, M. (1972). Education: At the crossroads of decision. In *Information technology: Some critical implications for decision makers* (pp. 112–117). New York: Conference Board.

Alper, B. (1975). Library automation. *Annual Revue of Information Science and Technology*, 10, 224–225.

Asheim, L. (1975). *Introduction to differentiating the media*. Chicago: University of Chicago Press.

Bass, D. (1969, September 15). Can this marriage be saved? *Library Journal*, 94, 3023–3025.

Before the Internet, librarians would "answer everything"—and still do. (2014, December 28). NPR. Retrieved from www.npr.org/2014/12/28/373268931/before-the-internet-librarians-would-answer-everything-and-still-do

Belson, W. A. (1959). *Television and the family*. London: British Broadcasting.

Bertot, J. C. (2009, June). Public access technologies in public libraries: Effects and implications. *Information Technology and Libraries*, 81–92.

Bohannon, J. (2013). Who's afraid of peer revue? *Science* 342(6154), 60–65.

Boisse, J. A., & Stoffle, C. J. (1978). *Epilogue in the information society: Issues and answers*. Phoenix, AZ: Oryx.

Boulding, K. (1967, January). *New York Times Book Review Section*.

Boyle, D. (1976, January). In the beginning was the word ... libraries and media. *Library Journal*, 125–129.

Bradbury, R. (1953). *Fahrenheit 451*. New York: Ballantine.

Bravy, G. J., & Feather, K. C. (2001). The impact of electronic access on basic library services: One academic law library's experience. *Law Library Journal, 93*(2), 261–268.

Breasted, J. H. (1926). *The conquest of civilization.* London: Harper & Brothers.

Bunge, M. (1970). *Causality: The place of the causal principle in modern science.* Cleveland, OH: Meridian.

Bush, V. (1945, July). As we may think. *Atlantic Monthly.*

Candela, L., Castelli, D., & Pagano, P. (2011). History, evolution, and impact of digital libraries. In I. Igelzakis, T. Synodinou, & S. Kapidakis (Eds.), *E-publishing and digital libraries: Legal and organizational issues.* Hershey, PA: IGI Global.

Cardi, J. (1961, August 26). Editorial. *Saturday Review, 44.*

Carpenter, R. (1933). The antiquity of the Greek alphabet. *American Journal of Archaeology, 37*(1), 8–29.

Carpenter, R. (1938). The Greek alphabet again. *American Journal of Archaeology, 42*(1), 58–69.

Carrol, C. E. (1972). Some problems of microform utilization in large university collections. *Microform Review, 19–24,* 208–212.

Chisholm, M. (1975). Introduction and rationale. In M. Chisholm (Ed.), *Reader in media technology and libraries.* Englewood, CO: Microcard.

Clark, H. F., & Sloan, H. S. (1960.) *Classrooms in the factories.* New York: New York University Press.

Clark, J. W. (1909). *The care of books.* Cambridge: Cambridge University Press.

Corbin, J. (1976, January). Library networks. *Library Journal, 101,* 203–207.

Crainfield, P. (1967). Retrieving the irretrievable? Proceedings of the First Annual Conference on Simulation, New York, American Statistical Association, New York Area Chapter.

Croneberger, R., & Luck, C. (1975, November). Defining information and referral service. *Library Journal.*

Culler, D. (1955). *The imperial intellect.* New Haven, CT: Yale University Press.

Curtius, E. R. (1953). *European literature and the Latin Middle Ages.* New York: Pantheon.

Dain, P. (1975, February). Ambivalence and paradox: The social bonds of the public library. *Library Journal.*

Davies, D. W. (1974). *Public libraries as culture and social centers.* Metuchen, NJ: Scarecrow.

de Bury, R. (1948). *The philobiblon.* Berkeley & Los Angeles: University of California Press.

De Gennaro, R. (1976, January). Library automation, changing patterns and new directions. *Library Journal,* 175–183.

Dewey, M. (1876). The profession. *American Library Journal, 1.*

Digital innovation hubs. (n.d.). Toronto Public Library. Retrieved from www.torontopubliclibrary.ca/using-the-library/computer-services/innovation-spaces

Dilworth, D. (2014, June 30). US publishing industry earned $27.01B in net revenues last year. GalleyCat. Retrieved from www.mediabistro.com/galleycat/us-publishing-industry-earned-27-01b-in-net- revenues-last-year_b87377

Diringer, D. (1947). *The alphabet: A key to the history of mankind.* New York: Philosophical Library.

Domínguez, J. (n.d.). Search DPLA and Europeana. Retrieved from http://dp.la/apps/2

Dougherty, R. M., & Blomquist, L. L. (1974). *Improving access to library resources: The influence of organization of library collections and of user attitudes toward innovative services.* Metuchen, NJ: Scarecrow.

Drake, S. (1970). Early science and the printed book: The spread of science beyond the universities. *Renaissance and Reformation*, 7(3), 43–52.

Edmonds, R., Guskin, E., Mitchell, A., & Jurkowitz, M. (2013, May 7). Newspapers: By the numbers. Pew Research Center's Project for Excellence in Journalism. Retrieved from http://www.stateofthemedia.org/2013/newspapers-stabilizing-but-still-threatened/newspapers-by-the-numbers

Egan, C. M. (1974, March). Establish a cassette program for a public library. *Illinois Libraries*, 239–243.

Eliot, T. S. (1922). *The waste land.* New York: Horace Liveright.

Eliot, T. S. (1933). *The use of poetry and the use of criticism.* Cambridge, MA: Harvard University Press.

Entralgo, L. (1970). *The therapy of the word in classical antiquity.* New Haven, CT, & London: Yale University Press.

Erman, A. (1923). *Literatur der Agypter.* Berlin: Akademie Verlag.

Eshelman, W. (1973, May 6). Audio-visual aids: Fallout from the McLuhan galaxy. *New York Times.*

Essif, A. (2015, May 28). The Internet can't replace libraries: Why they matter more than ever in the age of Google. Salon. Retrieved from http://www.salon.com/2015/05/28/the_internet_cant_replace_libraries_why_they_matter_more_than_ever_in_the_age_of_google_partner/

Feeley, J. (1967, December). The library environment. *University of Toronto Graduate.*

Fowler, G. A. (2014, August 12). Why the public library beats Amazon—for now. *Wall Street Journal.* Retrieved from www.wsj.com/articles/why-the-public-library-beats-amazonfor-now-1407863714

Frame, D. M. (1965). *Biography of Montaigne.* New York: Harcourt Brace.

Fraser, D. (1974). *African art as philosophy.* Uppsala, Sweden: Interbook.

Frederiksen, L., Cummings, J., Cummings, L., & Carroll, D. (2011). Ebooks and interlibrary loan: License to fill? *Journal of Interlibrary Loan, Document Delivery and Electronic Reserves*, 21(3), 117–131.

Fritz, B. (2014, January 7). Sales of digital movies surge. *Wall Street Journal.* Retrieved from http://www.wsj.com/articles/SB10001424052702304887104579306440621142958

Gelb, J. (1963). *Study of writing.* Chicago: University of Chicago Press.

Geller, E. (1971, June 15). This matter of media. *Library Journal*, 96(12), 2048–2053.

Glover, J. (1974). *Lighter side of the library.* Taunton, MA: William S. Sullwold.

Gombrich, E. H. (1975). *Art and illusion: A study in the psychology of pictorial representation.* New York: Pantheon.

Gore, D. (1975, September 15). The view from the Tower of Babel. *Library Journal*, 1599–1605.

Griffey, J. (2010). *Mobile technologies and libraries.* Chicago: Library & Information Technology Association.

Hall, M., & Hall, E. T. (1975). *The fourth dimension in architecture: The impact of building on man's behavior*. Santa Fe, NM: Sunstone.

Hamburg, M., Clelland, R. C., Brimmer, M. R. W., Ramist, L. E., & Whitfield, R. M. (1978). *Library planning and decision-making systems*. Cambridge, MA: MIT Press.

Havelock, E. (1963). *Preface to Plato*. Cambridge, MA: Harvard University Press.

Havelock, E. (1976). *Origins of Western literacy*. Toronto: Ontario Institute for Studies in Education.

"Have you watched a book today?" An experimental project of the Public Television Library. A final report. (1975). Public Television Library. Washington, DC: Eric Clearing House.

Hessel, Al. (1950). *A history of libraries*. New Brunswick, NJ: Scarecrow.

Himmelweit, H. T., Oppenheim, A. N., & Vince, P. (1958). *Television and the child: An empirical study of the effect of television on the young*. London: Oxford University Press.

Hoivikru, J. (2013). Global village: Mobile access to library resources. *Library Hi Tech, 31*(3), 467–477.

Huxley, A. (1964). Education on the non-verbal level. In A. de Grazia & D. A. Sohn (Eds.), *Revolution in teaching: New theory, technology, and curricula*. New York: Bantam.

Huxley, T. (1920). A liberal education. In C. Rinaker (Ed.), *Readings from Huxley*. New York: Harcourt, Brace & Howe.

Hyer, A. L. (1975). Educational technology. In M. Chisholm (Ed.), *Reader in media technology and libraries*. Englewood, CO: Microcard.

Innis, H. (1951). *The bias of communication*. Toronto: University of Toronto Press.

Innis, H. (1971). *Empire and communications*. Toronto: University of Toronto Press.

Jaynes, J. (1977). *The origin of consciousness in the breakdown of the bicameral mind*. Boston: Houghton Mifflin.

Johnson, A. (1954). *The effect of television set ownership upon public library use*. Master's Thesis University of Chicago.

Jones, C. S. (1976, January 1). The urban public library: Proving utility. *Library Journal*, 53–90.

Jovanovich, W. (1971, June). The universal Xerox life compiler machine. *American Scholar*, 249–255.

Joyce, J. (2000). *Finnegans wake*. New York: Penguin.

Korpela, S. (2005, September). Library 10: In tune with the times. Retrieved from http://finl and.fi/Public/default.aspx?contentid=160103&nodeid=37598&culture=en-US

Kramer, S. N. (1959). *History begins at Sumer*. Garden City, NY: Doubleday.

Lazarfeld, P. (1940). *Radio and the printed page: An introduction to the study of radio and its role in the communication of ideas*. New York: Duell, Sloan & Pearce.

Leavis, Q. D. (1965). *Fiction and the reading public*. New York: Russell & Russell.

Le Clercq, A. (1975). Collecting non-print media in academic libraries. *Tennessee Librarian, 28*, 84–87.

Lee, M. (2015, March 11). Public libraries, U. Wisconsin–Madison team up on climate change MOOC. *Library Journal*. Retrieved from http://lj.libraryjournal.com/2015/03/ed-tech/publ ic-libraries-u-wisconsin-madison-team-up-on-climate-change-mooc/#_

Leimkuhler, F. F., & Neville, A. E. (1968, September). The uncertain future of the library. *Wilson Library Bulletin*, pp. 30–38.

Licklider, J. C. R. (1965). *Libraries of the future.* Cambridge, MA: MIT Press.

Logan, R. K. (1979). *The poetry of physics and physics of poetry.* University of Toronto Lecture Notes. {*Now available as of 2010 in a published form from World Scientific Books in Singapore.*}

Logan, R. K. (1986/2004). *The alphabet effect: A media ecology understanding of the making of Western civilization.* Cresskill, NJ: Hampton.

Logan, R. K. (1995). *The fifth language: Learning a living in the computer age.* Toronto: Stoddart.

Logan, R. K. (2000/2004). *The sixth language: Learning a living in the Internet age.* Caldwell, NJ: Blackburn.

Logan, R. K. (2007). *The extended mind: The emergence of language, the human mind and culture.* Toronto: University of Toronto Press.

Logan, R. K. (2010a). *Understanding new media: Extending Marshall McLuhan.* New York: Peter Lang.

Logan, R. K. (2010b). Digitally augmented books: The eBook platform for books that are smart, readable, searchable, networked, updatable, and promote active reading. *Explorations Media Ecology, 9*(3).

Logan, R. K. (2010c). *The poetry of physics and physics of poetry.* Singapore: World Scientific.

Logan, R. K. (2013). *McLuhan misunderstood: Setting the record straight.* Toronto: Key.

Logan, R. K. (2014). *What is information?—Propagating organization in the biosphere, the symbolosphere, the technosphere and the econosphere.* Toronto: DEMO.

Logan, R. K., & Stokes, L. W. (2004). *Collaborate to compete: Driving profitability in the knowledge economy.* Toronto & New York: Wiley.

Logan, R. K., & White, N. W. (1981). Energy and health. In N. W. White (Ed.), *The health conundrum* (pp. 113–122). Toronto: TV Ontario.

Logsdon, R. N. (1970, September 15). Librarian and scholar: Eternal enemies. *Library Journal, 95,* 2871–2874.

Luria, A. R. (1970, March). The functional organization of the brain. *Scientific American, 222*(3), 66–73.

Maitland, F. W. (1897). *Domesday book and beyond.* Cambridge: Cambridge University Press.

Marks, S. (2015). About the OLRC. Retrieved from http://spotdocs.scholarsportal.info/display/ODLRC/About+the+OLRC

Marshall, J., & Emerick, T. (1972, February 15). Social responsibilities round table. *School Library Journal.*

Martin, S. (1976, January). Tools for the information community. *Library Journal.*

Mason, E. (1972, October). The sobering seventies: Prospects for change. *Library Journal,* 3115–3119.

McClintock, P. (2014, January 28.). Box office: Boom! Bust! Inside a wild $25 billion year overseas. *Hollywood Reporter.* Retrieved from http://www.hollywoodreporter.com/news/box-office-boom-bust-inside-674757

McGilchrist, I. (2012). *The master and his emissary: The divided brain and the making of the Western world.* New Haven, CT: Yale University Press.

McLuhan, M. (1951). *The mechanical bride: The folklore of industrial man.* New York: Vanguard.

McLuhan, M. (1962). *The Gutenberg galaxy: The making of typographic man.* Toronto: University of Toronto Press.

McLuhan, M. (1964). *Understanding media: Extensions of man*. New York: McGraw-Hill.

McLuhan, M. (1970). *Libraries: Past, present, future*, SUNY Geneseo Address, July 3.

McLuhan, M. (1975). Laws of the media (LOM). *Technology and Culture, 34*(1).

McLuhan, M. (1995). A McLuhan Sourcebook assembled by William Kuhns. In E. McLuhan & F. Zingrone (Eds.), *Essential McLuhan*. Concord, ON: Anansi.

McLuhan, M., Hutchon, K., & McLuhan, E. (1977). *City as classroom: Understanding language and media*. Agincourt, ON: Book Society of Canada.

McLuhan, M., & Logan, R. K. (1977). Alphabet, Mother of Invention. *Et Cetera, 34*, 373–383.

McLuhan, M., & McLuhan, E. (1988). *Laws of media: The new science*. Toronto: University of Toronto Press.

McLuhan, M., McLuhan, S., & Staines, D. (2003). *Understanding me: Lectures and interviews*. Toronto: McClelland & Stewart.

My Autobiography: A Fragment by F. Max Müllerit is available online at http://www.gutenberg.org/ebooks/30269

Needham, J. (1979). *The grand titration*. Toronto: University of Toronto Press.

A new kind of learning. (n.d.). University of Waterloo. Retrieved from uwaterloo.ca/stratford-campus

Newman, J. H. (1933). *On the scope and nature of university education*. New York: Everyman.

Nielsen, E. (1954). *Oral tradition: A modern problem in Old Testament*. Norwich, UK: SCM.

Nonaka, I., & Takeuchi, H. (1995). *The knowledge creation company*. New York: Oxford University Press.

Nyberg, H. S. (1935). *Studien zum Hoseabuche*. Uppsala: A. B. Lundequistska.

Ong, W. (1982/2002). *Orality and literacy: The technologizing of the word*. New York: Routledge.

Opie, I., & Opie, P. (1959/2000). *The lore and language of schoolchildren*. New York: New York Review Books.

Orr, J. M. (1977). *Libraries as communication systems*. London: Greenwood.

Otten, K. (1971, July–August). A hypothesis: Micro-form will become the major medium for "new information." *Journal of Micrographics, 4*, 265–273.

Owens, M. (1976, January). The state government and library. *Library Journal*, 9–18.

Palfrey, J. (2015). *BiblioTech: Why libraries matter more than ever in the age of Google*. New York: Basic.

Parker, E. B. (1961). *The impact of radio book review program on public library circulation*. Springfield: Illinois State Library.

Parker, E. B. (1971). Potential interrelationships between library and other mass media systems. In J. Becker (Ed.), *Proceedings of the Conference on Interlibrary Communications and Information Networks, Chicago ALA* (pp. 188–195).

Parker, J. S. (1974). International librarianship: A reconnaissance. *Journal of Librarianship, 6*, 219–232.

Pauling, L. (1960). *The nature of the chemical bond*. Ithaca, NY: Cornell University Press.

Peters, F. E. (1970). *The harvest of Hellenism*. New York: Simon & Schuster.

Peyser, J. (1973, April). Planning audiovisual services in public libraries. *Library Journal, 98*, 1342–1345.

Popper, K. (1959). *The logic of scientific discovery*. London: Routledge.

Powell, L. G. (1958). *A passion for books*. New York: World.

Puzo, M. (1969). *The Godfather*. New York: G. P. Putnam's & Sons.

Randal, W. M. (1946). Some principles for library planning. *College and Research Libraries*, 7(4), 319–325.

Reliabilty of Wikipedia. (n.d.). Wikipedia.com. Retrieved from en.wikipedia.org/wiki/Reliabili ty_of_Wikipedia

Richardson, E. G. (1914). *The beginnings of libraries*. Princeton, NJ: Princeton University Press.

Ringer, B. (1976). Copyright and the future of authorship. *Library Journal*, 101(1), 229–232.

Roberts, K. (2012). *Facing the future: A vision document for British Columbia's public libraries*. BC Government. Retrieved from http://commons.bclibraries.ca/wp-content/uploads/2012/12/ Facing-the-Future-A-Report-on-the-future-of-libraries-for-the-Province-of-British-Col umbia.pdf

Rosenwald, M. S. (2015, February 21). Why digital natives prefer reading in print. Yes, you read that right. *Washington Post*.

Ryan, F. (1971, November). Instructional television fixed service. *AV Instruction*, 16, 43–45.

Sartre, J.-P. (1950). *What is literature?* London: Methuen.

Schramm, W., Lyle, J., & Parker, E. B. (1961). *Television in the lives of our children*. Stanford, CA: Stanford University Press.

Schwartz, T. (1974). *The responsive chord*. New York: Doubleday.

Seeley, K. Q. (2014, March 7). Breaking out of the library mold, in Boston and beyond. *New York Times*. Retrieved from http://www.nytimes.com/2014/03/08/us/breaking-out-of-the- library-mold-in-boston-and-beyond.html?_r=0

Shera, J. H. (1969, September). The quiet stir of thought; or, what the computer cannot do. *Library Journal*, 94, 2875–2880.

Shera, J. H. (1971). *"The compleat librarian"; and other essays*. Cleveland, OH: Press of Case Western Reserve University.

Sherman, S. (2015, June 27). The New York Public Library wars: What went wrong at one of the world's eminent research institutions? *Chronicle of Higher Education*. Retrieved from chronicle.com/article/The-New-York-Public-Library/231127/

Sheviak, M. R. (1971). The message of media. *School Libraries*, 20(3), 17–20.

Shields, G. (1978). New role of the librarian in the information age. In E. J. Josey (Ed.), *The information society: Issues and answers*. Phoenix, AZ: Oryx.

Shlain, L. (1999). *The alphabet versus the goddess*. New York: Penguin.

Shores, L. (1955). Books: Continuous communicability. *Saturday Review*, 41(26).

Shores, L. (1968, Winter). Medium way. *Library College Journal*, 1, 10–17.

Snow, C. P. (1959). *The two cultures and the scientific revolution*. New York: Cambridge University Press.

Stein, L. (2014, August 25). Library without books debuts at Florida's newest college. Reuters. Retrieved from www.reuters.com/article/2014/08/25/us-usa-florida-library-idUSKB- N0GP0W620140825

Stone, C. W. (1967, October). The library function redefined. *Library Trends*, 181–196.

Stone, C. W. (1975). The use of media and technology and libraries. In M. Chisholm (Ed.), *Reader in media technology and libraries*. Englewood, CO: Microcard.

Stratford campus library services. (n.d.). University of Waterloo. Retrieved from http://uwaterl oo.ca/stratford-campus/resources-and-services

Tabor, J. (2014, August 17). Halifax looks forward to the opening of its very own library of the future. *Globe and Mail*. Retrieved from www.theglobeandmail.com/news/national/halifax-looks-forward-to-the-opening-of-its-very-own-library-of-the-future/article20090514/

Taylor, R. (1973). *Curriculum design for library and information science*. *Education and Curriculum Series No. 1*. Syracuse, NY: Syracuse University School of Library Science.

Teague, J., & Carroll, J. (1973). Opinion paper. Information in an informationless world; or The making of an information scientist. *Journal of the American Society for Information Science, 24*(1), 40–44.

Teplitz, A. (1970). Microfilm and reprography. In *Ann. Rev. of Info Science & Technology* (Vol. 5. Chicago: Encyclopedia Britannica.

Thoman, E., & Jolls, T. (2005). Media literacy education: Lessons from the center for media literacy. In G. Schwartz & P. U. Brown (Eds.), *Media literacy: Transforming curriculum and teaching, Vol. 104* (pp. 180–205). Malden, MA: National Society for the Study of Education.

Thorton, J. L. (1941). *The chronology of librarianship*. London: Grafton.

Trueswell, W. (1968). *Analysis of library user circulation requirements: Final report*. Amherst: Department of Industrial Engineering, University of Massachusetts.

Turner, A. (2015). McLuhan in the library. *Art Libraries Journal, 40*(1), 5–10.

2013 Internet ad revenues soar to $42.8 billion, hitting landmark high & surpassing broadcast television for the first time—Marks a 17% rise over record-setting revenues in 2012. (2014, April 10). Interactive Advertising Bureau. Retrieved from http://www.iab.net/about_the_iab/recent_press_release_archive/press_release/pr-041014

University of California Library Statistics. (2001, July). 7. Retrieved July 17, 2005, from http://www.slp.ucop.edu/stats/00-01.pdf Ucop.edu

University of California Library System. (2005). University of California Library Statistics 1990–91, University-wide Library Planning, University of California Office of the President (July 1991), 12.

University of California Library Statistics. (2004, July). 7. Retrieved July 17, 2005, from http://www.slp.ucop.edu/stats/03-04.pdf Ucop.edu

Unprecedented number of cuts to library programs in Canada. (2012). Ontario Library Association. Retrieved from www.accessola.org/web/OLAWEB/Home/SearchResults.aspx?q=unprecedented%20cuts x

Vagianos, L. (1976). Today is tomorrow: A look at the future information arena. *Library Journal, 101*(1), 147–156.

Vespasiano. (1926). *The Vespasiano memoirs: Lives of illustrious men of the XVth century by Vespasiano da Bisticci, bookseller* (W. George & E. Waters, Eds.). London: George Routledge & Sons.

Waddell, H. (1927). *The wandering scholars*. London: Constable.

Wall, M. (2014). Back to school: U of T library system ranked in top three with Harvard and Yale. Retrieved from http://news.utoronto.ca/back-school-u-t-library-system-ranked-top-three-harvard-and-yale

West, C. (1971, Summer). Stop! The print is killing me! *Synergy*, *33*, 2–5.

White, J. F. (1971). *New forms of worship*. Nashville, TN: Abingdon.

Wolchover, N. (2011, January 24). How accurate is Wikipedia? livescience.com. Retrieved from http://www.livescience.com/32950-how-accurate-is-wikipedia.html

Author Index

Subject Index

Lance Strate
General Editor

This series is devoted to scholarship relating to media ecology, a field of inquiry defined as the study of media as environments. Within this field, the term "medium" can be defined broadly to refer to any human technology or technique, code or symbol system, invention or innovation, system or environment. Media ecology scholarship typically focuses on how technology, media, and symbolic form relate to communication, consciousness, and culture, past, present and future. This series is looking to publish research that furthers the formal development of media ecology as a field; that brings a media ecology approach to bear on specific topics of interest, including research and theoretical or philosophical investigations concerning the nature and effects of media or a specific medium; that includes studies of new and emerging technologies and the contemporary media environment as well as historical studies of media, technology, and modes and codes of communication; scholarship regarding technique and the technological society; scholarship on specific types of media and culture (e.g., oral and literate cultures, image, etc.), or of specific aspects of culture such as religion, politics, education, journalism, etc.; critical analyses of art and popular culture; and studies of how physical and symbolic environments function as media.

For additional information about this series or for the submission of manuscripts, please contact:

Lance Strate or Mary Savigar
strate@fordham.edu | Mary.Savigar@plang.com

To order other books in this series, please contact our Customer Service Department:

(800) 770-LANG (within the U.S.)
(212) 647-7706 (outside the U.S.)
(212) 647-7707 FAX

Or browse online by series:
www.peterlang.com